CANADA'S INDIANS
Contemporary Conflicts

CANADA'S INDIANS
Contemporary Conflicts

James S. Frideres

Associate Professor
of Sociology
University of Calgary

p
Prentice-Hall ✦ of Canada Ltd.
Scarborough h Ontario

© 1974 by Prentice-Hall of Canada Ltd.
Scarborough, Ontario

PRENTICE-HALL, INC., ENGLEWOOD CLIFFS, NEW JERSEY
PRENTICE-HALL INTERNATIONAL, INC., LONDON
PRENTICE-HALL OF AUSTRALIA, PTY., LTD., SYDNEY
PRENTICE-HALL OF INDIA PVT., LTD., NEW DELHI
PRENTICE-HALL OF JAPAN, INC., TOKYO

Library of Congress Catalog Card No. 73–21083

ISBN
0–13–112755–1 (pa.)
0–13–112763–2 (cl.)

3 4 5   78 77

PRINTED IN CANADA

To my wife, Carol Anne and our children
Steffani and Jhohn Riel

Acknowledgements

IN WRITING this book, many people have helped and hindered its production. Unfortunately, I do not remember all those individuals and groups who have done so and would like to forget those who fall into the latter category. However, I express my apologies for not mentioning the names of all those who have helped. I would like to thank Doug Skoog and E. D. Boldt for their encouragement and for stimulating my thinking about a number of ideas when the manuscript was in its inception. A special expression of appreciation is due to Frank Molloy, Assistant Production Editor of Prentice-Hall of Canada, Ltd., who carefully read and edited the manuscript.

I would also like to thank Joan Ryan, Marlene Koch, and June Smith for reviewing a preliminary draft and suggesting changes and refinements, and Rosie Handy, who has patiently typed many drafts of the manuscript.

Contents

seven

eight

Preface

THIS BOOK reveals the current social conditions of Indians. It may lack the emotionalism some desire, but it reflects my basic orientation. We need to look at the facts as they are, neither glorifying one group nor condemning the other. Many books have been published castigating whites or Indians. But how does this help promote social change? Once the facts are faced, the question then becomes: Will we do anything to change them? My non-emotional orientation stems from two facts: (*i*) my academic training and (*ii*) living on a reserve for 21 years. I have experienced the everyday realities of Indian life and the emotionalism that sometimes accompanies it. I want to explicate the first and hold the latter in abeyance.

The solutions offered here are the result of academic and personal experience. The program outlined is directed specifically toward Indians, but perhaps it could be directed to any oppressed minority group in Canada. It calls for major changes in the dominant group's relation to Indians. It is not "new" in the sense that some changes have been advocated for many years. Its uniqueness lies in its attempt to pull together all those recommendations for change into a single theoretical context—colonialism. However, this does not absolve Indians (or their leaders) from also making changes. Too often in the past, books and articles in journals and magazines have treated the white as the "bad guy" and the Indian as the "good guy." The Indian is seen as noble and incapable of any wrongdoing. This myth is misleading and dangerous to native people wishing to change their position in the larger society. It is time to face realities. Whether Indians have suffered injusticies in the past is of little consequence in directing the proposed program. The important point is that the realities of the world are at work, directing their impact on both whites and Indians.

The overt hostility between status and non-status Indians may have been initiated and fostered by whites, but it must cease. Leaders of both groups must tackle this problem and stop the bickering which aggravates the diversity and disorganization of Indians. Too often Indians have perpetuated petty grievances and engaged in dialogues reflecting a "one-up-manship" attitude. Likewise, Indians must allow for some controlled outside help. To feel that they are self-sufficient is a healthy attitude, but to reject out of hand any help by any outside group is foolish and will result in continued subjugation. While we all, no doubt, would like to think of ourselves as self-sustaining units, capable of making major institutional changes, the harsh realities force us to act otherwise. Indians are not in a position to reject all outside help. These contributing factors to the splintering and internal conflict must be combated if there are to be meaningful changes. Thus, the reader will not find this book identifying with one group or castigating another. The historical data may seem one-sided, but it only reflects reality.

For those concerned with the fate of the Indians and in a more general sense, Canada as a nation, the analysis and solution of the Indian-white problem presented will be used to plan future action. Some, however, will feel that the plan is idealistic, unworkable and will reject it out of hand.

Others, undoubtedy, will laud the efforts and then, as they have always done, place it quietly beside other dust-covered, action-oriented books. The fate of this text remains to be seen, but the case is clearly stated.

JAMES S. FRIDERES

Introduction

THE ECONOMIC and social status of the Canadian Indian is one of abject poverty. The assistance that has been provided to Canadian Indians by the empowered groups has always had two serious drawbacks: (*i*) an explicit (or implicit) "wardship" orientation and (*ii*) it has been so minimal that its impact has been negligible on the life styles and chances of the native people throughout Canada. Both factors have been based on a single ideology—racism.

While some people may object to this claim, it is evident in the underlying ideology of the manifest policies regarding native-white relations throughout the history of Canada. I have chosen as one indicator, the proceedings of the federal parliament as the basis for this claim. As one reads the proceedings and the laws eventually enacted, one is struck by the blatant racist thought that has prevailed. Dosman (1972) points out that the Agents' Reports are inundated with racist comments, typical of the Euro-Canadian dominant group. The following is an example from Alexander Morris (1880), who arranged the initial treaties with native people:

Let us have Christianity and civilization to leaven the masses of heathenism and paganism among the Indian Tribes; let us have a wise and paternal government faithfully carrying out the provisions of our treaties.... They (native people) are wards of Canada, let us do our duty by them.... *(296–297)*

The Minister of the Interior stated, in 1902:

... our position with reference to the Indian is this: we have them with us, and we have to deal with them as wards of the country. There is no question that the method we have adopted of bringing these people to an improved state ... there is a difference between the savage and a person who has become civilized, though perhaps not of a high type. *Debate of the House of Commons, 2nd Session, 9th Parliament, 1902, Ottawa, 3046.)*

The reader may claim that these are isolated examples from a different era and that they have to be substantiated by "hard data." But they are representative of a much larger legal, academic, and literary scene. It might also be argued that people are more enlightened today. Again, many contemporary examples could be presented but discussion of this will be deferred.

While it may never be possible to quantify the degree of racism (both individual and institutional), the evidence examined unmistakably reveals the same central theme. Its blatancy may have been disguised, but the impact has still been the same. People still believe that natives are biologically and socially inferior and as a result, discrimination against Indians at both the individual and institutional level still has a sound, rational basis for most people.

Whites are continually amazed when there are confrontations and generally blame the native people. "Getting uppity," "trying to take advantage," *etc.* are disguised forms of saying that the blame lies with native people, not whites. Only people with a distorted and abbreviated view of history would make this claim.

Let me give an example. When natives clash with whites, most people tend to forget (or perhaps don't want to realize) that historical facts and existing structural relations all set the stage. But it is curious that no one looks at these. They focus upon the immediate situation. Thus, when the Indians "protest" via some overt behavior (*e.g.*, at St. Regis since the late fifties and at Cold Lake in the early seventies), they are seen as the troublemakers. Yet perhaps the reasons for the protest are because hundreds of native children die in their first year, because hundreds of native men are unable to get jobs, or because of the Indians' inability to get adequate housing. They are not necessarily the initiators. It shows a racist position to suggest that the "fault" lies with native people. It ignores the subtle violence that has been perpetrated against natives since the coming of the white man. Alternatively, it suggests that the people in power want to maintain their positions and accept the status quo. Clearly the former position allows them to do so. People in Canada should not be allowed to go hungry, or be uneducated. We are a nation of plenty—but only those who support the empowered groups will benefit in the harvest.

Some people will be angered by these claims, indignant that they should be labeled racist. They will say that other history books they have read have not made these claims. But history is man's way of recording past behavior. Man is susceptible to the political and social forces of the time the "history" is written. When were the natives allowed to write histories? When they did, why were they dismissed as fabrications?

An author's explanation of social events depends on his point of view. On this basis, the historian must infer the actors' motives since overt social behaviour can be interpreted in many different ways. For example, if a student saw his professor sitting in a pub late at night with a beautiful female student, he would probably infer many "motives" to the professor. They may, or may not, be accurate. So it is with history. Historians infer motives to groups as well as to individuals. Unfortunately, until recently, our historians have largely been Euro-Canadians, presenting similar views of social reality.

In the past, empowered groups have been able to define history and provide an explanation of the present. A good example is the portrayal of wars between Indians and whites by Canadian historians. Part of this bias in the recording of events is because Western civilization is based upon an "enemy concept". As Pelletier has pointed out, everything people do in white society must end in fighting—whether against crime, welfare or inflation. Thus, when Indians attacked a white village or fort and won, it was called a massacre, while if whites attacked an Indian village and won, it was described as a victory. Since the dominant group are able to make these interpretations and definitions, they are also able to keep others from initiating alternative explanations or definitions. Because history gives credence and legitimacy to a society's normative structure, it became necessary for the dominant group to reconstruct social history. By reconstructing history, these new definitions could be imposed and future generations would continue to associate "savage" and heinous behavior with Canadian natives. An example of this can be found in the comparison by Trudel and Jains (1970) of French-Canadian and English-Canadian history textbooks. After reading about, for example, the battle of the Plains of Abraham in an English and in a French text, one has the distinct feeling that they are not discussing the same event. As Patterson (1972) points out, alien history is pulled down and discredited, and national history replaces it. Continuity of tradition for any group is truncated when the communication channels are taken over by people who wish to change the information being transmitted (Lindesmith and Strauss, 1968). How often have we known something to be true at one point in history only to find out many years later that perhaps the government (or some other group) suppressed or distorted information which might have led us to believe something quite different? Brown (1971) and Andrist (1964) have vividly portrayed American-Indian history from an alternative point of view. Their information concerning Indian-white relations is quite dissimilar to that provided by "established" historians.

Readers have reacted quite differently to books by Cardinal (1969), Pelletier and Waubageshig (1970) compared to books by Morton (1963), McInnis (1959) and Lower (1957). The layman's typical reaction to the first three authors is that "they are biased, therefore it will interfere with the logic of their position and subsequent conclusion; consequently, I reject all they say." But the layman tends to accept the "explanations" provided by the second group of "established academic" authors. I am not attempting to suggest that the first are right or the second wrong. What I do suggest, however, is that people should allow themselves the "maneuverability" of ingesting both. It is a serious oversight not to realize that the "history" of Canada taught in grades 5–12 (and on into university) was written mainly by English speaking Euro-Canadians, specifically of British ethnicity. How easy to see then, why students disagree with Cardinal and Pelletier. The Ontario Education Commission, in a study of elementary Canadian history books, discovered that many historical events involving native people had not been recorded. In fact, the commission found that many history books did not discuss the role of Indians in Canadian history. From a preliminary study I have noticed the same omission from university history texts. Walker (1971) characterized Canadian historians in their analysis of Indians in Canada as ignorant, prejudiced and in some cases, dishonest. While one could argue that the positions taken in history books are idiosyncratic and simply reflect an individual viewpoint, when one analyzes the content of all history books, a common theme emerges. This does not imply that a history by a non-English-speaking Euro-Canadian would necessarily be objective, just that it may reflect a different view of reality. However, we do not have to attribute deliberate falsification to historians. In any reconstruction of the past, the interpretation of events is shaped by the way an author perceives them, by what he remembers, and where he stands in the social system. The important point is that a reshaping of the past occurs. History is no more factual than the bias of the writer.

If Indian-white relations do not change and the Indians are not allowed to attain self-control and plan their own destiny, there will be further conflict.

Indians at present are using the legal system in an attempt either to get back land that they claim is theirs or to be compensated for it. They regard as a precedent the legal battle between natives and the United States Government (in Alaska) in which Eskimos (Aleuts and Indians) received $942 million and 40 million acres of land in compensation for lands taken away (Harrison, 1972). However, regardless of the legal outcome, native people will win psychologically (if not economically). If the courts rule in their favor, they will be in an excellent position to become economically independent and subsequently a competitive force in Canadian society. They will be able to shake loose the "wardship" policy which has besieged them since the coming of the white man.

If they lose, their feeling that the white man has always discriminated against them will be reinforced. Stronger feelings of anger and hatred will emerge and there will be a tighter internal cohesion between native people. An evil image of whites will crystalize, leading to a bipolarization—all

Indians are good, all whites are bad. Radical and militant leaders will emerge. Indian leaders in BC expressed the possibility of these developments in a National Film Board film called *This Land*. The film, dealing with the land issue in BC during the late sixties, clearly demonstrates the increasing belligerency of Canadian Indians. Indians, again having seen the unfairness of the whites and lacking faith in the existing establishment procedures, will rise to the call of their militant leaders. A guerrilla-style war may result.

My central aim here is to give the student of Indian-white relations a new perspective on the problem. The situation is usually defined as an Indian problem and, generally is couched in an individualistic framework. Solutions offered are based on this perspective. In my view, it can be a white problem (although that does not exclude Indians from some "house cleaning"). To view Indian-white relations from an individualistic perspective will not provide solutions, for example, to integrating native people into the larger society.

Since the aim is to provide alternative views of reality, it is only fair to include the outlook of white academics as well as Indian leaders. Thus, four previously published papers concerning the relationship between natives and whites are included. They will not only add strength to the argument, but will also expose the reader to an Indian perspective.

Drucker's paper has been included because it specifically focuses on BC and its historical power relations with natives. The Canadian government's relationship with natives is fairly uniform except in relation to those in BC. Treaties were never negotiated with natives there (except the initial Douglas treaties of 1850–54). At the time when treaties were being drawn up and Indian lands taken over, whites did not feel they had to "negotiate." By the time the white man began to settle in BC in large numbers, it was economically expedient not to "deal" with the natives as the federal government had previously felt. Native people in the north were never recompensed for their surrender of the land encompassed by Treaty 11. Perhaps it is even more important that most Indians in the north have never signed a treaty with the government. Clearly because of the stage of economic and social-political development of Canada at the time BC was being settled, new and bold techniques of exploitation were adopted by the empowered whites when dealing with the native people. Their dealings with the natives provide a unique and distinctive element in Canada's history and an illegitimate and devastating force which has had many lasting repercussions for natives in this region. The paper attempts to show the historical forces (internal and external) which led the federal and BC governments to act as they did and why they succeeded.

Dunning's article has been selected for various reasons: (*i*) he attempts to show that there are differences in the structure and operation of reserves and that this distinction must be made before there can be a solution to the Indian-white problem; (*ii*) he tries to show some of the problems natives encountered in their attempts to adjust to living conditions in "white southern areas;" (*iii*) he attempts to place the reserve within the context of the larger social structure.

The other two articles selected have similar suggestions about the future relations between natives and whites. Both authors are Canadian Indians. Stewart attempts to show "another side" to white Canadians. He is one of the few Indian writers who is read by white Canadians. We are constantly being told about the Indian problem, but almost always from a white point of view. Stewart attempts to give his definition of the "problem"—one he hopes is representative of Indians. His diagnosis is that (*a*) it is not a total "Indian problem" and (*b*) conflict should be regarded as possible. He claims that the "power structure" in Canada has done very little to allow natives to attain self-control of their destiny and, as a result, Indians see that changes will come only from their efforts.

Pelletier discusses the techniques Indians must use to survive in an "alien" environment. He also gives an Indian outlook on the white educational system and its subsequent impact on the Indian children forced to attend schools. His discussion of differential aspects between Indian and white culture and of some unique adaptations shows significant insight.

CANADA'S INDIANS
Contemporary Conflicts

1

Contemporary Indians

WHILE MANY STUDIES have been made of native
people, no-one has yet compiled relevant statistics on Canadian Indians as a whole. In the past
there have been a series of "individual" studies
of various bands, tribes or reserves. But they did
not give a total picture of the "social state" of the
Indians. The aim of this chapter is to present
data reflecting the social characteristics of all Canadian Indians at present.

INDIANS AND HISTORY

First we have to make a distinction between
several different legal and quasi-legal categories
of Canadian Indians. Then we can trace a short
history of the Indian-white relationships. It is no
easy matter to determine who is an Indian and who
is not. The problem involves historical factors as
well as definitions. The definition of an Indian
has changed with time. Initially whites defined
natives as Indian if they exhibited a certain way
of life. However, after a time, during which
miscegenation occurred between Indians and
whites (specifically the French), a distinct ethnic
group called the Metis emerged. Thus for some
time a distinction was made between Indians

and Metis. Both groups were legally recognized as ethnically separate and distinct by the dominant group.

But later, more importance was given to Indians and the dominant group downgraded the use of Metis as a symbol for a distinct ethnic group. Thus in the censuses before 1941, the ethnic origin was traced through the mother. Since eastern Indian tribes are matrilocal, this seemed to be a satisfactory means to delineate Indians from other ethnic groups. If the mother was Indian before 1941, the children were also defined as Indian.

However, this was only true for those people who had been previously defined as Indian under the British North America Act. Statistics Canada still made a distinction between Indian and "mixed origin" until 1941, when the definition was changed so that the father's ethnic group determined that of his children. However, this rule was used only for "off reserve" Indians. For those who lived on the reserve, both mother's and father's lineages were used to classify a person Indian (Romaniuk and Piché, 1972).

In 1951 a more complex legal definition was introduced, stating that only those individuals who fell under the Indian Act would be classified as "Indians."[1] Today, while the federal government only legally recognizes any obligation to status or registered Indians, it nominally recognizes the ethnic group referred to as Metis. On the other hand, certain provinces, such as Alberta, have formally recognized the Metis and have established Metis colonies.

As shown above, culture or race no longer affect the definition of an Indian—today's definition is a legal one. While someone may exhibit all the racial and cultural attributes traditionally associated with "Indianness," if he does not come under the terms of the Indian Act, he is not (in the eyes of the federal and provincial governments) an Indian. Below is a list explaining the government typology:

1. *Registered Treaty On and Off Reserve Indian*—This group is considered to consist of the natives whose ancestors made agreements (or "treaties") with the Crown. These Indians surrendered their land in return for a reserve, a small annuity and an initial cost outlay. They are considered to be under the regulations as specified by the BNA Act of 1867 and later, the Indian Act of 1951. The original Indian Act has continually been changed by the federal government since its conception. "Indian" means a person who, pursuant to this act, is registered as an Indian or is entitled to be registered as an Indian. Of the just over 250,000 registered Indians in Canada in 1971, about half were in this category. Of these, about 70 per cent live on the reserve. The remainder live in large metropolitan areas throughout Canada although a small percentage live in smaller communities across the country. To maintain their "treaty" or registered status, they must live on the reserve, maintain a residence on the reserve, and/or return to live on the reserve for a specified period every three years. If they fail to do this, they can lose their "treaty" or "registered" status and thus be struck from the roll.

[1]In 1939 Duplessis was able to get northern Quebec Eskimos re-defined as Indians so that they came under federal, instead of provincial, control (Richardson, 1972).

2. *Registered Non-Treaty Indians*—Indians in Quebec, the Maritimes, parts of the NWT and in most of BC did not carry on negotiations with the federal government and therefore are not considered "treaty" Indians, although in some cases they were given crown land. The Iroquois of Brantford and Tyendingaga and certain other groups who migrated from the US are also in this group, considered to be "registered" Indians.

Like those in group 1, they are defined as Indians in the legal sense of the word. The important point here is that a person can be a "registered" (legal) Indian and subject to all the provisions of the Indian Act, even though his band or tribe has not signed a treaty with the government. It also shows that residence on a reserve is not necessary to maintain this status because in many cases Indians (regardless of whether they signed a treaty) were not given land in return.

3. *Non-Registered Indian*—People in this group may exhibit all the cultural and/or racial attributes of "Indianness," but they are not defined as Indians in the legal sense. Although they are not considered "registered" Indians (because they refused—or were not allowed—to make agreements with the Crown) they share most of the social and physical characteristics of treaty Indians. Included in this category are those Indians who have undergone "enfranchisement." They may have lost their Indian status in several ways. For example, until 1960 an Indian had to give up his legal status if he wanted to vote in a federal election. Today an Indian can apply for enfranchisement if he wants to renounce his Indian status. An Indian may choose to give up his Indian status by applying formally to Ottawa. If he does so, all heirs are excluded from being Indian. He also forfeits all rights and obligations of an Indian. Since 1955 about 700 Indians per year have been enfranchised (see Table 1). Even today, an Indian woman and her children will lose their Indian status if she marries a non-Indian. In 1970, 652 were enfranchised. Of these, 615 resulted from marriages of Indian women to non-Indian men.

4. *Metis*—Members of this group are defined as having "mixed" ancestry. Initially the title meant a half "mixture" of French and Indian, although it has now been broadened to include almost all people with at least some Indian ancestry. These people, as well as those in group 3, are not subject to the regulations of the Indian Act.

Metis have historically been defined and treated as a legal entity. The federal government, between 1870 and 1875, recognized the treaty and aboriginal rights of Metis. Metis were given land, scrip (valued between $160 and $240 or 240 acres of land) and medical and educational subsidies, just as the "status" Indians now receive. They also could choose to "take treaty" and become registered Indians. In addition, crown lands were given to the provinces to set up colonies for them. But in 1940, the Indian Affairs Branch (IAB) changed its position and refused to acknowledge the existence of the Metis as a legal entity. At present they are re-emerging as an ethnic group, with only informal—not legal—recognition by the federal government.

What is the reason for these distinctions? Those in power are aware that making such nominal distinctions between Canadian natives has a "di-

Table 1. Community Affairs Branch Enfranchisements, 1969–70

	Adult Indians enfranchised upon application together with minor unmarried children		Indian women enfranchised after marriage to non-Indians together with minor unmarried children		Total Indians enfranchised
	Adults	Children	Women	Children	
Nova Scotia	–	–	2	–	2
PEI	–	–	–	–	–
New Brunswick	–	–	1	–	1
Québec	1	–	30	–	31
Ontario	20	13	164	24	221
Manitoba	6	2	72	9	89
Saskatchewan	4	–	70	24	98
Alberta	7	4	61	21	93
BC	3	–	137	27	167
District of MacKenzie	–	–	9	–	9
Yukon	–	–	1	2	3
	41	19	547	107	714

Indian Enfranchisements 1955–70

1955–56	192	130	337	97	756
1956–57	192	145	389	113	839
1957–58	169	149	305	50	673
1958–59	138	52	612	–	802
1959–60	221	248	433	221	1,123
1960–61	125	70	592	167	954
1961–62	94	47	435	140	716
1962–63	90	50	404	109	653
1963–64	46	38	287	102	473
1964–65	46	34	480	176	736
1965–66	38	18	435	147	638
1966–67	31	22	457	148	658
1967–68	62	28	470	56	616
1968–69	37	20	531	197	785
1969–70	41	19	547	107	714

vide and conquer" effect. The problem of controlling Indians is eased because they begin to fight between themselves. This is particularly noticeable between the Metis and the registered Indians. They are given different privileges, different amounts of money from different sources, and different "powers." However, Red Power advocates are now attempting to point this out and to suggest ways of counteracting its influence. What is being suggested is that "status" does not matter when there is discrimination. The distinction between registered and non-registered Indians cannot be made visually. Thus, in daily interaction, Euro-Canadians cannot and do not distinguish between the various Indian groups. If the person "looks Indian" he is often treated according to the stereotype predominant in Canada, *e.g.*, that he is lazy, drunk, happy-go-lucky. Many Indians, though legally defined as members of separate groups, will exhibit similar life styles. Thus, the similarities can sometimes overshadow the legal differences. (See Davis, 1968, for a similar argument.)

In general, the policy toward native people by the dominant groups has been two-sided. It publicly proclaimed "respect for native people's rights," while privately denying them any rights, such as to vote and choose their "reserve" (Anderson and Wright, 1971; Washburn, 1965). Since an extended historical review of Indian-white relations is beyond the scope of this book, the reader should consult the following sources for a thorough explanation: Patterson, 1972; Jenness, 1937; *Report on the Affairs of the Indians in Canada*, 1844; Stanley, 1952.

We will briefly examine the policy of the two dominant groups in their relations with natives, considering first the French policy, then the British. Conclusions will be based on documents and histories written during the time of contact. The technique for gathering information used here is referred to as a content analysis. I have attempted to analyze formal and informal documents relevant to the times, including personal correspondence between government officials.

We will initially consider French-Indian relations both in Canada and the United States and then turn specifically to Canada. A quite thorough review of the documents available on the attitudes of the French settlers to the Indians reveals no well defined policy on how they were to act toward the natives. Generally, the French were attempting to "exploit" the land and continue the "pseudo-colonization" of North America. However, initially they did not mean to settle New France with any large stable population. Because of the mainly mercantilistic philosophy,[2] the small number of French people wishing to emigrate to New France, and the strong influence of Roman Catholicism, a policy of cultural and/or physical genocide was not invoked. The initial relationship of the French to the Indians can best be described as one of total dependency, but this soon changed to a "symbiotic" one. Intermarriage ("wintering in") between French trappers and Indians became common practice and was encouraged by French authorities. The French wanted to stabilize good relations with the Indians so that the fur trade would continue. It is important to point out that these sexual relationships between French men and Indian women were not meant to be "exploitive." The relations were stable and the father was considered to be responsible for his "wife" and offspring. When war broke out with England, the demand for fur decreased and the French mercantilistic phil-

---

[2]Mercantilism was a prevailing economic thought which held two basic tenets: (*i*) the mother country was to have great wealth, *i.e.* there was a desire to accumulate wealth in any form, and (*ii*) the mother country was to "exploit" other regions and import raw materials to be refined and sell them, *i.e.* the mother country was supposed to keep a favorable balance of trade.

osophy came to an end. This also brought a change in the French policy
toward the Indians. In France's new relationship with native people, the
natives' land rights began to be systematically ignored (Harper, 1947:131).
Evidence for this can be found in letters Louis XV gave to companies coming to New France. These letters state that "the land, coasts, ports, havens,
etc. are the full property of the company and they have full right to dispose
of them in any way they desire" (B.F. French, 1851). Similar provisions
can be found in the privileges, power and requirements given to the Company of One Hundred Associates by Cardinal Richelieu nearly a century
before. (See I. G. Shea, *Charlevoix's History of New France*, Vol. 2, p. 39.)

When the French moved to a new area to settle, they tried to do so
peacefully. (They were generally successful since the agricultural style of
life only minimally disrupted native life.)[3] Following the settlement, the Indians were asked to join in a "treaty" to acknowledge their submission to
the king of France. Though very little land was actually expropriated by
the French, the settlements were not established without the frequent use
of force. When the Marquis de Tacy was placed in charge of the government of Canada in 1663, one sees within the commissions set forth an indication that "arms" were to be used to subjugate the natives if necessary.
(For a more thorough discussion on this issue see Cummings and Mickenberg, 1972).

The two strong influences in New France at the time were Roman
Catholicism, and mercantilism which was at its height. Rather than treat
the Indians as "distinct and inferior," the French policy was to make them
one with their own people, at least in Canada. This "ideology" is very clear
in the correspondence between Colbert and Talon.[4]

Colbert, writing to Talon, April 6, 1666, said:

> In order to strengthen the Colony in the manner you propose, by
> bringing the isolated settlements into parishes, it appears to me with-
> out waiting to depend on the new colonists who may be sent from
> France, nothing would contribute more to it than to endeavor to civil-
> ize the Algonquins, the Hurons and other Indians who have embraced
> Christianity, and to induce them to come and settle in common with
> the French, to live with them and raise their children according to
> our manners and customs.

In his reply, some seven months later, Talon told Colbert that he had
endeavored to put his suggestions into practical operation under police regulations.

In another letter dated April 9, 1667, Colbert wrote to Talon:

[3]Because the seigneur system of agriculture was used, the French always remained
near major waterways and did not intrude into the interior of New France.

[4]Two additional factors which contributed to the "good" relations between the
French and Indians were: (*i*) the "military" alliance of the Huron, Algonquin and
French; (*ii*) the fact that the area where the French settled was occupied by the Algonquin Indians who were "primitive migratory hunters" (Jenness, 1967) and had no
real tribal organization (having been in the area only 70 years) (Cummings, 1972).

Recommendation to mold the Indians, settled near us, after our manners and language.

I confess that I agreed with you that very little regard has been paid, up to the present time, in New France, to the police and civilization of the Algonquins and Hurons (who were a long time ago subjected to the King's domination) through our neglect to detach them from their savage customs and to obligate them to adopt ours, especially to become acquainted with our language. On the countrary, to carry on some traffic with them, our French have been necessitated to attract those people, especially such as have embraced Christiantiy, to the vicinity of our settlements, if possible to mingle there with them, in order that through course of time, having only but one law and one master, they might likewise constitute only one people and one race.

That this was the policy favored by the king is expressly stated by Du Chesneau in his letter to de Signelay, November 10, 1679:

I communicated to the Religious communities, both male and female, and even to private persons, the King's and your intentions regarding the Frenchification of the Indians. They all promised me to use their best efforts to execute them, and I hope to let you have some news thereof next year. I shall begin by setting the example, and will take some young Indians to have them instructed.

In another letter from Duchesneau to de Signelay dated November 13, 1681, he wrote:

Amidst all the plans presented to me to attract the Indians among us and to accustom them to our manners, that from which most success may be anticipated, without fearing the inconveniences common to all the others, is to establish villages of those people in our midst.

Thomas, commenting on this letter by Duchesneau, says:

That the same policy was in vogue as late as 1704 is shown by the fact that at this time the Abnaki was taken under French protection and placed, as the records say, "in the center of the colony." (*1896: 544*)

One can then see why the French were able to maintain rather amiable relationships with natives for quite some time.

For the English, however, the relationship was quite different, and mostly of a negative character. But, it should be pointed out that there were differences between the official English government policy and the methods and policies of the individual settlements. It should also be noted that different "structural" variables were in operation when the English made a serious bid to control New France. First, mercantilism as an economic theory had been discarded, the importance of the fur trade was dwindling, and colonization in the true sense was now important. In addition, the religious idelogy of the British had a very different basis to that of the French. Manifest destiny and the Hamlite rationalization[5]pervaded the British secular way of life, exemplified in the Protestant ethic that hard work and no play would bring salvation.

A review of the documents relevant to the initial contact period between the English and the Indians reveals that the native people were completely overlooked and ignored. Little control was exerted over the British settlers as their westward expansion began. For example, the Indians were not mentioned in discussions when land was given to companies.

> For example, the letters patent of James I to Sir Thomas Gage and others for 'two several colonies,' dated April 10, 1606, although granting away two vast areas of territory greater than England, inhabited by thousands of Indians, a fact of which the King had knowledge both officially and unofficially, do not contain therein the slightest allusion to them. (*Thomas, 1896:550*)

Later charters, however, recognized the existence of natives but the recognition reflected the basic racist ideology. In the charters of Charles I, this statement is typical of several:

> ... to collect troops and wage wars on the 'barbarians,' and to pursue them even beyond the limits of their province and if God shall grant it, to vanquish and captivate them; and the captive put to death. ...

Until 1755, the English followed a policy of expediency. At first they chose to ignore the Indians, but when this was no longer feasible (because of westward expansion), they chose to isolate them (through the reserve system) or to annihilate them (as in the case of the Beothuk Indians of Newfoundland). In 1755, the "Indian agents" (today referred to as superintendents) were appointed and the "ward" policy of Canada toward the native people was formally established. It is important to note that the Indian agents initially placed in control of the reserves were always military men.

In 1830, the federal government was questioning the value of the Indian. Invasion from the south by the US was no longer an immediate and direct threat (although fear of US invasion did continue all through the nineteenth century) and there were no other potential attackers. As a result, there was no likelihood of Indians being needed for support in a battle. The Indian had lost his value to the white man. Thus by 1830, Indian Affairs ceased being a branch of the military and became part of the public service (Surtees, 1969). With this change the British adopted a humanitarian attitude to the Indian.

In terms of Canadian policy after confederation, the first Indian Act was passed in 1876 and was first revised in 1880. Some minor alterations

[5]Manifest destiny, though it varied considerably, was the belief that "whites" should control the world, or at least large parts of it. The Hamlite rationalization was the belief (taken from the Bible) that Ham was cursed by God, turned into a non-white person, "and he and his descendants should remain cursed and be subservient to whites from then on!" Indians were obviously then, descendants of Ham.

were also made in 1884 and 1885, and there was a "major" revision in 1951 (which left the act essentially in its present form). Interestingly enough, there is a remarkable similarity between the 1880 version of the act and the present one, indicating that the IAB has not undergone any major ideological shifts in the past hundred years of dealing with the Indians.

The policy toward Indians historically differed in administration between east and west. In Ontario and Quebec, until 1860, the Imperial Government handled all the affairs and expenses of native Canadians. However, at that time, a Crown Lands Department was established and a commissioner appointed. He assumed the role of chief superintendent of Indian Affairs. In other areas of Canada, the Indian Affairs office was administered by the various provincial or colonial governments.

Included in the BNA Act of 1867 was a special provision allowing for the administration of Indian Affairs to come under the control of the Government of Canada. Initially Indian Affairs was the responsibility of the Department of the Secretary of State, but in 1873 it was transferred to the Department of Interior. In 1880 a separate Department of Indian Affairs was formed but in 1936 it fell under the jurisdiction of the Department of Mines and Resources. Then in 1950, it was once again shifted to become part of the Department of Citizenship and Immigration. From 1953 to 1966 it was handled by the Northern Affairs and National Resources Department. Since 1966 this has been called the Department of Indian Affairs and Northern Development. Hence the administration of Indian Affairs has flitted from one department to another, with the result that it has been able to develop little continuity.

The process of establishing formal treaties with native people began with the Douglas Treaty in BC in 1850. This was considered a Province of Canada Treaty. In the same year the Robinson Superior and Huron treaties were signed. The last were made with the Mississauga Indians of Rice Lake, Mud Lake, Scugog Lake and Alderville—just north of Lake Ontario—in 1923. This was a post-confederation treaty. No treaties were ever made with the Inuit except at the Moravian mission in Labrador in 1769. The map (Figure 1) shows the areas Indians surrendered for each treaty.

All the treaties showed several similarities which can be grouped in four categories,

● *Indian Promises*—These were promises made to the British by the Indians. They ranged from "maintaining peace" to "not to molest persons or property."

● *Government Obligations*—These ranged from "the setting up of Reserves" to "commissions to take census."

● *Annuities*—These were given to members of the band which agreed to the treaty. They ranged from $3 per person per year to triennial suits of clothes to each headman.

● *Treaty Presents*—These were gifts to members of the band who signed the treaty. They ranged from medals and flags to miscellaneous hunting and fishing equipment.

However, the privileges and goods offered to the Indians decreased substantially from the Robinson Superior Treaty (1850) to Treaty 11

(1921). For example, in Treaty 11, no land concessions (reserves) were made. In addition, the obligations of the federal government correspondingly decreased in the later treaties. The cuts were in the form of smaller allotments per Indian family and smaller annuities.

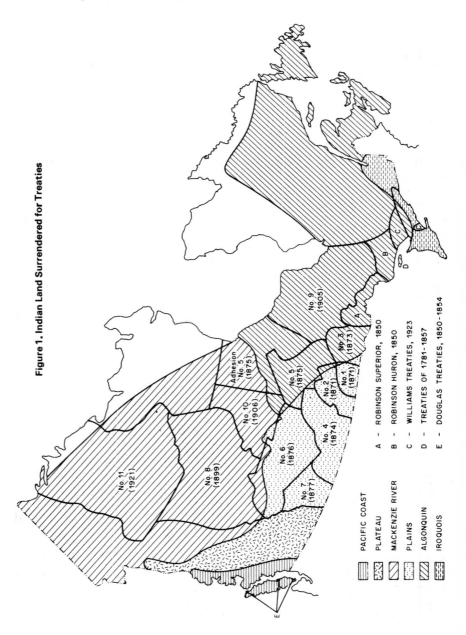

Figure 1. Indian Land Surrendered for Treaties

Table 2. Reserve Land Registry

	No. of bands	No. of reserves and/or settlements	Approx. acreage	No. of reserves with completed registers	No. of confirmed registers	Acreage under registration
PEI	1	4	1,646	3	1	1,400
Nova Scotia	12	38	25,552	37	1	68
New Brunswick	15	22	37,579	22	–	–
Quebec	41	39	188,207	39	–	–
Ontario	111	171	1,541,288	168	3	22,324
Manitoba	61	103	541,550	102	1	13,350
Saskatchewan	68	124	1,256,495	124	–	–
Alberta	42	96	1,607,478	95	1	14,720
BC	196	1,629	843,161	1,592	37	3,903
Yukon	16	26	4,877	–	–	–
NWT	13	29	2,153	–	–	–
Total	576	2,281	6,049,986	2,182	44	55,765

   The land concessions ranged from 16,700 square miles in the Robinson Superior Treaty to 372,000 square miles in Treaty 11. Each of the treaties was made with one or several bands—a group of Indians who share a common interest in land and money and have historical connection *as defined by the Indian administration.*[6] At present over 100,000 natives live on reserves and they belong to 550 different bands, the largest being the Six Nations (near Brantford, Ontario) with a population of 8,200.[7] There are some 2,241 reserves in Canada, although this number is also controversial. Reserves can vary in size and there is no minimum, though 160 acres per person is the maximum. For example, some reserves in BC cover only a few acres. The largest reserve is 500 square miles. In Eastern Canada there is generally one reserve to a band while in the West, one band may hold several reserves. BC has over 1,600 reserves, but less than 200 bands. Table 2 shows the number of bands, reserves and approximate acreage by province.

   Almost half of the entire treaty or registered Indian population live in Ontario and BC. A total of a little over 6 million acres are now legally defined as reserves.[8] This means there are about 30 acres per capita, or 100 acres per family (Allan, 1943).

   What is the membership of each of the four groups previously defined? Unfortunately, the numbers vary with different books (as will be seen by comparing tables in this text). Estimates of the total Registered Indian population varies from 220,000 to 260,000. An additional 200,000 to 250,000 are classed as non-registered Indians. Estimates of the number of Metis range from 60,000 to 600,000. According to briefs submitted by the Metis Association, 40,000 reside in Alberta, 20,000 in Manitoba and 30,000 in Saskatchewan. The remainder are spread throughout the remaining provinces, with Quebec having the largest proportion.

   Two further criteria that can be used to characterize Indians are language and cultural life styles. Ten traditional linguistic groups have been delineated: Algonquin, Iroquois, Sioux, Athabasca, Kootenay, Saliash, Wakash, Tsimish, Haida, and Tlingt. Six major cultural areas have also been established: Algonquin, Iroquois, Plains, Plateaus, Pacific Coast and MacKenzie River. There is, of course, a considerable overlap between the two categories. However, with time, the white man has systematically ob-

---

[6] A band is a political label applied to natives by the dominant group. It may, or may not, cut across traditional cultural differences. It is important to realize that the minister can "create" and "destroy" bands. Thus, the number of bands in existence will vary from year to year. When this politically convenient label was attached to various Indian tribes, there was very little concern about its impact on Indian culture. For example, some Indian tribes were matrilineal (tracing descent through the mother's side), while others were patrilineal. When various bands were established, both matrilineal and patrilineal tribes were considered as a single band and treated as patrilineal. This produced serious social disorganization within the cultures of the tribes.

[7] Each band is administered by an agency. At present there are 87 agencies across Canada. Sometimes one agency handles only one band, such as the Caughnawaga, but agencies can handle more than one band. The New Westminister agency handles 32.

[8] Originally nearly 7 million acres of land was defined as reserves, but through federal expropriation, the total acreage is continually decreasing.

literated some of the native cultural and linguistic distinctions. Forced migration of some groups with a distinct language from one area to another caused cultural and linguistic mixing. For example, the Ojibway were originally from southeast Quebec and eastern Ontario. By 1750 they had moved into an area west of the Great Lakes and by 1805 were established in Saskatchewan. Other groups such as the Assiniboine and Chipewyan have split, with one group moving north, the other south.

SOCIAL AND DEMOGRAPHIC CHARACTERISTICS

Caution should be used when interpreting the data in this chapter. First, much of it comes from one source—the IAB. Hence, it is liable to represent a vested interest. Second, and perhaps more important, is the question: "Who is an Indian?" As already pointed out, labelling a person Indian or non-Indian can be problematic. Thus, as the material is from many sources whose definition of an Indian may differ, the tables will not always correspond perfectly. This problem of interpretation is most acute when attempting to ascertain if "short term trends" are occurring (or reversal of trends). The trends may reflect a change in the definition or at other times, simply the inclusion of a geographical area which had not previously been included, *e.g.*, the Yukon and NWT. For example, looking at Table 1, one notices that with time the Indian population vacillates tremendously. This varied growth and decline is due largely to the different definitions that were attached to the label "Indian." If one included non-status Indians as well as Metis in Table 3, the number of Indians would increase by well over 5 per cent.

Table 3. Canadian Native Population, 1881–1970

	Population	% Of total population
1881	108,547	2.5
1901	127,941	2.4
1911	105,611	1.5
1921	113,724	1.3
1931	128,890	1.2
1941	125,521	1.1
1951	165,607	1.2
1961	220,161	1.2
1970	250,781	1.3

Source: Statistics Canada, 1961 Census, series 1.2–5 — Population. Reproduced by permission of Information Canada

Apart from the problems discussed above, Table 3 shows that there appears to have been a steady increase in the absolute number of Indians since early this century. Until 1960 the percentage of Indians relative to the total Canadian population was decreasing significantly. Since 1960, however, the relative percentage has been increasingly slightly. Beginning in the late 1950s the natural increase rate for Indians has hovered around 3 per cent and by 1968 the rate of increase had risen to over 3.4 per cent per year. However, by 1970, the rate of increase had dropped again to 2.8 per cent, compared to the 1.5 per cent rate of increase in the general Canadian population.

Table 4 alludes to specific changes in population since 1954. In addition the figures show the rate of increase for specific years. The data reveal that since 1954, the total native population has nearly doubled, a statistic which contrasts with those for most other ethnic groups. The fast rate of increase reflects changes in several factors: the definition of an Indian, lower mortality rates, higher fertility rates and longer life span.

Thus, while the relative percentage of Indians in Canada decreased until 1950 and then remained stable, the figures obscure the fast increase taking place in absolute numbers. As the increase in the general Canadian

Figure 2. Indian Population in Canada

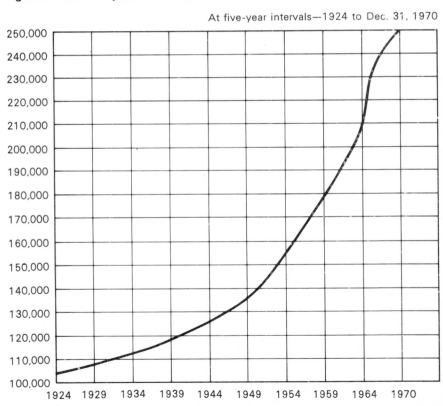

At five-year intervals—1924 to Dec. 31, 1970

Source : Department of Indian Affairs and Northern Development, *Annual Report*, 1969–70, p. 69.

Table 4. Indian Population Changes, 1954–69

	Population						% Of total population 1967	% Rate of change 1965–67	% Rate of change 1967–69	% Of non-resident population 1967	Estimated 1978 population
	1954	1959	1965	1967	1968	1969					
PEI	272	341	373	399	418	435	0.4	7.0	4.1	–	547
Nova Scotia	3,002	3,561	4,040	4,275	4,411	4,512	0.6	5.8	2.3	28	5,439
New Brunswick	2,629	3,183	3,783	3,984	4,156	4,274	0.6	6.6	2.8	22	5,620
Quebec	17,574	20,453	20,246	22,300	26,302	27,050	0.4	10.1	2.9	16	34,253
Ontario	37,255	42,668	49,391	52,832	52,981	54,052	0.7	7.0	2.0	34	67,237
Manitoba	19,684	23,658	28,979	31,095	33,358	34,342	3.4	7.3	3.1	18	49,603
Sask.	18,750	23,280	30,012	31,189	33,852	35,062	3.4	3.9	3.6	15	51,559
Alberta	15,715	19,287	23,403	26,591	27,322	28,443	1.8	13.6	4.1	19	43,566
BC	31,086	36,229	40,940	42,780	46,046	47,138	2.3	4.5	2.4	27	5,968
Yukon	1,568	1,868	3,216	2,711	2,562	2,484	14.8	-15.7	-3.0	24	3,517
NWT	4,023	4,598	5,569	5,911	6,082	6,271	23.4	1.4	3.1	–	8,218
	151,558	179,126	189,952	224,067	237,490	244,063	1.7	6.8	2.8	23	275,527

Source:　Background documentation for AIC Conference on Indians at Jasper, Alberta, October, 1968.

population begins to level off, Indians will again make up an increasingly larger proportion of the population. The data also reveal that Indians make up sizeable percentages of the general population of the Prairie provinces, BC and the North.

The tables show that about a quarter of the Indians in Canada today reside in Ontario, 20 per cent in BC and 14 per cent each in Manitoba and Saskatchewan, while Alberta and Quebec each have 11 per cent. The remainder of Indians are equally spread over the other provinces and territories. The increase in Indian population since 1954 has been highest for Alberta, with a 13.6 per cent increase between 1965 and 1967, and a 4.1 per cent increase in 1968–69. However, in Yukon Territory there has been a decrease in the growth of the native population. The reason for this seems to be that many Indians migrate to adjacent provinces. All other provinces seem to show the approximate 3 per cent increase previously mentioned.

Table 4 also presents information on the percentage of Indian population considered "non-resident" in 1967. It shows that the range is quite wide, with 34 per cent of Ontario Indians not living on the reserve compared to 15 per cent of those in Saskatchewan. On the average it shows that fewer than a quarter of the Indian population were considered non-resident in 1967. To demonstrate the extreme changes in the past four years, Walsh (1971) shows that nearly 30 per cent of Indians are now considered non-resident. While the increase in non-residents is dramatic, it still shows that over 70 per cent of the Indian population wish to remain on the reserve. This strongly suggests that the reserve still provides security and maintains its "lure" for Indian people. The reserve still remains home for most Indians. It is where they have grown up, where their friends and family are and where, if things get tough, they can retreat to if necessary. These factors, combined with a strong white prejudicial attitude toward them, lend a strong internal pull and external push for most of them to remain on the reserve. As projected in Table 4, by the end of the decade, nearly 300,000 Indians will be legally defined as non-resident.

Even if the number of Indians who leave the reserve increases, the absolute population of those who remain will show a sizeable increase.[9] This of course is not what the existing political dominant group wants. Reserves are potential "hot beds" for political and social discontent. If the Indians become economically developed they could pose a competitive threat to some Canadian corporate structures. An example of this has already happened in BC, where a group of Indians built high rise apartments on their reserve next to Vancouver. They were opposed by local businessmen. Politically, natives could, and to some extent have already, become a formidable adversary. The reserve—a closed, spatial area—could precipitate increasing Indian identity, augmented by an ease of communications between natives and a lessening in communication with outsiders.

When communication takes place only within a group, contrast con-

---

[9]These people— nearly 300,000 — will be asked to remain on the six million acres now designated as reserve land.

ceptions of other groups will emerge. Thus, one's own group will begin to be seen as "good" while the other group will be seen as "bad." If no outside communication is allowed (nor engaged in), internal communications are sanctioned. That is, members are not allowed to say anything "bad" about their own group nor "good" about the other group. Should an Indian suggest that perhaps the federal government's white paper might contain some good and/or legitimate points, he would become suspect of complicity or of being duped. The result is that information which might change the stereotypic and negative evaluation of the "other" group cannot be processed. To point out that one's own group is not faultless is to invite severe negative sanctions. These reserves could then become a "center" for radical-militant activities—clearly another reason why the government would like to see them abolished.

Tables 5 and 6 show the crude birth and mortality rates for natives. Table 6 shows that the birth rate for natives is nearly twice as high as the overall Canadian rate, and that it increased until 1965. If we compare the fertility rates of Indian women, we find a clear regional disparity. Eastern Indian women are quite similar in their fertility rates to their white counterparts whereas Prairie Indian women have fertility rates more than twice as high as women in Western Canada generally. Overall in 1960 the crude birth rate per thousand was 41.9, and by 1965 it had increased to 43.5. It has since however, slowly decreased so that in 1969, the birth rate was similar to the 1960 level. This rate is extraordinarily high compared to the birth rate for the overall Canadian population (which peaked in 1963 at 25.3 per thousand and is currently 17.6. Regional differences are important, however. Indians in the eastern provinces have birth rates not unlike the overall provincial rates. Their infant mortality as well as average crude death rates are also quite similar to the overall provincial data. Indians on the central plains, however, are characterized by extremely high birth rates and high mortality rates. For example, one band in northern Saskatchewan alone contributes 10 per cent of all Indian births in Canada.

Table 5. Indian Crude Birth Rates

	No. of Births	Births/1000
1911	2,647	25.5
1921	2,853	26.9
1955	6,038	39.2
1960	7,751	41.9
1965	8,710	43.5
1969	7,950	41.0

Source: Department of Indian Affairs and Northern Development, *Annual Report*, 1970–71. Reproduced by permission of Information Canada.

Table 6. Trend in Indian Mortality, 1960–64

	Males			Females			Both sexes		
	Estimated mid-year population	Deaths reported	Crude death rate per 1,000 population	Estimated mid-year population	Deaths reported	Crude death rate per 1,000 population	Estimated mid-year population	Deaths reported	Crude death rate per 1,000 population
1960	95,061	1,127	11.86	90,108	863	9.58	185,169	1,990	10.75
1961	96,718	1,094	11.31	91,721	792	8.63	188,439	1,886	10.01
1962	100,038	1,097	10.97	95,061	934	9.83	195,099	2,031	10.41
1963	103,394	1,155	11.17	98,192	887	9.03	201,586	2,042	10.12
1964	106,747	1,105	10.35	101,456	825	8.13	208,203	1,930	9.27

Trend in Infant Mortality 1960–64

	Males			Females			Both sexes		
	Live births registered	Deaths under 1 year of age	Infant mortality rate per 1,000 live births	Live births registered	Deaths under 1 year of age	Infant mortality rate per 1,000 live births	Live births registered	Deaths under 1 year of age	Infant mortality rate per 1,000 live births
1960	3,832	356	92.90	3,690	261	70.73	7,522	617	82.03
1961	3,978	334	83.96	3,829	262	68.43	7,807	596	76.34
1962	3,926	314	79.98	3,928	274	69.75	7,854	588	74.87
1963	4,044	323	79.87	4,027	245	60.84	8,071	568	70.37
1964	4,229	298	70.46	4,021	210	52.23	8,250	508	61.58

Source: Department of Indian Affairs and Northern Development, Annual Report, 1970–71. Reproduced by permission of Information Canada.

Table 6 specifically addresses the mortality rates for Canadian Indians during the period 1960–64. First, the overall scene depicted in Table 6 reveals that the mortality rate for Indians is much higher than for whites. In 1955 the infant mortality rate was 103 per 1,000 live births while for whites it was 31. By 1960 the rate had decreased to 79 for Indians and 27 per thousand for whites. Again, while proportionately there has been a great decrease in Indian infant mortality, it still remains absolutely quite high. In 1968 the mortality rate again decreased to 62 per 1,000 for Indians, but the figure should be viewed in perspective with the white infant mortality rate of 20.1 per thousand. Thus, when we compare the mortality rates for children in their first year, we find that the rate for Indians is nearly three times that for the white population. If we compare the mortality rates for babies in the 0–2 year old category, we find that the Indian mortality rate is eight times that of the white population.

Looking at the overall trend in Indian mortality, we find that in 1960 the crude death rate per thousand was about 11 and that it only decreased to 9.3 four years later. Again, region variations are noticeable. While Indians in BC have average Indian birth and fertility rates, they have the highest infant mortality rates in Canada. The death rates for adult Indians there also is second highest in Canada—generally due to accidents. This is much higher than the national death rate per thousand for all Canadians in 1965 of 7.6. By 1968 it was 7.1. Using this data, one is able to estimate the average life span for these groups. The expected average life span of an Indian in 1970 was 34 years (33.67 for males, 36.82 for females) while for the average white, the expected life span was nearly 72 (69.04 for males, 75.60 for females). However, if an Indian passes the first two years of life, the expected life span for males and females rises to 50 and 53 years respectively. Respiratory diseases and accidents are the chief causes of death for adult Indians, accounting for nearly half of all Indian deaths in the past five years. However, the harsh fact still remains that Indians will on average live nearly 40 years less than their white counterparts and even if they survive their first two years, they will still on average live 20 years less. This is a sad commentary on the "just society" promised to Canadians in the twentieth century.

What are the residential patterns of Canadian Indians? As pointed out previously, the recent trend indicates that increasingly more Indians are moving to urban areas. Of those who have moved to urban areas, over half are relocating in large metropolitan areas of more than 100,000. Two explanations can be given for the migration to larger areas. First, unskilled employment is easier to obtain in large metropolitan areas than in small towns and second, large "Indian ghettos" are being built up in various urban centers such as Winnipeg, Toronto, and Edmonton. Once a sizeable population of an ethnic group resides in an area, it becomes easier for other members of that group to move to that area. Table 7 also shows the phenomenal increase in the number of Indians migrating to the large urban areas. However, more will be said of this in the chapter on urbanization.

Indians still maintain a high degree of adherence to their mother tongue. However, this too is slowly being eroded by English. In 1941,

Table 7. Indian Population by Selected Cities

	Indians			Total Population
	1951	*1961*	*1970*	*1961*
Calgary	62	335	5,000	249,641
Edmonton	116	995	10,000	281,027
Montreal	296	507	3,000	1,191,062
Ottawa	–	180	930	268,206
Quebec City	29	58	–	171,979
Regina	116	539	1,640	160,247
Toronto	–	1,196	24,000	672,407
Vancouver	239	530	3,820	561,950
Winnipeg	210	1,082	20,000	265,429

Source: Statistics Canada, 1961 Census, series 1.2—Population Bulletin 1.2–5, Table 38. Reproduced by permission of Information Canada.
Note: 1970 figures are estimates based on local sources.

fewer than 10 per cent claimed English as their mother tongue. The figure reached 15 per cent in 1951 and by 1961 well over a quarter of the Indian population acknowledged English as their mother tongue. Fewer than 2 per cent claimed French as their mother tongue. For those who claimed English as their mother tongue, fewer than 5 per cent were bilingual and for the remaining 70 per cent who claimed an Indian dialect as their mother tongue, more than 40 per cent were "somewhat" bilingual. This of course suggests that the "Indian" mother tongue is dying fairly rapidly.[10] But the local Indian dialect is being revived in many areas and many Indians are still bilingual. They have learned (just as other immigrants) that to integrate into the larger society, they must speak English. Thus, to a certain extent, the decreasing number of people with local Indian dialect as their mother tongue reflects the increasing number moving to the city. However, this is not to suggest that other factors such as the educational process have not contributed to the rise in the number speaking English (as the only language and/or as a second tongue). Virtually all formal education lessons are given to Indians in English at present. Because of the high Indian drop-out rate at elementary levels, the impact on language has been reduced. However, as education—in English—becomes a tool used more and more by Indians, their dialects will disappear even more rapidly.

Examination of the religious affiliations of natives shows the conservative influence they have had on the Indians' view of reality. Just as French Canada has been historically influenced by Roman Catholicism, so have the native people. Present statistics indicate that over half (56 per cent) of the Indians of Canada are Catholics. This, of course, reflects the extent of

[10]Statistics Canada defines "mother tongue" as the language a person first learns in childhood and still understands.

Table 8. Indian Population by Age and Sex, December 31, 1964

	0–5		6–15		16–20		21–64	
	Males	Females	Males	Females	Males	Females	Males	Females
PEI	23	40	47	43	15	15	90	83
Nova Scotia	341	324	522	522	220	198	872	756
New Brunswick	354	368	541	492	182	188	764	662
Quebec	2,155	2,149	2,807	2,777	1,094	1,114	5,323	4,887
Ontario	4,485	4,367	6,245	6,068	2,455	2,392	10,233	9,226
Manitoba	3,531	3,481	3,930	3,899	1,439	1,391	5,374	4,620
Saskatchewan	3,754	3,699	4,053	4,040	1,318	1,315	5,058	4,630
Alberta	2,997	2,934	3,290	3,322	1,144	1,148	4,120	3,760
BC	4,743	4,772	5,791	5,720	2,144	2,094	8,089	7,054
Yukon	286	253	259	284	111	110	426	367
NWT	546	587	649	662	261	235	1,120	974
Canada	23,215	22,974	28,134	27,829	10,383	10,200	41,469	37,019

	65–69		70 and over		Not stated		All ages	
	Males	Females	Males	Females	Males	Females	Males	Females
PEI	3	2	2	4	3	6	183	193
Nova Scotia	26	21	56	47	35	54	2,072	1,922
New Brunswick	30	14	45	37	15	25	1,931	1,786
Quebec	209	208	428	375	42	141	12,058	11,651
Ontario	475	360	809	749	186	415	24,888	23,577
Manitoba	230	148	370	341	12	67	14,886	13,947
Saskatchewan	186	162	364	280	6	49	14,739	14,175
Alberta	166	112	309	229	36	75	12,062	11,580
BC	399	248	552	471	7	57	21,725	20,416
Yukon	14	10	40	53	–	2	1,136	1,079
NWT	57	53	102	100	14	23	2,749	2,634
Canada	1,795	1,338	3,077	2,686	356	914	108,429	102,960

Source: Statistics Canada, 1961 Census, series 1.3—Bulletin 1.3–2, Table 82. Reproduced by permission of Information Canada.

the Jesuit and Oblate mission work among Indians. The second largest Indian religious group (coincidently quite close to Roman Catholic ideology) is the Anglican (25 per cent). Twelve per cent belong to the United Church of Canada. Together, members of these three religious groups comprise 93 per cent of the total Indian population. The remaining 7 per cent are evenly distributed between the other Christian churches in Canada. Since the above information has been collected by Statistics Canada, it presents a picture of official statistics. However, an important question not answered by the figures is whether the Indians have accepted the beliefs of the religious groups. Generally they have not. But religious groups have still made a definite impact on native culture and thought.

Table 8 shows the age distribution of native people relative to the total Canadian population. It is interesting to note that almost half of the native population are younger than 15. Two-thirds of the Indian population are younger than 25. Only about one-third of the overall population are in the age range of 0–15. Clearly, there is a growing concentration of young Indians in the overall native population. The percentage of Indians relative to the total Canadian population in the 15–44 age category is quite similar—37 per cent and 41 per cent respectively. However, if we compare the percentages in the 45–64 category we find fewer than 10 per cent of Indians but nearly 20 per cent of the overall population included in this group. The 65 and older group displays further similarities, with 5 per cent of the Indian population represented, and 8 per cent of the whites. What do these figures reflect? First, that there is a "stable" Indian population growth rate, meaning continued high growth. Second, that as the death rate decreases (unless birth rates decrease), more and more Indians will be in the age category 15–40, which is the prime employment category. Thus, as more and more Indians are concentrated in this age category, the demand for jobs will increase.

Figures on the marital status of natives do not support the stereotype that almost all Indian families are "broken." The data in Table 9 shows that the occurrence of broken homes among Indians is less frequent than among the overall white population—6.7 per cent compared to 7 per cent respectively.

There are three alternative explanations: (i) The claim that Indian families have higher "broken marriages" than other ethnic groups is just a myth. (ii) Native people are poor. Since divorces involve court costs, alimony, etc., they do not go through the formal processes but rather "separate" or desert. (iii) Many women, even though they live with a man and bear several children, never get married officially. This means they may have common law marriages or in some cases they may be married according to Indian laws. Since 1957, the federal government has refused to acknowledge Indian marriages as legal. Indians have learned that unmarried women with children receive a fairly substantial income through the "baby bonus" scheme. For example, an unmarried Indian woman with three children would receive about three times as much money in social welfare than a married (yet separated) Indian woman with three children. In addition, the unmarried Indian woman would be eligible for several "educational and vocational training programs" not available to the married woman.

Table 9. Marital Status of Indians and Total Population

	Indians			
	Single	Married	Widowed and divorced	
15–19	19,702	1,987	17	
20–24	9,219	8,053	58	
25–34	6,354	19,837	353	
35–44	2,214	15,589	720	
45–54	1,086	11,612	1,203	
55–64	613	7,398	1,757	
65+	456	5,331	3,737	
	39,644	69,807	7,845	117,296
	33.3%	60%	6.7%	100%
	All Canada			
	Single	Married	Widowed and divorced	
15–19	1,361,734	70,395	430	
20–24	649,440	531,833	2,373	
25–34	451,417	2,101,900	18,790	
35–45	251,747	2,087,405	50,733	
45–54	191,438	1,585,916	101,150	
55–64	140,054	980,370	169,046	
65+	145,376	757,485	488,293	
	3,191,206	8,115,304	830,815	12,137,325
	26%	67%	7%	100%

Source: Statistics Canada, Marital Status by Ethnic Groups, Bulletin 1.3–7, Table 106, 1961. Reproduced by permission of Information Canada.

Using a sociological interpretation coupled with other relevant research, the second and third alternatives seem the more plausible. Thus, we would conclude that even though "officially" the divorce rate of natives is similar to that of the total population, it should not be used as an indicator of family stability. Some anthropologists have legitimately argued that the white standards of family stability should be used only with whites (and white North American families), not with other cultures. To project one's definition of what constitutes a stable marriage or family on to another culture simply demonstrates ignorance and inability to escape ethnocentric biases.

The above analysis is somewhat reflected when viewing the marriage figures. About 60 per cent of the total native population are technically married and 67 per cent of the overall population of Canada are married. Corresponding differences are readily noticeable for the "single" category. The preceding analysis has further application in regard to the illegitimacy rate. In 1965, 32 per cent of all Indian children were illegitimate, markedly in excess of the national rate.

Considering the above data, the picture of Canadian Indians is rather dismal. We have seen that the population is increasing at very high rates, yet below what we would expect by just viewing the crude birth rates. This seemingly contradictory picture is explained by the phenomenally high death rates. As a result of the high birth rate, we find that two-thirds of the Indian population are younger than 25. As these young people migrate to the city (or remain on the reserves), they will be seeking a firm position in the occupational and social structure within Canadian society. To date we know that they have not found such a niche.

What will be the consequences? Traditionally the defeated Indian has returned to—or remained on—the reserve. He has internalized his defeat and has attempted to isolate himself further from white society. To admit defeat and acknowledge that one has been discriminated against leaves a lasting impression on one's self identity. In the case of the Indian, bitterness has turned to resentment but the resentment has been turned inward. Tomorrow the turning process may be reversed. The young Indian may no longer be willing to castigate himself but may strike out against a real or perceived agent. The increased amount of activity within native organizations may provide a clue to what we can soon expect.

SOCIO-ECONOMIC STATUS

We will choose three traditional measures of socio-economic status (SES)—income, occupation, and education—to evaluate the current status of natives in comparison to other groups in Canada.

Income

Hawthorn *et al.*, (1966) show that the "per capita income per year" for natives is about $300, and about $1,400 for Euro-Canadians. There is a similar discrepancy between the two groups in yearly earnings per worker. For Indians the figure is $1,361; for Euro-Canadians it is $4,000. Table 10 shows the annual income for a sample of bands across Canada.

If one could view the range of per capita annual income of various bands, they would be seen to vary from well over $4,000 to a low of $55. This means, with few exceptions, that as the per capita income decreases, the percentage of people receiving welfare increases. However, the amount of welfare actually provided to Indians depends on each Indian superintendent's attitude, *i.e.*, if he takes a liberal view more welfare will be granted. Thus, the actual amount earned by each Indian family is not accurately reflected in Table 10.

Using the standard set by the federal government as a measure of poverty ($3,500), the above table shows that over 80 per cent of the native people could be considered living in poverty.

Table 10. Band Ranking by Average Per Capita Real Income from Gainful
Employment

	Average annual earnings per worker ($)	Average monthly earnings per worker ($)
Skidegate	4,642	438
Caughnawaga	4,554	495
Walpole Island	2,048	332.5
Sheshaht, V.I.	4,400	411
Lorette	3,529	336
Squamish	3,427	428
Tyendinaga	3,818	459
Six Nations	2,660	308
Curve Lake	2,222	304
Mistassini	1,853	331
Masset	1,428	370
Dog Rib Rae	1,546	273
Port Simpson	2,729	395
Kamloops	2,037	214
Sarcee	1,354	202
Fort William	2,334	288
Williams Lake	1,708	228
Moose Factory	2,256	361
Fort Alexander	1,992	279
River Desert	836	—
St. Mary's	1,320	181
Attawapiskat	1,400	—
Pointe Bleue	1,800	290
Tobique	2,050	193
Pekangikum	779	124
Shubenacadie	809	201
Oak River, Man.	770	214
Rupert House	810	253
Cold Lake	1,840	—
Fort St. John	931	186
The Pas	1,283	194
James Smith	1,143	173
Peguis	480	104
Big Cove	734	105

Source: Hawthorn, H., et al., A Survey of Contemporary Indians of Canada,
Indian Affairs Branch, Vol. I, 1967. Reproduced by permission of Information Canada.

Figures derived from Housing Survey, Indian Affairs Branch, Ottawa, January
1965.

When the income level is broken down by province (Table 11) an even clearer picture emerges. It shows (*i*) that in only three provinces more than 20 per cent of the total native population make more than $3,000, and (*ii*) that nearly half of the natives earn less than $1,000.

Table 11. Income of Reserve Indian Families, 1967

	$1,000 or less (%)	$1,000 – 3,000 (%)	$3,000 or more (%)
PEI	64.4	31.2	4.2
Nova Scotia	65.5	26.4	8.1
New Brunswick	49.4	42.4	8.2
Quebec	47.5	32.2	20.3
Ontario	24.3	53.7	22.0
Manitoba	60.8	34.3	4.4
Saskatchewan	57.3	35.8	6.9
Alberta	33.2	50.3	16.5
BC	29.3	44.6	26.1
	40.5	43.0	16.5

Occupation

Table 12 shows the degree of "over-under" representation of natives in various occupational categories. To make the data more meaningful, a comparative ethnic group (British) has been included. First, however, let us look at the degree of over-under representation of natives in each category.

There is a substantial over-representation of natives in the "primary and unskilled" group. The data also show that from 1931 to 1961, the over-representation in this area has not decreased substantially.[11] An assessment of the degree of under-representation shows that natives are consistently under-represented in white collar occupations. From 1931 to 1961, there has even been an increase in under-representation.

The second group (British—the charter group), included to allow for comparisons, shows an opposite trend. The under-representation increases for "low prestige" jobs and decreases for those with "higher status." Similarly, the over-representation for occupations in the professional and financial category since 1931 increased from 1.6 per cent to 2 per cent. The table seems to substantiate that "the rich get richer and the poor get poorer."

[11]The data presented show the percentage points that each group is either over or under the labor force distinction. That is, if ethnicity was not a factor in placing people into various occupations, we should find similar proportions of ethnic groups in each occupational category as are in the total population. For instance, if natives make up 3 per cent of the total population, we should find similar percentage distributions in each occupational category. Thus, the per cent-over-under-representation should hover round zero.

The specific composition of Indians in the labor force shows that 20 per cent are classified as farmers or farm workers. An additional 36 per cent are evenly split between traditional activities (*e.g.* hunting and trapping) and production work. Fifteen per cent are loggers. The remaining 27 per cent have low status jobs except for the 3 per cent in managerial and professional activities. Their representation in this last category can be better viewed in relation to the British (12 per cent), Jews (40 per cent) and French (8 per cent).

Another indicator of a group's position in society (related to occupation) is duration of employment. Average duration of employment per year for natives is 4.8 months. Looking at the specific length of time Indians have been employed, Hawthorn *et al.*, (1966) show that about a quarter of the employable males worked less than two months. Two-thirds of the employable males worked less than six months while an additional 10 per cent were employed for six to nine months in a year. Only 28 per cent of the total employable native population were employed longer than nine

Table 12. Over-Under Representation of Male Labor Force

	British	Indian and Eskimo
1931		
Professional and financial	+1.6	−4.5
Clerical	+1.5	−3.7
Personal service	−.3	−3.1
Primary and unskilled	−4.6	+45.3
Agriculture	−3.0	−4.9
All others	+4.8	−29.1
1951		
Professional and financial	+1.6	−5.2
Clerical	+1.6	−5.2
Personal service	−.3	−.6
Primary and unskilled	−2.2	+47.0
Agriculture	−3.2	−7.8
All others	2.5	−28.2
1961		
Professional and financial	+2.0	−7.5
Clerical	+1.3	−5.9
Personal service	−.9	+1.3
Primary and unskilled	−2.3	+34.7
Agriculture	−1.5	+6.9
All others	+1.4	−29.5

Sources: Census of Canada, 1931, monograph 4, Table 67, and Vol. 7, Table 40; Census of Canada, 1951, Vol. 4, Table 12; and Census of Canada, 1961, Vol. 3.1–15, Table 21. Reproduced by permission of Information Canada.

months. For example, Buckley, Kew and Hawley (1963) found that of the 2,200 northern Saskatchewan Indians and Metis in the labor force, fewer than 200 had year-round jobs.

The above figures do not make a bright picture for Indians attempting to enter the work force. Natives are hired for short term, low pay jobs requiring minimum skills. So even if they worked full time, their income would still be low.

Many registered and non-registered Indians gave evidence to the 1970 Special Senate Committee on Poverty and information in the report will be used to discuss Indian employment further.

Table 13 shows the total Indian labor force and employment rates and compares them to the total Canadian labor force and employment. The Indian employment rate seems to be quite high in contradiction to the data in Table 14. However, a closer look at these tables shows the effect of discrimination and the reason for the discrepancy.

Table 13 shows that the total rate of unemployment for natives is 12.29 per cent and 3.9 per cent for the total Canadian population. This shows the Indian unemployment rate is over three times greater but another interpretation can be made with further analysis. The participation rate for natives is consistently 20 per cent lower than that for the total Canadian population. Thus Table 13 shows that even though one fifth of the native

Table 13. Indian and Canadian Labor Force and Employment (On and Off the Reserve, 1961)

	Rate of employment		Participation rate		Labor force*	
	Indian	Canadian	Indian	Canadian	Indian	Canadian
Newfoundland	95.8	91.4	22.2	42.7	72	113,771
PEI	96.0	97.4	19.3	51.3	25	34,339
Nova Scotia	83.6	95.7	24.2	49.7	415	238,750
New Brunswick	89.7	94.1	25.2	48.5	362	179,702
Quebec	79.7	95.5	30.5	52.4	3,259	1,178,710
Ontario	90.3	96.6	34.4	56.8	9,264	2,404,812
Manitoba	84.5	97.2	25.8	55.3	3,868	343,938
Saskatchewan	90.6	98.0	29.1	53.5	4,462	326,736
Alberta	91.5	97.2	32.6	56.9	4,746	491,487
BC	84.7	94.7	28.4	51.9	5,847	581,395
Yukon	74.6	94.9	34.0	66.9	418	6,257
NWT	95.0	97.8	30.9	54.2	911	7,463
Canada	87.7	96.1	30.3	54.0	33,649	5,907,360

Source: Department of Indian Affairs and Northern Development; Brief to Special Senate Committee on Poverty 1970, 14:170–71. Reproduced by permission of Information Canada.

*Number of people 15 and older employed or seeking employment during the *week before* enumeration.

Table 14. Indian Labor Force and Employment, by Residence, 1961

	On reserve			Off reserve		
	Labor force	Employment rate	Participation rate	Labor force	Employment rate	Participation rate
Newfoundland	–	–	–	72	95.8	22.3
PEI	22	95.4	17.2	3	100.0	–
Nova Scotia	296	81.1	20.9	119	89.9	40.2
New Brunswick	307	88.5	23.9	55	96.4	35.5
Quebec	3,152	80.3	31.3	107	63.6	17.2
Ontario	5,009	88.9	28.8	4,255	91.9	44.4
Manitoba	2,464	80.7	23.4	1,404	91.2	31.6
Saskatchewan	2,712	89.1	21.3	1,750	92.9	34.3
Alberta	2,673	90.1	31.0	2,073	92.3	34.8
BC	4,464	86.9	27.8	1,383	77.7	30.6
Yukon	27	77.7	38.6	391	74.7	33.7
NWT	–	–	–	911	95.1	30.9
Canada	21,126	86.3	27.9	12,523	88.4	35.7

Source: Department of Indian Affairs and Northern Development; Brief to Special Senate Committee on Poverty 1970, 14:172–73. Reproduced by permission of Information Canada.

population (which is theoretically eligible for employment) does not participate, of those who do, over 12 per cent will remain unemployed. Also, the validity of the criteria used to determine the active "labor" force is dubious. Finally, the time of year has an additional impact on the employment rate since primary and unskilled jobs are most affected by seasonal factors, especially by winter. However, even without these rather serious criticisms, the fact remains that native unemployment is three times higher than the rate for the total Canadian labor force.

Table 14 shows a breakdown of employment rates by residence for natives. The data reveal that the participation rate for natives off the reserve is not much higher than for those on the reserve—35.7 per cent to 27.9 per cent. However, the higher participation rate of reserve natives is not balanced by a corresponding increment in the employment rate. In fact the increase in employment is less than half of the participation increase. Clearly then, only about half of those who move off the reserve can expect to find employment.

The Indian employment rate is about the same for males and females.

Because Indians mostly have seasonal and/or part-time occupations, they have little job security. And even when they apply for seasonal jobs, the placement of Indians has always been low. La Rusic (1968) shows that highly skilled Indian men employed by mining exploration companies as line cutters and stakers never received the same high pay or working conditions as whites. Thus, the low income does not merely indicate that Indians engage only in seasonal jobs.

Education

It has become a cliché today to think of education in terms of "the only way to make it." Young people who do not show academic ability are usually looked on as "not having it." The cliché's validity is dubious but it does reflect the most pronounced Canadian cultural bias. Education is important because of its impact on life style and life chances. If it is so important for success it would seem likely that most people would use it as effectively as possible. And if in fact all Canadians did take this attitude, it would also reflect a basic egalatarianism. Our aim is to compare the education of natives with that of the general Canadian population.

The federal government does appear to have fulfilled its responsibility to the Indians in the area of finance for education (Frideres, 1972). Federal expenditure for Indian education was $13.5 million in 1956 and this had increased to $52 million by 1967. By 1970, well over $125 million was allocated for their education. However, less than 1 per cent of this money went directly to Indian communities for them to control. Most was spent on federal (white) civil servants in various administrative and bureaucratic positions or on capital grants to provincial and local governments to purchase "seats" in non-Indian schools. As a result, Indian people have had little control over how money for their education is spent. The above figures point out that while a huge increase in educational funding has taken place, this has not solved the problem of involving Indians in the educational process. While lack of control over spending is certainly a problem, a more crucial one lies in the teaching process itself. Therefore, any improvement in the situation would probably need to involve a review of the curriculum used by the Indian children in the provincial schools. The curriculum is regulated by provincial governments and is the same one used by "white-urban-middle class" students in other provincial schools (Waubageshig, 1970).

The general thesis presented in this chapter hinges on three related aspects of native education:

1. *Education of natives was initially handled by the military and until recently was left to religious leaders*, e.g. *missionaries*. For many years after Britain took control of Canada, Indian education was under the control of the military. While the actual power was vested in the government in England, the day to day activities were left to the military, until the colonial governments assumed the responsibility in 1830.

In 1824 it was agreed that a fund should be established for Indian education but this did not happen until 1848. However, as the IAB has pointed out:

> There was no widespread concern for the Indian people among the local residents and the new nation was too occupied with other matters. In a few instances where the population was sparse, the enrolment of Indian pupils was essential to the establishment of provincial schools and this did lead to limited acceptance of them in the common schools but as these areas became more heavily settled, the Indians became a less significant part of the population and were no longer needed or welcomed. *(1965:4)*

The federal government was reluctant to run these schools so it passed the responsibility to other agencies—mainly religious institutions.

2. *Education was viewed as the best way to segregate and subsequently acculturate native people.* The religious missionaries who began to "educate" the Indians brought with them foreign culture and values. Since it was generally felt at the time that Indians would live in isolation, the missionaries underemphasized the quality of the education they needed to provide and put too much emphasis on religion.

> Paying little attention to the multitude of linguistic and other cultural differences among the tribes, and the varied traditions of child rearing in preparation for adulthood in the tribal communities, the government entered the school business with a vigor that caused consternation among the Indians. The package deal that accompanied literacy included continuing efforts to 'civilize the natives' ... children were removed—some times forcibly—long distances from their homes, the use of Indian languages by children was forbidden under threat of corporal punishment, students were boarded out to white families during vacation times, and native religions were suppressed. *(Fuchs, 1970:55)*

3. *The education now provided for natives—as in the past—is irrelevant and consequently useless to them.*

The over-riding concern of all the schools was the provision of a religious
education; the creation of a 'religious feeling' in each (Indian) student.
(Kaegi, 1972: 12)

Let us begin by considering the educational process for Indians in a
historical context.

As already mentioned, before confederation Indian education was the
responsibility of the military. Then legislation was passed and the provincial and/or local governments assumed the duty.

Several legislatures had made provision for the attendance of Indians at
schools serving non-Indian children, including the payment to local authorities in both Upper and Lower Canada for the incorporation of Indian
reserves into established school districts or school sections and some provision had been made in the statutes for the financing of Indian education. *(Special Senate Hearing on Poverty, 1970:14, 59)*

However, with passage of the British North America Act, Canada's Parliament was given the power to administer Indian affairs, which included
"education." In 1876, the Indian Act was passed and this provided the legal
basis for federal administration of Indian affairs.

In addition to legislation affecting Indian education, most treaties
signed after 1871 contained a commitment:

To maintain schools for instruction on the reserve and whenever the Indians of the reserve shall desire it or to make such provision as may from
time to time be deemed advisable for the education of the Indian children.

Indian schooling—until 1945—was "education in isolation."

During this period, schools, and hostels for Indian children were established, but scant attention was paid to developing a curriculum geared
to either their language difficulties or their sociological needs. A few Indian bands established schools for their children on the reserves, but the
majority of them had neither the financial nor leadership resources to
establish and operate their own schools. Provincial governments were
too preoccupied with their own priorities to become involved in Indian
education. Missionaries provided a modicum of services, but their 'noble
savage' philosophy effectively insulated the Indians from the mainstream
of society. *(Special Senate Hearing on Poverty, 1970:14, 59)*

Federal and provincial government policy on Indian education can
be considered in two phases. The first (1867–1945) has been labeled the
"Paternalistic Ideology" while the second (1945 to the present) has been
called the "Democratic Ideology" (Hawthorn *et al.*, 1967). The second
phase simply refers to an "open door policy" which enabled natives to attend school off the reserve. This was a radical departure from the earlier
policy of isolation.

The paternalistic policy was warmly advocated and perpetuated by
the various religious orders in Canada. The first schools for natives were

quasi-educational institutions set up by religious groups. Under Sections 113–22 of the Indian Act, the federal government is legally free to enter into contracts with the provincial governments and religious organizations for providing Indian children with an education. Again, this underscores the complete lack of control Indians have over their own education (Hawthorn *et al.*, 1967:31–32). Four churches—the Roman Catholic, Anglican, United and Presbyterian—have always expressed interest in "educating" the Indians in their denominational or residential schools.[12] Together, Roman Catholic and Anglican denominational (residential) schools account for two-thirds of Canada's church schools. The Catholics and Anglicans have had the greatest historical impact on natives in Canada . . . and they still have the greatest impact today.

Their interest in "educating" natives has overtones of paternalism and moral salvation and they indoctrinate conservative attitudes. For example, a basic tenet in Roman Catholicism is that poverty is not necessarily bad and that people should not attempt to produce social change in society to upgrade their position. By enduring their poverty they will be showing humility and making penance for their sins as an appeasement to God. The "after" life is of much more concern than what happens on earth. This is summed up in the proverb used by Catholics to place the "after" life in perspective: The first shall be last and the last shall be first. Acceptance of this ideology precludes using "force" to bring social change—it even precludes desiring change. It is easy to see why the government was willing to allow the churches to manage the "education" of Indians. Churches operating schools were given land, per capita grants and other material rewards for their efforts.[13] "Education" for the natives meant "moral" admonishments, cultural genocide and material exploitation by the churches. The concern of these "educators" for "profits" and maintenance of property instead of for the natives is sometimes striking. Their continued opposition to integrated joint schools and unwillingness to support native teachers, use of native tongue, *etc.* all lead one to suspect the motives of the churches.

As Hawthorn *et al.* point out:

> We note that the greater the educational resources possessed by a church or the greater its investment in Indian education, the greater its anxiety to maintain the status quo. On the contrary, the faiths having the least material interests in Indian education are much more open to innovation. *(1967:61)*

It has been previously mentioned that well over half of Canada's natives today are "Catholic." The advantages of this are apparent from the interpretation a special joint Senate-House of Commons Committee made of Sections 113–22 of the Indian Act. Their interpretation was that when the majority of the members of a band belong to one religious denomination, teaching in the school must be done by someone of the same religion.

[12]Schools founded and operated by a particular religious group.
[13]Religious schools receive a fixed amount proportional to the number of pupils for the administration, maintenance and repair of the buildings.

These factors point to continued involvement by religious groups having no real interest in natives becoming independent and subsequently defining and controlling their destiny.

Before looking at the Indians' current educational standards it may prove helpful to discuss the impact of the residential schools on native children. In the past, they were almost all built in the country, far from white settlements. They had the effect of reducing contact between children and their parents. The schools were regimented and showed little concern for the individual; the focus was on conformity. Since there were few adults, the children did not have normal adult-child relations and the possibility of this was reduced further because most staff were non-Indian.

Few of the teachers were well qualified or educated themselves. They neither stimulated the children nor acted as "role models" for their students to emulate. The average annual staff turnover until 1964 was never less than 21 per cent and in 1964 it was nearly 30 per cent. The percentage of Indian children attending these schools has reduced drastically in the past twenty years and it should be no surprise that they were unpopular. (See Caldwell, 1967 and *The Canadian Superintendent*, 1965.)

Today, Indians can attend federal schools or integrated joint schools. There are three types of federal schools: (*a*) denominational (sometimes called residential and/or religious); (*b*) day; (*c*) boarding and hospital.

Denominational schools are those founded and still operated by a religious group. Day schools, the biggest group under federal control, are those located on the reserve. They provide education only for those Indians on the reserve and for non-Indian children there, such as teachers' children, *etc.* Boarding schools are for native orphans or children from broken homes.[14] These schools may or may not be on the reserve. Hospital schools, for Indians in government hospitals provide classes from pre-school level through to adult education. All "boarding" schools are presently under church control, mainly Roman Catholic. These schools, while technically integrated so that white and Indian children can attend, have a big majority of Indian students. The federal government provides finance to the churches to operate these schools.

Integrated joint schools, which have lately become more important in Indian education, have mixed classes for Indians and non-Indians. In most cases they are part of the existing provincial school system. The only real difference between this type of school and a non-integrated one is in financing. At integrated joint schools, the federal government pays for each Indian student who attends. Table 15 shows the distribution of natives in each of the different types of schools. Table 16 also breaks the distribution into secondary and elementary and adds two additional categories—"special" and "absent from the reserve."

Table 15 shows that about 70 per cent of the native population were attending federal schools in 1963–64. Table 16 shows the distribution from 1961 to 1966, so comparing the two, we can see the trend for native chil-

---

[14]All of these schools were founded by the federal government but are operated by religious orders.

Table 15. Indian Enrolment by School, 1963–64

Federal school		
Day	32,331	Indian
	1,200	Non-Indian
Residential	7,234	Indian
	993	Non-Indian
Hospital	238	Indian
Joint integrated	15,672	
	57,668	

dren to attend non-federal schools. In 1961, a majority of native students went to federal schools. However, by 1966, 52 per cent were attending federal schools and 48 per cent non-federal. By 1971 the pendulum had swung and 61 per cent of Indian children (from kindergarten to grade 13) were enrolled in provincial schools. This trend is expected to continue, with an even greater increase in the percentage for provincial schools. Since most Indian pupils transfer to provincial schools at grade six, the above figures would show an even smaller attendance at federal schools if enrolments were available for Indians aged over 12.

The statistics show that until grade 6, most native children attend federal schools then switch for secondary education. Fewer than 10 per cent continue in the federal school system. The remainder are forced to attend non-federal schools out of necessity, not choice, because there is a great shortage of federal secondary schools. For example, Manitoba has only one federal secondary school—in Cranberry Portage, nearly 700 miles north of Winnipeg!

The switch from one type of school system to another has a serious disruptive influence on the educational and social development of native children. The change of social milieu has the greatest impact. Initially these children enter the federal school as a distinct cultural group and with a minimal knowledge of English. However, no individual (or group) is at an advantage because they each have a similar social status. They are among their own "kind." When they transfer, the students are broken up and sent to different schools—depending on where they live.

The second disrupting factor in their lives is discrimination. Lyon et al. (1970) present ample data showing that other students as well as teachers discriminate against Indian students. Living on the reserve, they would already have been subjected to much institutionalized discrimination without being immediately and directly aware of it. But moving to an integrated school means daily exposure to direct discrimination. Their self concepts can be seriously and permanently distorted. The short-term effect of discrimination can be reflected in lower marks and eventually it can lead to dropping out.

Table 16. Indian Enrolment by School and Grade

Year and Type of School	Grade				Special	Absent from reserve*	Total
	Pre–1	1–6	7–8	9–13			
1961–62	3,560	32,746	5,698	3,381	739	1,616	47,740
Federal	3,403	24,256	3,361	596	739	–	32,355
Non-federal	157	8,490	2,337	2,785	–	1,616	15,385
1962–63	3,759	34,035	5,772	3,830	590	1,924	49,910
Federal	3,407	24,262	3,004	737	590	–	32,000
Non-federal	352	9,773	2,768	3,093	–	1,924	17,910
1963–64	3,897	35,453	6,161	4,065	770	4,575	54,921
Federal	3,575	24,791	3,089	750	506	–	32,711
Non-federal	322	10,662	3,072	3,315	264	4,575	22,210
1964–65	4,027	36,229	6,758	4,761	804	4,686	57,265
Federal	3,422	24,067	3,292	768	509	–	32,058
Non-federal	605	12,162	3,466	3,993	295	4,686	25,207
1965–66	3,660	38,929	7,107	5,220	1,013	5,466	61,395
Federal	3,093	24,566	3,203	716	462	–	32,040
Non-federal	567	14,363	3,904	4,504	551	5,466	29,355
1970–71							
Federal	4,551	19,043	2,625	174	–	–	26,393
Non-federal	–	–	–	–	–	–	41,042

Source: *Canada Year Book*, p. 208. Reproduced by permission of Information Canada.
*Pupils (and parents) living off the reserves in communities with educational facilities usually attend non-federal schools but school records are not maintained by the Indian Affairs Branch.

Two additional disrupting factors—age differences and competition—are suggested by Elliott (1970). As Hawthorn *et al.* (1967:132) point out, only 12 per cent of Indian students are in their proper age grade.[15] The average native student is generally about two-and-a-half years younger than his non-Indian classmate. This age difference does not affect Indian students at federal schools since all students in any one classroom—*i.e.*, grade level—are in the same condition, but it does have serious repercussions in an "integrated" school. In other words, while Indian students in any one grade level at a federal school are older than their white counterparts, the impact is minimized because all the Indian students at that level are of a similar "over age" status. Elliott claims that the competition for achievement is greater in integrated (non-federal) schools than in federal schools. Competition may make a child psychologically uncomfortable and adversely affect his academic performance. The Indian child does not get adequate counseling when he is placed in this new environment. The disruptions eventually result in a high drop-out rate among Indian children.

Figure 3 gives a graphic regional comparison of the distribution of native children attending federal and non-federal schools. It shows that with the exception of Manitoba, native children in the western provinces mainly attend non-federal schools. The situation in Manitoba is rather curious since in 1964, the schools agreed with the provincial government to set a uniform tuition fee which is paid by the IAB. Manitoba has also passed legislation guaranteeing natives the right to attend the school of their choice—federal or non-federal. The data suggest that if natives are given a choice, they will choose the federal school, on the reserve. But since Manitoba has only one federal high school, it suggests that those in power do not really want Indian students to stay at federal schools.

Table 17 shows Indian student enrolment between 1964 and 1969 and also the annual percentage increase. The figures present a very fluctuating picture. For grades 9–13, the percentage increase in enrolment dropped between 1964 and 1967. Since then the increase has been nearly as much as in 1964. But despite the drop in percentage increase an ever-growing number of native children are attending school. Considering actual enrolment figures and the number of Indians aged from six to 15, the fluctuations can be easily accounted for. Almost 56,000 natives are aged from six to 15 and the school enrolment is 56,642. So the percentage increase is dwindling because attendance has almost reached the optimum level.

Table 18 compares the percentage enrolment of native students to enrolment for the general Canadian population. The table is somewhat difficult to interpret because the age distribution for the two groups differs. However, there is a rather pronounced trend. Compared to the general Canadian population, the percentage of native children attending school is about half. This is particularly striking since a greater proportion of the native population is in the 15–19 age group.

Table 19 compares non-Indian enrolment with Indian enrolment at federal schools (which makes up only little more than half of the total In-

---

[15]Students aged six should be in grade 1, those aged seven in grade 2, *etc.*

Figure 3. Elementary and Secondary Regional School Enrolment, January, 1968

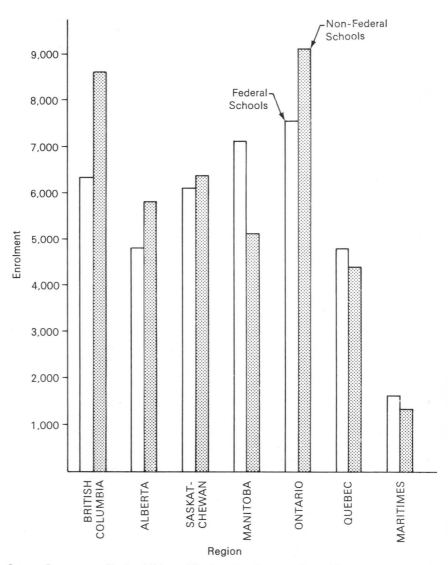

Source : Department of Indian Affairs and Northern Development, *Annual Report,* 1967–68.

dian school population—see Table 16). However, Table 19 does enable the relative distribution of Indian and non-Indian students to be compared. Nearly a fifth of the native students are in grade 1. Grades 1–3 Indian students make up nearly half of the total. This contrasts to the non-Indian

Table 17. Indian Enrolments, Grades 9–13 with Annual Percentage Increases

Grade	1964–65	% increase from 1963	1965–66	% increase	1966–67	% increase	1967–68	% increase	1968–69	% increase
9	2,309	17.86	2,474	7.15	2,590	4.69	2,808	8.42	3,091	10.08
10	1,212	6.32	1,423	17.40	1,520	6.82	1,784	17.37	1,949	9.07
11	726	16.77	777	7.02	897	15.44	952	6.13	1,246	30.74
12	481	53.18	499	3.53	478	-4.39	560	17.15	691	23.17
13	33	3.13	47	42.42	25	-46.81	31	24.00	37	19.35
Gr. 9–13	4,761	17.12	5,220	9.22	5,510	5.55	6,135	11.34	7,014	14.90
Total Gr. 1–13	47,748	4.53	51,256	7.35	53,371	4.13	56,120	5.15	56,642	0.93
% Of Total, Gr. 9–13	9.94		10.16		10.30		10.93		12.38	

Source: Department of Indian Affairs and Northern Development; Brief to Special Senate Committee on Poverty, 1970, 14:63. Reproduced by permission of Information Canada.

Table 18. Percentage of Indian and Canadian Enrolments by Grade

Grade	1964–65		1965–66		1966–67		1967–68		1968–69	
	Indian	*Canada*	*Indian*	*Canada*	*Indian*	*Canada*	*Indian*	*Canada*	*Indian*	*Canada*
	%	%	%	%	%	%	%	%	%	%
9	4.83	7.6	4.82	7.7	4.85	7.9	5.00	7.9	5.46	—
10	2.53	6.6	2.77	6.6	2.84	6.8	3.18	7.0	3.44	—
11	1.52	5.4	1.51	5.6	1.68	5.7	1.70	5.9	2.20	—
12	1.00	3.2	.97	3.4	.89	3.3	.99	3.4	1.22	—
13	.06	0.9	.09	0.9	.04	0.8	.06	0.9	.06	—
Total	9.94	23.7	10.16	24.2	10.30	24.5	10.93	25.1	12.38	

Source: Department of Indian Affairs and Northern Development; Brief to Special Senate Committee on Poverty, 1970, 14:63. Reproduced by permission of Information Canada.

Table 19. Comparison of Non-Indian and Indian School Enrolment, 1960–61

Grade	Non-Indian enrolment (Public, private schools)		Indian enrolment (Federal schools)	
	No.	%	No.	%
1	468,470	11.8	6,974	18.8
2	436,425	11.0	5,811	15.0
3	425,914	10.7	5,566	14.4
4	404,168	10.1	4,863	12.6
5	393,902	9.9	4,325	11.2
6	381,081	9.6	3,686	9.5
7	367,120	9.3	2,784	9.7
8	332,429	8.4	1,967	5.1
9	290,146	7.3	1,294	3.3
10	209,528	5.3	691	1.8
11	156,796	3.9	417	1.7
12	99,841	2.5	261	.7

Source: *Canada Year Book*, 1962, for public and private school enrolment; Indian Affairs Branch *Annual Report*, 1962, for enrolment in federal schools. Reproduced by permission of Information Canada.

population distribution. The figures also show that most native students are in primary grades whereas the non-Indian students are mainly distributed evenly in all grades (with the exception of the last two years of high school). In general, Table 19 suggests again that native children do not complete their education.

Table 20 shows that most of the federal schools are in Ontario, where there are also the greatest number of Indian students. The distribution of schools to students is nearly perfect. That is, most federal schools are in provinces with the biggest native student population. This table indicates how federal schools have been cut back by over one hundred since 1965, with only the NWT and the Yukon getting more. This is evidence of the federal government's policy of "integration."

The student-teacher ratio for federal schools is shown to vary from a low of 1:18 (in Quebec) to a high of 1:28 (in the Yukon and NWT). The national average is 1:12. It should be noted that fewer than 1 per cent of the teachers and administrators currently hired for federal schools are Indians themselves. This means that native children are being educated on or near the reserve by non-Indians with little intrinsic interest in the community. Although over 90 per cent of the instructors in Indian schools are "qualified" teachers, only 13 per cent are university graduates.

From Table 21, which shows a breakdown of Indian educational attainment, it can be seen that in 1961, nearly a quarter of the existing native population had no formal education. An additional quarter have had less than five years of formal education. The data also suggest that the younger people are spending more years on education but that they still lag far be-

Table 20. Indian Schools by Enrolment and Province

	Federal schools 1964–65	Federal schools 1970–71	Teachers	Pupils
Newfoundland	0		0	0
PEI	1		2	43
Nova Scotia	8	12	33	818
New Brunswick	9		25	686
Quebec	25	21	141	2,532
Ontario	100	78	271	7,266
Manitoba	72	35	233	6,069
Saskatchewan	71	51	221	5,475
Alberta	32	22	178	3,836
BC	78	47	228	5,934
Yukon and NWT	1	4	5	141
Total	397	270	1,337	32,800

Source: Statistics Canada, 1961, Census of Canada. Reproduced by permission of Information Canada.

Table 21. Educational Achievement of Indians 15 and Older, 1961 — Percentage

Age	None	Elementary 1–4	Elementary 5+	Secondary	University
15–34	10.4	18.5	50.6	20.1	0.4
34–55	26.3	27.4	38.2	7.8	0.3
55+	48.2	29.0	19.7	3.0	0.2
Total 15+	21.0	22.7	42.0	13.8	0.3

Source: Statistics Canada, 1961, Census of Canada. Reproduced by permission of Information Canada.

hind their Euro-Canadian counterparts. For those in the 15–34 age group, only 10 per cent have had no formal education compared to almost 50 per cent for those in the 55 and older category. The table shows that nearly 90 per cent of natives have not matriculated.

By presenting comparative data, we can judge the degree of under-over representation for school attendance. It shows quite clearly that the native is becoming increasingly under-represented in the educational system while the reverse applies to the British (comparative) group. Indian children in the 5–24 age group were under-represented by 12.5 per cent in 1951. By 1961 this had increased to 13.5 per cent. If we compare this data to the British ethnic group, we find a reversal. In 1951 their over-

Table 22. Indian Students in Post-Secondary and Vocational Courses, 1965–66

Course of study	PEI	NS	NB	Que.	Ont.	Man.	Sask.	Alta.	BC	YT	NWT	Canada
University	–	14	3	39	18	4	9	11	32	1	–	131
Teacher training colleges	–	–	1	10	7	–	–	–	–	–	–	18
Nurse training	–	1	1	3	10	–	3	2	4	–	–	24
Vocational	1	25	15	181	389	135	114	49	294	40	1	1,244
Upgrading	2	–	12	2	352	144	52	10	135	17	–	726
Total	3	40	32	235	776	283	178	72	465	58	1	2,143

Source: *Canada Year Book*, 1972, p. 208. Reproduced by permission of Information Canada.

representativeness was only 3 per cent, but this had increased to over 4 per cent by 1961. The data then suggest that instead of the "educational gap" closing, it is in fact widening.

Our data so far has shown that like other Canadian children, a high percentage of native children attend elementary school. This is where any similarity in school attendance ends. As Table 21 shows, fewer than 1 per cent of Indians attend university, whereas nearly 7 per cent of the general population reach tertiary level. But what of other "post secondary" and vocational schools? Table 22 shows that the largest concentration of native people (60 per cent) taking "secondary" education are involved in "vocational training." These programs include training in carpentry, sheetmetal work, motor mechanics and farming. A third of the native "post secondary" students are classed as doing "upgrading" courses. This is a "catch all" category and can mean anything from "a course on canning preserves" to "a course on advanced mathematics." However, it seems clear that nearly all natives are being prepared to accept jobs at the semi-skilled level or lower.

Table 23, which is more specific in its breakdown of "post secondary" education available to Indians, shows that generally enrolment for these courses is increasing. However, there is no indication yet whether this will result in a better social position for the Indian. It appears that the dominant group are now able to argue that they are providing better educational facilities for native people, by pointing to figures such as the $125 million expenditure in 1971. They can argue that they are doing their part in the battle against poverty. However, they fail to point out that there is no large scale program to channel natives into "highly skilled," managerial or professional occupations. Only one Canadian university (Trent) has an Indian studies program and has actively recruited native people either as teachers or students.

Why have our great "liberal" and hallowed academic institutions refused to establish such programs? The reasons are generally divided into two arguments—money and qualifications. Some say that such special programs would cost the taxpayer hundreds of thousands of dollars to set up. They contend that the present facilities are adequate. The second argument is generally used by academics themselves. To allow students who have not matriculated into university would be lowering the standard or cheapening the degree, they say.

A counter argument to the first claim is that no-one objects when university staff receive up to $600 a year each for "travel" and other monetary and non-monetary benefits. The second argument hinges on a myth of equality in our society. We will consider this fallacy in the last chapter.

With the figures available on retention rates, we can see how many native students matriculate and of those, how many go on to university and graduation. We can see that in a 12-year school cycle (Table 24), 94 per cent of the native students did not graduate. Some regional statistics depict an even worse situation. Fisher (1969) shows, that in a study completed in 1965 in Alberta, 95 per cent of the native students left school before completing grade 9. The national "drop out" rate is 12 per cent, so obviously

Table 23. Indian Enrolment in Professional and Vocational Courses

	1967–68	1968–69	1969–70	1970–71
Adult education				
Basic literacy	2,224	3,415	4,388	5,471
Other adult programs	6,833	9,652	11,964	14,638
Total	9,057	13,067	16,352	20,109
Vocational training				
Pre-vocational	598	1,443	3,888	4,285
Vocational skills	1,029	1,393	2,114	1,778
Technology	274	364	414	529
University	180	235	321	459
Teacher training	27	38	49	48
Nursing	18	20	24	24
Other	180	340	2,007*	2,248*
Total	2,306	3,833	8,817	9,371
Employment relocation				
Short term	8,135	8,676	6,292	6,236
Regular	3,206	3,460	5,697	5,966
In-service training	144	330	218	218
On-the-job training	95	257	269	530
Family relocations	287	509	502	416
Apprenticeship	–	–	73	125

Source: Department of Indian Affairs and Northern Development, *Annual Report,* 1969–70; 1970–71. Reproduced by permission of Information Canada.
*All courses shorter than four months.

Table 24. Progress of Indian Students Through 12-Year School Cycle

Grade	Year	Enrolment	Loss (no.)	Loss (%)
1	1951	8,782	–	–
2	1952	4,544	4,238	48.2
3	1953	3,430	614	13.5
4	1954	3,652	278	7.1
5	1955	3,088	564	15.5
6	1956	2,641	447	14.5
7	1957	2,090	551	21.7
8	1958	1,536	554	26.5
9	1959	1,149	387	25.5
10	1960	730	419	36.5
11	1961	482	248	34.0
12	1962	341	141	29.3

Source: Hawthorn, H., *et al., A Survey of Contemporary Indians of Canada,* Vol. 2, Indian Affairs Branch, 1967. Reproduced by permission of Information Canada.

the Indians are not using or accepting the prevailing Canadian school system.

Turning to distribution figures we find that out of the Indians who are students, 90 per cent are at elementary school, 9 per cent at secondary school and fewer than 1 per cent at universities and colleges. For non-Indian students the figures are: 71 per cent at elementary school, 24 per cent at secondary school and 5 per cent at universities and colleges.

Table 25. Indian Students Enrolled in Post-Secondary Programs, 1953–71

	1953–54	1955–56	1957–58	1959–60	1961–62	1962–63	1970–71
University							
1st year	3	12	15	18	–	25	200
2nd year	8	4	8	12	9	12	108
3rd year	1	2	1	5	8	2	67
4th year	1	1	2	4	4	5	57
Law	–	–	–	–	2	1	–
Medicine	–	–	–	–	2	2	–
Teacher-training	9	18	21	33	25	20	–
Nursing	28	30	36	25	20	20	–

Table 26. Performance of Indian University Students

	1964–65	1965–66	1966–67	1967–68
Enrolment	88	131	150	156
Graduates	5	8	13	10
Completed course	57	76	79	97
Failed course	5	7	15	23
Withdrew	21	40	43	26

Source: Department of Indian Affairs and Northern Development; Brief to Special Senate Committee on Poverty, 1970, 14:65. Reproduced by permission of Information Canada.

Table 25 shows that native enrolments for university are increasing. Between 1953 and 1963, only 25 natives enrolled for first year university and out of that number only five reached their fourth year. Higher education has a short history among natives. Retention rate figures are even more dismal. According to the figures for 1967–68 (Table 26), we find that 156 natives were enrolled for university. If Indians were equally represented in the educational system on a population basis, the figure would be over 2,500. Of those, only 6 per cent graduated. An additional 17 per cent withdrew voluntarily during the year. Of the remaining three quarters, 20 per cent failed one or more courses which generally means automatic exclusion under the terms of their special entry program. The remainder passed all their courses. In 1970, 432 students were enrolled at university. The native's chances of finishing university are still quite small because he is not given special consideration and is treated "as an equal" when he is not. Language and cultural differences and the effects of discrimination put him at a disadvantage to white students. These factors are ignored by the university administration. The dominant group's attitude seems to be: "Talk a lot about the Indian problem, but don't ask us to do anything." If any universities had made serious attempts to meet the problem in the past ten years, the results would certainly be reflected in native enrolment figures.

The question being raised is: Why the high drop out rate? The Indian is now being exposed to the educational system. Why is he not pursuing a basic course of action which other Canadians know is "the right way to go"? The answer is simple. The educational system that has been developed and refined within Canada is for white, urban, middle class citizens. It is alien when placed in the context of a reserve (Fisher, 1969). It is irrelevant to the native child's everyday life. Also, the teachers are almost always non-Indians. Only 7.4 per cent of the teachers hired by the Department of Indian Affairs in 1965 were Indians. By 1970, 10 per cent were Indian. The teachers in these communities show a remarkable lack of involvement and have little or not contact with the local people. In this situation where the school system is using a curriculum which has not been developed by the local people and is irrelevant for the students and community, it is to be expected that there will not be very good participation or involvement.

As Castellano points out:

> But the distorted reflection of himself which is presented to the Indian child is not even the chief source of the sense of incongruity which most Indian children experience in the white school system. Far more significant and handicapping is the fact that the verbal symbols and the theoretical constructions which the Indian child is asked to manipulate bear little or no relation to the social environment with which he is most familiar. *(1970:53)*

Another crucial issue is the "image" of Indians projected by the mass media, including films and books used in the schools. A recent study on grades 1–8 social studies texts revealed that native people were generally portrayed (if even acknowledged) as savages, evil or non-entities (VanderBurgh, 1968). This has a serious impact on the Indians' personal development. As Kardiner and Ovesey (1951) point out, if a person is continually told he has negative traits, he will eventually begin to incorporate them into his "identity." If someone is continually told that he is homely or stupid, he will eventually believe it.

Hawthorn *et al.* (1967), Elliott (1970) and others have argued that lack of parental support is an additional factor in the drop-out rate. This is a rather naive and over-simplified explanation. Because native people have no influence in deciding their children's curriculum, and no control over choice of textbooks or staff, it is easy to see why they regard the education system as an "outside" institution. Until there are changes, it will continue to be viewed as another white racist institution to be tolerated but not supported. Indians still cannot be school board members in certain provinces.[16] Only when individual natives who live on the reserve are allowed to hold teaching and administrative positions will there be active adult community support. Thus, it is rather naive to "blame" the parents for the high drop-out rates. Only when the structural variables affecting the Indians are considered can it be seen that their reaction to the education system is not one of ignorance but of active rejection.

SOCIAL WELFARE

In our discussion here we will consider three sub-sections: living conditions, welfare and general health.

Living Conditions

There has never been a legal housing commitment by the federal government to native people. Studies on Indian housing go back only ten years.

Table 27. Housing Conditions on Indian Reserves for Selected Agencies

	(a) Condition of house			(b)	
	Good	Fair	Poor	Total houses	Total families
PEI	46.7	31.1	22.2	45	48
Nova Scotia	57.0	30.1	12.9	505	591
New Brunswick	58.3	27.3	14.4	506	571
Quebec	65.2	21.9	12.9	2,854	4,055
Ontario	45.6	29.2	25.2	9,271	9,884
Manitoba	48.2	22.1	29.7	3,966	4,602
Saskatchewan	44.2	26.1	29.7	3,713	4,293
Alberta	58.8	23.8	17.4	3,696	3,998
BC	43.5	32.9	23.6	5,270	5,879
Yukon	34.7	24.9	40.3	285	343
	49.5	26.9	23.6	30,111	34,264

Table 27 gives a distribution of the "adequacy" of present native housing. Nearly a quarter is classified as poor.[17] Less than half is considered to be good quality. Though Quebec professes to have the highest percent-

[16]This policy of exclusion is now under review. Indians now utilize school committees as a vehicle for communicating their desires and objections. These committees are set up by the band council and authorized to act on behalf of the Indian community but under regulations drawn up by the IAB.

[17]For a more detailed description of how these were established, see *Special Senate Committee Hearing on Poverty, 1970*, Vol. 14, p. 70. However, it should be pointed out that the size of family per house per Indian is set at 5.5 members.

Table 28. Indian Housing and Facilities

Region	Year	Type of Housing		No. of Rooms in Existing Houses							Total	Electricity	Sewer or Septic Tank	Running Water	Indoor Toilet	Indoor Bath	Telephone
		Frame	Log	1Rm.	2Rms.	3Rms.	4Rms.	5Rms.	6Rms.	Over 6Rms.							
Maritimes	1962-63	998	—	8	32	72	302	360	152	67	993	860	125	334	92	51	1,223
	1964-65	1,016	—	10	33	111	343	293	159	67	1,016	855	136	408	101	74	132
	1966-67	1,056	—	8	24	99	303	279	234	109	1,056	1,016	306	580	283	192	245
	1968-69	1,145	—	—	13	76	250	422	256	123	1,145	1,138	540	842	495	388	325
Quebec	1962-63	2,458	65	190	208	279	770	628	318	130	2,523	1,900	865	864	815	648	708
	1964-65	2,566	80	63	210	368	860	641	315	189	2,646	2,016	960	1,222	328	644	849
	1966-67	2,766	88	45	107	459	870	772	398	203	2,854	2,096	1,249	1,449	1,039	855	1,165
	1968-69	3,077	107	53	326	706	828	687	316	268	3,184	2,695	1,798	2,056	1,554	1,273	1,510
Ontario	1962-63	5,287	1,152	632	971	1,527	1,564	1,075	410	160	6,349	3,478	244	365	249	229	1,071
	1964-65	5,204	1,557	703	1,031	1,380	1,592	1,282	469	304	6,761	3,588	346	453	333	304	1,577
	1966-67	5,513	1,357	681	1,053	1,085	1,801	1,465	593	192	6,870	4,063	441	629	424	382	2,142
	1968-69	5,840	1,199	687	856	1,144	1,671	1,692	730	259	7,039	4,627	760	1,069	760	730	2,599
Manitoba	1962-63	1,313	2,176	1,169	1,020	885	216	156	33	10	3,489	644	3	2	18	21	47
	1964-65	1,658	2,130	1,267	877	883	360	304	89	8	3,788	999	3	3	64	5	124
	1966-67	2,384	1,582	987	690	955	499	485	344	6	3,966	1,567	8	8	65	9	178
	1968-69	2,894	1,245	803	614	771	605	713	551	85	4,142	2,369	57	57	348	55	280
Saskatchewan	1962-63	1,914	1,307	966	786	1,129	174	140	11	15	3,221	180	6	5	11	11	10
	1964-65	2,175	1,361	931	840	1,230	231	276	14	14	3,536	375	9	7	11	15	10
	1966-67	2,657	1,056	796	643	1,169	483	457	141	24	3,713	855	7	10	8	9	16
	1968-69	3,314	712	612	531	993	685	852	307	46	4,026	2,761	25	29	45	20	20
Alberta	1962-63	2,281	855	657	851	680	236	645	53	4	3,136	1,303	36	34	28	32	31
	1964-65	2,701	801	662	921	677	425	749	56	12	3,502	1,578	90	86	73	74	64
	1966-67	2,961	735	726	848	631	442	881	152	16	3,696	2,193	136	171	124	129	35
	1968-69	2,895	541	515	412	569	608	1,052	245	35	3,436	2,808	303	350	333	331	170
BC and Yukon	1962-63	4,859	460	456	719	973	1,406	951	500	314	5,319	2,819	929	1,832	1,079	737	509
	1964-65	4,854	466	358	681	937	1,500	1,042	526	276	5,320	3,289	1,132	1,933	1,137	903	662
	1966-67	5,098	457	361	605	917	1,629	1,160	583	300	5,555	3,956	1,298	2,438	1,317	1,166	745
	1968-69	4,941	485	262	510	304	1,496	1,473	661	220	5,426	4,405	1,765	3,141	1,764	1,587	1,138
Total	1962-63	19,286	6,500	4,225	4,849	5,762	4,695	4,077	1,477	700	25,786*	11,330	2,496	3,437	2,347	1,728	2,507
	1964-65	20,174	6,395	3,994	4,593	5,536	5,311	4,587	1,628	870	26,569	12,700	2,676	4,112	2,547	2,019	3,408
	1966-67	22,435	5,275	3,504	3,970	5,315	6,027	5,499	2,445	850	27,710	15,746	3,445	5,285	3,310	2,742	4,526
	1968-69	24,109	4,289	2,932	3,267	5,063	6,143	6,891	3,065	1,036	28,398	20,703	5,278	7,544	5,299	4,384	6,042
	1962-63	74.8%	25.2%	15%	19%	22%	18%	18%	6%	3%		44%	8%	13%	8%	7%	10%
	1964-65	75%	24%	15%	18%	21%	20%	17%	6%	3%		47%	10%	15%	10%	5%	13%
	1966-67	81%	19%	13%	14%	19%	22%	20%	9%	3%		57%	12%	19%	12%	10%	16%
	1968-69	85%	15%	10%	11%	18%	22%	24%	11%	4%		73%	19%	27%	19%	15%	21%
Based on a national total of 5,394,000 Houses as of May, 1968. Yukon and NWT not included.		Not known		1.3	2.5	8.6	17.2	25.2	21.8	23.4		98.6	Not known	96	93.5	91.2	94.2

* The totals for 1962-63 include 666 houses in the District of MacKenzie but in subsequent years the MacKenzie is not included.

Source: Department of Indian Affairs and Northern Development; Brief to Special Senate Committee on Poverty 1970, 14:81. Reproduced by permission of Information Canada.

age of "good" native houses, aspects of the data are misleading. Section (b) gives a comparison of the number of families to the number of houses. In Quebec there are 4,055 families but only 2,854 houses. This means, of course, that each of these "leftover families" must double up with another family. Thus, while 65 per cent of Quebec native housing is "good" it does not reflect the other part of the table which shows that nearly twice as many houses are needed for native people. Almost every house contains two families. Prince Edward Island comes closest to providing all of its Indian population—fewer than 50 families—with good housing. However, over half are considered "fair" to "poor."

Table 28 shows other details on native housing. Using an index based on electricity, sewage, running water and indoor plumbing, the Maritimes clearly show the highest housing standards. Manitoba, Ontario and Saskatchewan have the lowest. The data also show that over 90 per cent of the housing in the Maritimes has electricity (compared with 23 per cent in Saskatchewan), and 20 per cent have indoor toilets (0.9 per cent in Alberta). Overall, a little less than three-quarters of native houses have electricity, 27 per cent have running water, 19 per cent have indoor toilets and 21 per cent have telephones.

The internal structure of Indian housing generally is representative of lower class. For example, as Table 29 shows, in 1968–69 nearly 20 per cent of the houses in Manitoba and 15 per cent in Saskatchewan had one room. While this is a great decrease since 1962–63 for the two provinces (33 per cent and 30 per cent respectively), it is still well above the national average of 2 per cent. Table 28 shows that in 1968–69 10 per cent of the homes were one room, with an average of 5.5 people per household. The average are area of new Canadian houses is just over 1,000 square feet, but 90 per cent of average Indian houses have less than half this area. Over half the houses are smaller than 500 square feet. The federal government has now taken steps to "remedy" this situation by setting 600 square feet as a minimum. The age of Indian housing can also be used to indicate the standard. About 20 per cent were built before 1950, 20 per cent between 1950 and 1960, and the remainder since 1960.

Reserve housing is generally of low quality (in regard to facilities such as electricity, heating, *etc.*). The houses are mostly old and overcrowded. According to Statistics Canada, overcrowding occurs when the number of people per house exceeds the number of rooms. Using this standard, over 80 per cent of Indian homes can be defined as overcrowded. As pointed out in *Wahbung* (1971), overcrowding has serious social and interpersonal implications and it is indicative that violence is often responsible for deaths among Indians.

Table 29 shows present housing needs and those for 1974. This estimate takes into consideration natural population increase, migration and the number and types of existing houses.
Assuming each new house will cost about the same as it did in 1969, about $250 million will be needed to meet the projected figures. If the cost of housing increases, the projected total would be much higher.

Table 29. Indian Housing Needs

Housing requirements	March 31 1969 (survey)	March 31 1974 (forecast)
Reserve population	161,695	171,742
(a) No. of family units (based on 5.5 per unit)	29,399	31,225

Housing available

No. of good units (minimum CMHC standard)	14,166	14,166
No. of fair units (requiring renovations)	7,488	7,488
(b) Total houses available	21,654	21,654
No. of new houses required (a-b)	7,745	9,571

Source: Department of Indian Affairs and Northern Development; Brief to Special Senate Committee on Poverty, 1970, 14:70. Reproduced by permission of Information Canada.

Welfare and Child Maintenance

The federal welfare program has three general components:
1. Social security and public assistance.
2. Agreements with provincial and private social agencies.
3. Community development.

Under 1, only two programs have been set up to help natives directly —family allowance and old age security. There are more programs under 2, but if an Indian moves from one province to another, welfare will vary. For example only in Ontario may women receive the mothers' allowance or assistance to widows and unmarried women. The trend seems to be toward programs totally under provincial responsibility.

The following figures show the relative expenditures on social welfare for natives by the federal and provincial governments between 1967 and 1972. They are for the three IAB groups.

Indians received $18 million in social assistance in 1967 and $25 million in 1970. The amount for child maintenance nearly doubled in three years—to over $8 million in 1970. "Adult care"—welfare paid to anyone over 16 who cannot properly care for himself, nor get anyone to care for him—increased from $308,000 in 1967 to $485,000 in 1970. More will be spent as Indians live longer. Health services for Indians cost an estimated $40 million in 1973 and these figures do not include administration costs. More and more money is being drained into health costs because Indians are not allowed to participate in the larger society.

What has been the proportional increase in welfare payments? Figure 4 shows the relative increase in social assistance over five years. It

shows that even though the Indian population is increasing at about 3 per
cent, assistance has increased about seven times as fast. At present, over a
third (41 per cent) of the native people are receiving welfare, compared to
the national rate of 3.7 per cent. In 1961 about 56,000 were receiving public assistance. Eight years later there were nearly 70,000 recipients. In
Winnipeg, for example, Indians make up 3 per cent of the population and
12 per cent of the welfare cases. The high rate of public assistance reflects
a changing "dependency ration," *i.e.*, those people unable to compete actively in the labor force. Usually people under 15 and over 65 are considered "dependent" on the remainder of the population. In 1961, the depen-

Figure 4. Indian Affairs Branch Social Assistance Program 1962-63—1967-68

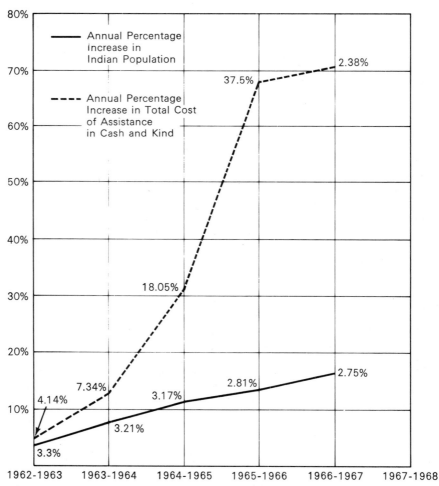

Source : Department of Indian Affairs and Northern Develoment, *Annual Report*, pp. 77–78.

dency rate for Indians was over 51 per cent compared to 40 per cent for the general population.

Figure 5 shows the relationship between population growth and the percentage increase in people receiving welfare (total and adults). It also suggests that the number of recipients is increasing at about 7 per cent per year. There was an 87 per cent increase in the number of cases under child maintenance and protection services between 1960 and 1963, followed by a 15 per cent reduction in 1964, and by a 27 per cent increase in 1965. Thus, between 1960 and 1967, the increase was nearly 100 per cent. We also find that the cost involved in child maintenance has gone up pheno-

Figure 5. Indian Affairs Branch Social Assistance Program 1962-1963—1967-68

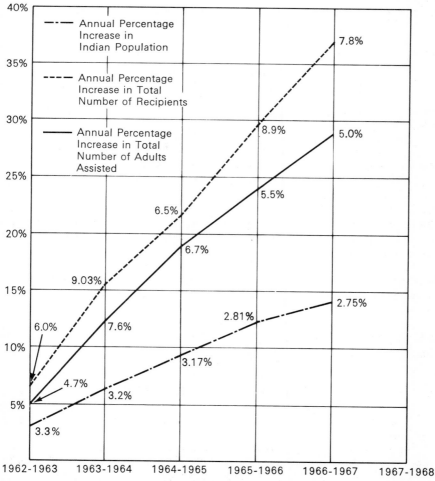

Source : Department of Indian Affairs and Northern Development, *Annual Report,* pp. 77–78.

menally by 12 per cent between 1960 and 1967. Since we have previously shown that the amount of money being used for "social assistance" is not increasing very fast, this suggests that more Indians are going to receive proportionately less than Indians received a decade ago.

Table 30, which gives a breakdown of the numbers of natives receiving welfare, shows that there was a slight increase in the number receiving aid between 1961 and 1964. It also shows that nearly a third of the recipients were considered adults. This group then is quite different from those considered "dependents." Nearly half the adults receiving aid were employable, suggesting that nearly 14 per cent of the welfare recipients resident on reserves were employable adults—a dismal picture. In 1960 the maintenance of "indigent" Indians—adults and children—cost the government about $850,000 and by 1966 this figure had tripled. The table (30) shows that the Maritimes, Manitoba and Saskatchewan provided welfare for over half of the native "resident" population. Those receiving welfare at the time of the survey would have been doing so for the past year. This suggests that there is a large pool of welfare recipients within the native population.

Health Problems

Until the age of 35, Indians generally have a much higher death rate than the national level, but after 35 the rate becomes very similar to the rest of the population.

In a publication by National Health and Welfare (1960), Cummings attempts to show the influence of native people on various Canadian statistics. His data show that in 1966, Canadian Indians had the effect of increasing deaths in infancy by 5.4 per cent, the national infant mortality rate by 3.1 per cent, the illegitimate birth rate by 10.9 per cent and death from all causes by 1.3 per cent. The conclusion is that since Indians made up only 1.2 per cent of the population in 1966, they contributed disproportionately to the statistics. With one exception, the figures for Indians were similar in most provinces. However, the Yukon consistently contributed well above the average. For example, the death rate in the Yukon was increased by over 20 per cent by Indians. Though Indians make up only a fifth of the population there, they virtually determined the territory's statistics.

Table 31, which gives the relative incidence of tuberculosis in Canada for 1967 and 1969, shows that while the overall incidence is decreasing, cases among Indians and Eskimos are increasing.

SELECTED SOCIAL PROBLEMS

Two further problems facing Indians which should be discussed here are crime and alcohol.

The crime rate among Indians is extremely high. Laing, in his much quoted *Indians and the Law*, says that 28 per cent of all male inmates and

Table 30. Natives Receiving Welfare

| | Total relief recipients | | Adults | | Employable adults | | | Heads of households | | | Frequency of assistance | |
| | | | | | | | | Adult recipients who were heads of households | | | Employable heads of households who received help each month in previous 11 months or more | |
National total	No.	% Of resident popula- tion*	Total adults assisted	% Of resi- dent adult population assisted†	Adult reci- pients who were employ- able	% Of adults assist- ed who were employ- able	% Of adults resi- dent on reserves who were employ- able and received assis- tance	Total	Employable No.	Employable %	No.	% Of heads of households assisted
Maritimes	3,705	56.5	1,403	44.1	597	42.6	18.8	681	483	70.9	282	41.4
Quebec	4,843	30.9	2,133	25.8	982	46.0	11.9	1,051	894	85.1	467	44.4
Southern Ontario	1,106	19.7	377	13.6	133	35.3	4.8	183	122	66.7	41	22.4
Northern Ontario	5,369	29.7	2,296	25.5	874	38.1	9.7	1,228	847	69.0	199	16.2
Manitoba	12,921	50.3	5,040	42.8	1,936	38.4	16.4	2,453	1,630	66.4	529	21.6
Saskatchewan	16,072	60.8	6,398	55.1	3,021	47.2	26.0	3,185	2,342	73.5	845	26.5
Alberta	8,667	42.7	3,519	38.8	1,423	40.4	15.7	1,474	1,109	75.2	368	25.0
BC & Yukon	8,857	22.4	3,506	18.7	1,322	37.7	7.1	1,918	1,117	58.2	262	13.7
Dist. MacKenzie	1,135	22.1	512	19.0	237	46.3	8.8	324	234	72.2	93	28.7
Canada (1965)	62,675	38.5	25,184	32.7	10,525	41.8	13.7	12,497	8,778	70.2	3,086	24.7
Canada												
1961	56,011	38.1	25,730		10,829			13,004	8,290	63.7		
1962	50,816	36.0	20,942		8,362			10,617	6,935	65.3		
1963	53,876	35.1	21,931		8,903			11,001	7,172	65.3		
1964	58,860	37.4	25,184		9,653			11,471	7,694	67.0		

Source: Department of Indian Affairs and Northern Development; Brief to Special Senate Committee on Poverty, 1970, 14:160. Reproduced by permission of Information Canada.
*Resident population: 162,942 (including 1,537 "off reserve" in the Yukon Agency).
†Resident adult population (reserve and crown land): 77,105 (including 765 "off reserve" in the Yukon Agency).

Table 31. Notification of New, Active and Reactivated Cases of TB

| | 1967 | | 1969 | |
	No.	*%*	*No.*	*%*
Registered Indian	431	8	629	12
Non-Registered Indian	119	2		
Eskimo	166	3	193	4
Other	4,711	87	4,296	84
Total	5,427	100	5,118	100

Source: Statistics Canada, Vols. 7, 9, "Incidence of TB." Reproduced by permission of Information Canada.

about 25 per cent of female inmates at Canadian prisons are Indians or Metis. The numbers in federal penitentiaries varies by province but they are always disproportionately high. For example, Lysyk (1969) points out that in Saskatchewan, while Indians make up only 3 per cent of the population, 80 per cent of the female prisoners are Indians. In Manitoba during 1965, 22 per cent of those incarcerated were of Indian ancestry. One simple explanation (to which I do not subscribe) is that Indians are inherently more prone to commit acts of defiance. Other social scientists also doubt this and suggest an alternative explanation. They say that because of Indians' low social status and society's negative stereotyped view of them, they are more conspicuous and more likely to be picked up by white police, charged and given prison sentences than whites. For example, 0.97 per cent of Indians have been convicted of indictable offenses compared to 0.18 per cent of whites. In a study by Bienvenue and Latif (1973) concerning arrest rates of Indians in Winnipeg, they found that for Indians and Metis, the rates are far greater than expected on the basis of their representation in the population.

The Indian crime rate can be considered in a similar light to the crime rate in lower class white areas compared to middle and upper class areas. The lower class white crime rates are also much higher because of society's negative stereotyped view of them and the fact that they are more readily seen by the police. In addition, most police (RCMP) are whites who are not accountable to the Indian community and thus do not attempt to ameliorate problems that might arise. It is much easier for them simply to charge the person involved. If a prison sentence is imposed, this not only removes the person from the community (and subsequently reduces the police work load) but also shows that they are "doing their job."

Institutionalized racism in the area of justice only begins with the arresting officer. At the time of the Laing Report (1967) there were 46 Indian constables, but by 1971 there were only seven. Moreover, the jobs of these "constables" vary from police work to janitorial duties. Thus, at the lowest level of justice, Indians are scarcely represented and this continues through the judiciary process. Juries are almost always white even though the alleged crime may have been committed on a reserve. Perhaps this is most clearly illustrated by a case in BC involving two RCMP officers and the death of an Indian, Fred Quill. An all white jury decided that the Indian's death was natural and accidental.

Indians are discriminated against when they seek parole: in BC from 1963 to 68, fewer than 8 per cent of Indians who applied for parole obtained it. This rate in comparison to whites (nearly 20 per cent) is much lower and is even more significant considering the disproportionate number of Indians in jails.

As a final comment, Laing in his 1967 report, made 17 recommendations for changes in the way the law is enforced on natives. Today, none of these recommendations has been taken seriously and implemented. For example, Laing points out that more Indian constables are needed and there should be special programs to bring this about. As shown above, the opposite has happened.

It is not uncommon to see RCMP wagons waiting at rear exists of township hotels at closing time. As Indians leave the almost totally segregated bars in these towns, they are put into the wagons and taken to jail. Alcohol is certainly linked to the "crime rate" of Indians. However, it can also be seen as a separate problem affecting social behavior.

The rate of alcoholism among Indians has been estimated at 15–25 per cent. While the definition of "alcoholism" used in the different studies has varied, the figures clearly suggest that the rate is much higher than that of the general population. But again, white society has chosen to consider the alcoholism rate as just another manifestation of the inherent inferiority of Indians, instead of seeing it as their way of handling and/or escaping from their hostile social environment.

Summary

Indian education is in a dismal state at present but there are promising signs. More and more young Indians are becoming educated both in the white man's way and in their own. Indian communities, stirred up by Red Power advocates, are becoming increasingly interested in the importance of education for their children. More and more young Indians are returning to the reserve as teachers and are contributing significantly to its development.

As for Indian social conditions, if the trend in society of individual entrepreneurship over community ownership and control continues, little improvement can be expected. People on welfare at present can expect to find their children joining them as they become adults, continuing the poverty-welfare cycle.

Provincial and federal governments and most whites bemoan the fact that more and more is being spent each year for the social welfare of Indians. This is not denied. The suggested alternative is community owner-ship and control. In the short term it may cost the government more but in the long term investment in human resources is by far the best we can make. To date, because of the control of the political arena by the econo-mic sector of our society, this has been strongly resisted.

2

Some Problems of Reserve Indian Communities: A Case Study

R. W. DUNNING

THE ANALYSIS of Canadian reserve Indian communities which have become dependently attached to the national socio-economic system through wages, trade and subsidies seems best conceptuzalized as two polar types.[1] These are of course abstractions or ideal types selected from what might be called an adjustment continuum. All reserve communities are to a degree interdependent with or dependently attached to the national society. However seeing them as extreme types permits an hypothesis about the nature of their dependency relations.

*From *Anthropologica*, 6, No. 1, 1964. Reprinted with permission.

[1] A draft of this paper was read at the Indian-Eskimo Association of Canada Conference, Kingston, Ontario, June, 1960.

Type A—The northern reserve community: a remote and isolated society which in some cases appears to be functioning with reference to its indigenous social structures and norms.[2] Adjustment to the national civilization is minimal. There is an inadequate knowledge of the national language and culture. The bolstered economy of subsidies allows some selective acceptance of external norms, particularly economic development but without the necessity of losing completely the indigenous social norms. See Dunning, 1959, where I have discussed this with special reference to kinship and marriage. Elsewhere (1959a) I have discussed one area of adjustment, the transfer from traditional authority to that of the non-Indian outsider.

Type B—The southern reserve community presents problems of adjustment which appear rather different. Perhaps it would be justified to draw a horizontal (very approximately) line across the country to separate the remote, non-English (or French) speaking peoples—Type A from those with a considerable history of contact together with a knowledge of the national language and culture—Type B. This dichotomy is no doubt dramatized by seeing in the northern areas some groupings whose social systems are flourishing and maintained by their sanction systems, whereas in the south the indigenous sanction systems of some communities appear to have disappeared.

This paper will concentrate on the problems of adjustment in the southern area. And as a certain degree of depth is required for a presentation of these problems, this paper will be limited to a consideration of data from one southern community.[3] There is moreover, the assumption of limited functionalism, *i.e.*, a degree of consistency and interrelatedness of social institutions or behavioural norms within a given community.

In the section which follows elements of social behaviour have been described which are easily observable and which could be collected in a short field trip. The purpose of this superficial ethnography is to attempt to demonstrate the degree of traditional or contemporary Indianness observed in public or social behaviour. In no sense therefore is the following an adequate ethnography of the society. What has been attempted instead is the documentation of behavioural norms sufficient to permit an hypothesis about Indianness in an Indian community. And the relevant aspect of Indianness in this paper is its part in either creating or maintaining a social identity for a given population. By the terms of the Indian Act the governmental administration is committed to supervise people of Indian status. And it is Indianness or a way of life which is either recognized or admitted by the people which provides the *raison d'être* for the Indian Affairs Branch.

[2]See Eggan, 1955:494, who makes the point that social structures may offer more resistance to borrowing than would be true of cultural elements. Murdock, 1949:192 makes much the same point. With respect to this Type A community in the north, it seems reasonable that individual cultural items may be accepted without taking over social norms, at least as long as they remain isolated.

[3]I wish to acknowledge the help I have received from H. M. Jones, Director. Indian Affairs Branch, and H. J. Featherston, Indian Agency Superintendent. A grant in aid of research from the Canada Council provided funds for the field work in this paper.

I BRIEF ETHNOGRAPHY OF THE PINE TREE OJIBWA

Origin of the Band

The people living on Pine Tree[4] Island are descendants of Chippewa (Ojibwa) Indians, who migrated from Lake Superior and occupied a vast area surrounding Georgian Bay, part of Lake Huron and Lakes Simcoe and Couchiching in the early years of the 19th century. The Indians then referred to as the Chippewas of Lakes Huron and Simcoe surrendered the larger part of this area to the Crown, so that by 1830, little land was left to them. This prompted Lieutenant Governor Sir John Colborne to appropriate a Reserve for their use containing about 9,800 acres in Pine Tree Township. In 1836, the Indians surrendered the whole of the Reserve for sale, following which time they split into four groups. One of these groups went to Cedar Point and thence to Pine Tree Island. We are not aware of the exact date of the move to Pine Tree Island, but it probably started sometime between 1836 and 1842 and continued during the next several years.

Pine Tree Island was recognized as Indian reserve land by the Crown prior to Confederation. Following Confederation, and under the terms of Section 91 (24) of the British North America Act, all Indian reserve lands including Pine Tree Island came within the exclusive legislative authority of the Parliament of Canada.[5]

One senior man said his grandfather was born at Cedar Point in 1833. And in 1856 when the latter surveyed Pine Tree Island there were three families living there. (It was claimed that this man's wife's father had been in the War of 1812).

Another senior man stated that there had been three chiefs who separated in 1837 to form three bands, one of which moved to Pine Tree Island and its attachment at Cedar Point. At this time there was only one farm in the neighbourhood (600 acres) settled by a United Empire Loyalist family.

In general the early demography and residence pattern seemed to consist of a very extensive use of the land by small family units—probably a man and his married sons and/or daughters who moved their campsites continually, both seasonally and from year to year.[6] It is clear from comments of the elders that the government had tried at this time to get the Indian people to agree to live together at a place consisting largely of marshland and presumed to be good trapping country. The people rejected this plan however, preferring extensive movement in small family units. It was largely due to the cumulative encroachment of settlers on homesteads which probably exerted sufficient pressure for the Indians to concentrate eventually at Pine Tree Island.

---

[4]The identity of the reserve and of individual persons in the band have been disguised.

[5]Letter from H. M. Jones, Director of I.A.B. 30.10.58.

[6]See Dunning 1959-b for the typical residence patterns of the hunting and collecting Ojibwa of Ontario.

Demography

The reserve situated on an inland lake in Southern Ontario consists of about 4,000 acres of land, 75% wooded, accessible only by boat and situated about 1½ hours drive from a major Ontario city. An additional tract of land at Cedar Point which is not suitable for farming has been largely subdivided into lots and leased to cottagers.

A few non-Indian men joined the band from time to time and were eventually integrated as full Indian members. A few persons whose mothers were band members but whose fathers were non-Indian and moved away were gradually absorbed into the band. During World War I five or six men in this category were given band membership by government action. The view was expressed that as the Indian population was going down at the turn of the century the government allowed some non-Indians to join the band.

The residence pattern has changed therefore from one of small units consisting of small extended families living at trapping and fishing grounds around the lake in the mid nineteenth century to that of the whole band living at Pine Tree. The older men described nostalgically the demographic pattern of the first two decades of this century. Houses were at that time spread out on the island both on the main road and the back bush road. Table 32 gives an indication of the amount of general farming done in 1916. It was arduous work. The grain had to be rowed over to the mainland and up the river several miles to the mill. The major problem seemed to be to get sufficient capital to purchase a team of horses and harness, as well as some livestock and poultry. Some of the men said they went north into the bush to work as loggers for a time. Photographs of the time, which show the present grand-parental generation as youngsters, give a picture of fairly well equipped farming people with some equipment and well dressed in the costume of the day, the women wearing the "Gibson Girl" type of headdress. In dress and comportment they would appear indistinguishable from any such Ontario rural community.

The total number registered as band members has increased from 107 in 1917, 120 in 1924, 157 in 1944 to 170 in 1958. Of this number approximately 135 or 75% live permanently at Pine Tree. Some of the non-residents are working away temporarily while others are permanent residents of cities and towns in various parts of the country. At present the houses on the bush road have been abandoned, the people having built houses fairly well spread along the length of the gravelled road, a distance of about three miles. The houses are mostly frame, a few being the older squared log with dovetailed corners, and nine are one-storey insulbrik covered bungalows built in recent years by the government for pensioners and persons unable to provide for themselves. A telephone line runs the length of the road and electricity was installed in the autumn of 1958. A few houses have wells from which several families get their water.

Economics

Out of a total of 28 resident households two had gardens of a small size containing mixed vegetables, and two others had some poultry (during the time of field work, summer 1958). A few persons raised beef cattle, but the majority of the cattle was owned by one person. A bull was band owned and serviced the individually owned herd gratis. A few horses were raised for sale. No crops of any kind were cultivated. There was a minimum of fencing and the cattle and horses roamed freely throughout the reserve.

Table 32 compares the total agricultural activity at the present time with that contained in the Department of Indian Affairs Annual Report for 1917. It is interesting to note that several of the older persons spoke nostalgically of the old days when every household had a team of horses, grew grain and hay as well as raising poultry and pigs.

Table 32.

	1917	1958
Population	107	(135 residents)
Acres in wheat	40	0
Acres in oats	35	0
Other grains	9	0
Peas, beans, etc.	1	0
Potatoes	1	0
Hay (acres)	80	40?
Wild hay	4	?
Other fodder	5	?
Geldings and mares	28	20–30
Foals	2	
Bulls	0	1
Milch cows	18	0
Young steers	17	100?
Other	20	
Poultry	294	50?

Although some fishing is done and the occasional animal is killed in the bush, neither occupation produced sufficient food to be counted in the economy of the reserve. The major part of the economy which is based on cash income, comes from wages and government payments. The Revolving Fund Loan represented a negligible but potential source of capital funds. This is used for the purchase of equipment, usually motor boats. No loans were made during the 1956–7 financial year, and two loans were made for the 1957–8 year, totalling $700.

Following is a list of total dollar value of government monies paid to reserve persons.

It is worth comparing per capita annual payments from Indian Band funds with that of per capita (estimated) annual costs of I.A.B. administration deriving from parliamentary appropriations. Per capita band fund interest payments for the year under review were approximately $25.00. For the same year per capita relief payments from band funds amounted to $10.76 (for 1956–7 financial year $9.05). Therefore band fund payments

Table 33.

Family allowances:	74 children,	averaging $6.50 per month	
		Total:	$5,772.00
Old age pensions:	20 persons,	$55 per month	
(including 3 aged pensioners in nursing homes)			
		Total:	13,200.00
Compensation:	1 person	$50 per month	
		Total:	600.00
Relief payments:	1956–7	Band funds	
		Total:	1,075.55
Relief payments:	1957–8	Band funds	
		Total:	1,453.55

Medical treatment and hospitalization in calendar year: No total cost available. 14 cases in addition to 6 confinements

amounted to approximately $35.00 per capita. The 1959–60 Indian Affairs Branch Budget estimate (submitted to Parliament, 5–2–59) amounted to $41,447,455.00. Construction and Equipment was $7,362,500. Indian Health Services; operation and maintenance was $20,729,052, construction and equipment was $3,100,500. This represents a total of $72,639,507, or approximately $430 per capita. Therefore the total costs of services to Indian status persons in the community under study (on a per capita basis) were about ten times that paid out of band fund interest and relief payments.

Wages—Some persons are living away almost permanently and their wages would be spent largely outside the reserve area. Regarding resident wage earners, there are 22 who worked consistently at nearby settlements mostly in maintenance or unskilled labouring jobs. In addition there were some who did not work continuously, but preferred to take up occasional labour and remain for periods on the reserve or in a state of travelling to a nearby settlement in search of work. Some of these men reported from time to time that they were to get a driving job the next day for which they would earn high wages for a few days. This did not eventuate, however, although some of them were seen often in possession of wines which were consumed along the reserve road.

A further source of income is that of the tourist business. A few men have built fishhuts (12) which are rented by the day to tourists, for fishing parties. During the summer holiday season as many as five households have at one time or another entertained guests. During this summer only two were doing so. The difficulty of this kind of occupation is the low earning potential and uncertain clientele. The wife of the man who has continued in this occupation, admitted to me when referring to a newly arrived guest, that he was a good boy and paid for his meals. The husband claimed his reason for entertaining so many people was that "they drop a lot of money" (meaning that they give gratuities occasionally). This man was in a good position to conduct business as he had rented the unused church manse, a solid concrete block house for $5.00 per month, and consequently had more room than most for tourists.[7] It is difficult therefore to assess the amount of income from this type of business, although I suspect it is rather small. One or two of the older men occasionally act as guides to tourists for fishing. This appeared to be rather rare, none having guided during the time of the fieldwork. Two older women made a few baskets for sale. Complaints were voiced by these persons that none of the younger women would make baskets and they feared that soon the craft would be lost to the band.

One man operated a small motor launch as ferry boat, carried the mail, occasionally hired his launch out to tourist parties, and ran a few head of cattle on the island. He occasionally made a speech on Indianism for a fee. His position was unique in the band. Having married a non-Ojibwa Indian status woman who had an inheritance of saleable lands from another reserve, he had an economic position shared by no others in the community. Moreover he had spent a couple of years together with his two sons working in the mines in Northern Ontario in order to obtain capital for his business enterprise.

Although most of the land remains under communal ownership, 96 parcels of land were individually owned and inherited by members of the band.[8] One or two of the owners of waterfront land were trying to lease cottage lots to outsiders. Up to the end of 1958 several lots had been leased but no cottages had been built. The opinion was expressed that this would provide work for the islanders in the form of construction and maintenance.

Use of Language

In the use of a language, English is almost the only language used. Ojibwa is used only on occasion, such as a meeting or at a social occasion for special purposes such as humour, and usually only between two persons. Although most of the older persons could speak Ojibwa, there was one person who was always referred to as the expert. (He was brought up by his widowed grandmother, a noted magico-medical expert who maintained the old traditional life). Often he spoke to other men in Ojibwa and they re-

[7]His wife however objected to many of the clients because of their drinking parties. Others on the reserve, complained about this. They said it should be stopped. During my residence there, there were several late drinking parties which became rowdy, and on one occasion his guests, four men and one woman, left suddenly at dawn. It was at this time that his daughter-in-law was taken suddenly to the city hospital for emergency treatment.

[8]One of these persons complained to the ethnographer that he had no paper (deed or title) to prove his ownership.

sponded by a smile or nod, but rarely conversed with him in other than
English. Day school has been conducted continuously since the mission
school of the latter 19th century whose effects in establishing English as the
single language no doubt have been considerable. Moreover the idiomatic
use of English leaves no question as to which language claimed dominance.
Regarding the men, the latter language was used in many forms of idiom,
slang and obscenity.

Kinship

In the belief that the older persons would be more knowledgeable
about traditional ways of life, several senior persons were questioned about
Ojibwa terms for different categories of kin. Three men and two women
were elderly but not senile, besides being interested in discussing Ojibwa
traditions. One man and one woman were helped by their spouses, and a
further older woman was not included because she did not know any of the
Ojibwa language. One additional person questioned was of middle age.
Using traditional Ojibwa kin categories *i.e.*, cross and parallel relatives,
the persons were asked for the Ojibwa equivalent of the English kin category. Following is a table of the responses.

Thus approximately 35% of the major kin terms were known to the senior and consequently more conservative adults in the population. These
answers were in some cases given only after some reflection. It should be
noted moreover that a few responses (see asterisks) differ from the normal
kin categories *e.g.*,
bro.in-law: one response is *opposite-sexed* (m.s.) cross-cousin/sibling-in-
law term;
sis.dau: only one response to this and it is the normal term for daughter
with first person prefix and third person suffix;
sis.son: one response only; giving the term for daughter with a suffix;
bro.: one response is same-sexed cross-cousin / sibling-in-law (m.s.);
sis: one response is the younger sibling of either sex.
It seems reasonable to assume—and this was verified in observed behaviour wherever possible—that the actual use of kin terms by the people
was even less than the table shows. As far as could be seen younger children spoke English almost exclusively, including the use of kin terms. Moreover in several cases persons asked the ethnographer what terms should be
used for persons outside the nuclear family.

In terms of behaviour such as visiting, reciprocal or obligatory gift
giving or presentations of any kind, kinship appears to play a negligible
part. Some brothers do recognize a slight preference for one another, but
this appears to be no more than would be true for the average rural Ontario
family.

As previously implied, the residence pattern is almost exclusively that
of the nuclear family or incomplete family where there is no male parent.
Usually the grandparents live separately nearby. There is extremely little
social interaction between senior age mates. Some spoke of loneliness and
expressed eagerness about visits from an outsider. In discussions some of

Table 34.

	Total no. of terms	Same terms	Total responses Alternative terms or different	Unknown
G.g.fa.	2	2	1	3
G.g.mo.	2	4	1	2
G.fa.	1	5	–	1
G.mo.	2	2	2	2
Fa.	2	5	2	1
Mo.	4	3		2
		3	1	
		2		
Fa.bro.	1	2	–	4
Mo.bro.	2	2		3
Mo.sis.	1	1		5
Fa.sis.	0	0		6
Bro.(m.s.)	2	3	1*	2
Sis.(m.s.)	2	3	1*	2
Sis.(f.s.)	1	3		3
Y.sibl.	1	1		5
Son	1	3		3
Dau.	1	3		3
Child	2	1		5
Bro.son				
Sis.son	1	1*		5
Bro.dau.	1	1		5
Sis.dau.	1	1*	5	
G.child	1	4		2
Affines				
Husband	1	5		1
Wife	3	3	2	1
Fa.-in-law	1	2	1 (general	3
Mo.-in-law	1	1	term)	5
Bro.-in-law	2	3	1*	2
" (f.s.)	1	1		5
Sis.-in-law (m.s.)	1	2		4
Sis.-in-law (f.s.)	0			6
Son-in-law	1	3		3
Dau.-in-law	1	1		5
Totals Percentage 36.4%	43	76	18	99

the elders said nothing about their equals while others talked about seeing so few people and how they did not like the others. One or two would meet at church meetings and others at general band meetings or council meetings. Youngsters associated with their immediate neighbours who tended to be closely related. Adults tended to express some fraternal solidarity in associations. The general social pattern appeared similar to that of Odanah, described by Barnett and Baerreis (1956:65).

Genealogies

The genealogies show a long history of non-Indian interaction. In terms of marriage it is notable that traditional Ojibwa patterns expressed the legal status of marriage only by community recognition of the state of living together. Consequently non-Indians were free to move into the area and if accepted were permitted to live with a woman who thereby claimed married status in the community. A few of these persons remained, but the majority stayed only a short time, with the result that a number of children were brought up in the community by their deserted mothers. Legally they were non-Indians, but following the recruitment programme of World War I several of these had served in the services and were later admitted to Indian status by the Minister. Some of these took the totemic identification of their mothers, while others "forgot" their totems. At present very few of the middle aged and elderly persons knew their totems.

In the genealogies showing from two generations above the present middle aged persons to the present time approximately 20% of persons are recognized as illegitimates.[9] Following are two genealogies which show something of the illegitimacy pattern. Within recent years there have been eleven births to unmarried women. When the total number of post-pubertal unmarried women is considered (1949 census gives 8 women aged 16 to 20 inclusive) this proportion of non socially sanctioned issue represents an important proportion of the total population. Of these eleven births, so far five have been given Indian status under the New Indian Act. It is notable also that no paternity suits have been initiated by the Indian administration (letter from Indian superintendent, 24–2–60).

Various statements were made by members of the community in this regard. One senior man called the new Indian legislation (Section 11E, Indian Act 1951) "race suicide", and regarding the problem of illegitimacy through non-Indian paternity: "We just about had it licked" (until the new Act came into force). Another said three or four girls went to town to high school and all returned the same year pregnant.

A point of importance in this situation appears to be the security with which Indian status and consequently band membership is held by the adolescent women. Marriage—if such were considered by the non-Indian man —would mean leaving home and community; whereas liaisons outside marriage which result in issue simply mean that the women concerned may stay home and accept welfare benefits as well as the probability of their children being accepted by the band. As one person who was aware of the

[9]Speaking of children in this category in Jamaica, Rodman says: "It is unfortunate that more emphasis has not been placed upon the distinction between children that have resulted from a current union and 'outside' children—the actual distinction that is usually made within the lower class". Hyman Rodman, "On Understanding Lower-Class Behaviour," *Social and Economic Studies*, 8, No. 4 (Dec. 1959), 445. See also Edith Clarke, *My Mother Who Fathered Me*, London, 1957.

implications of this development said: "we could vote them out of the band in council, but it is hard to do that and we feel sorry for the child". Moreover the previous generation has a high incidence of illegitimacy which serves as a precedent for the present generation.[10]

These senior persons were apparently not held in disrepute, but were considered as normal members of the community. Moreover there were two non-Indian men who were at the time of field work living with two women of the community. One of the women was unmarried and of child bearing age. She had recently borne two illegitimate children, one of whom had been given Indian status by the administration. The fact of these two men openly living with community women did draw reactions from some persons. Several persons informed the ethnographer that they did not like the procedure (one said, "I hate that man"), and when asked why they did not take action, replied that the Agent required a report from the chief. Furthermore it was alleged that when the agent or policeman visited the island, the men would simply run into the bush for an hour or so, thereby escaping detection by the administration.

In both genealogies the women (EGO) have married in middle life. One has held the position of councillor of the band.

Supernatural Belief System

Several of the elders reminisced about the traditional beliefs and practices. There were two grandfathers of present day elders who had been noted conjuring and *mide* specialists. These men both became converted to the Methodist denomination of Christianity and became travelling lay preachers in the latter part of the nineteenth century. The conjuring lodge was described to some extent, although no one had knowledge of the shaking of the lodge. They knew only of the isolation and singing preparatory to the conjuring performance.[11] There was no knowledge (admitted) of the *Nanibush* or *Weskayjak* folklore. The *mide* was understood by the elders as a general power for good or evil, but there was no memory of rituals or any practices. One or two persons described vaguely accounts of individual persons performing feats. One man entered the water like a serpent and came up about a half mile out, returning later exuding a fishy odour. He was subsequently able to perform curing and seeing feats. The grandmother of one man had been a noted *mide* practitioner and there had been great fear evidenced towards her medicine bundle after her death. One female pensioner who is at present in a nursing home in the town had inherited the war medicine—*megasum-shkiki*. With this medicine she had once

[10]Note the recent brief to the Parliamentary Committee by the Alberta Indian Association (as reported on the C.B.C. 11.5.60.) regarding women from wealthy bands who do not marry. It was claimed that they rejected marriage and kept their illegitimate children at home in order to keep them in their own bands. The brief suggested that the children should belong to the father's band.

[11]In his attempt to establish rapport by informing some persons that he had seen the conjuring performance in northern Ontario, the ethnographer may have unwittingly influenced the situation. Several of the elders expressed a keen interest in hearing about it as well as a wish to visit those areas.

Figure 6.

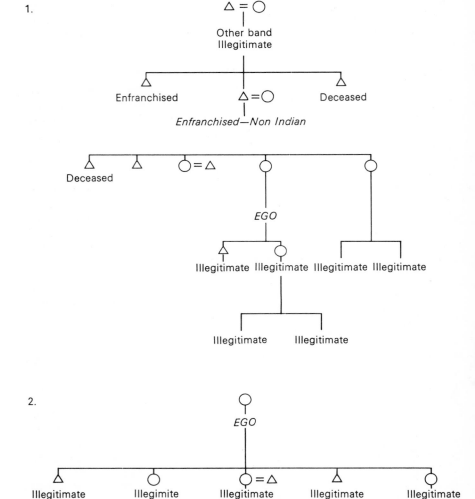

cured a mortally wounded dog. She presently refused to pass on the medicine to anyone—perhaps because no one is willing to have her live with
them. One woman while in hospital in the city talked with a person from
a northern band. The latter told so many stories about the evils of the *mide*
practices at present going on that the informant asked her to stop. She
claimed she was afraid.

It appears that the elders have a general but vague knowledge of the traditional supernatural practices. Their knowledge of them seems to be sufficiently unclear that these supernatural traditions would have no significance as supernatural sanctions or perhaps even as cultural values for the present adult generation and even less for the younger generation.

Movement, Migration and Social Interaction

Since 1954 (until 1958) a few persons have become enfranchised. These were two nuclear families, one single man and four women who married non-Indians. In the latter case women became enfranchised upon marriage to non-Indian status persons. For men however it is necessary to demonstrate to the superintendent their ability to maintain themselves financially for one year before their request is recognized. A few persons at present totalling 35 (including children) work and live away from the reserve. And it is from this group that an occasional recruit for enfranchisement comes. These enfranchisable persons who live and work away from the reserve population do not offer much incentive for others to follow suit. More immediate is the example set by the occasional worker whose lot is not much above subsistence level (with one or two exceptions). It is this type of person spending his time on the reserve or in the nearby town who makes up the bulk of the residential working population.

A few persons have either moved away to another band area or have joined this band. This is normally a result of interband marriage and post-marital residential status. In this way a few persons have established ties of affinity and visiting relationships with members of some other bands. A few have maintained semi-permanent or permanent residence with ultimate transfer of band membership. Regarding inter-band visiting it was pointed out that the government permitted Indian visitors only two weeks' time to visit his kin. This was spoken of in the context of the non-Indian visitors who stayed for lengthy visits and were apparently not sent away.

Within the band social interaction is selective. All movement is along the road to the post office or ferry. People call out as they pass along or stop to chat with certain close relatives. They were observed to ignore members of some families who were sitting out in front of their houses. There appears to be a minimum of informal interaction between persons not closely related. One family remains more formal than the others. This is the family of the ferryman and postmaster. He operates a small soft drink business in his dining room adjoining his post office. He has the position of collecting fares from the ferry business and generally conducting a business involving credit. His relations and those of his family with the others remain polite but formal. His daughter goes away to boarding school. Although they often entertain visitors from outside they diplomatically restrict interaction with other members of the band.

During social gatherings such as church or school evenings a few adults, mostly women and their younger children attend, sitting inconspicuously and passively as the teacher or minister organize a performance or discussion. During the period of fieldwork the latter two visited some homes occasionally, mostly contacting the women of the household.

Political Activity and Social Sanctions

The band elects a chief and two councillors. In the early days it was a lifetime chief. This person was variously spoken of as a leader who got things done and represented his people in a responsible way; and alternatively some said he was a land grabber who acted to dispossess unfortunate people in order to amass more wealth. At the present time it is a three year term.

Council Meetings—None was held during the time of field work—apparently deal mostly with problems of employment, housing, relief and band loans. It appears that the price of election as chief or councillor is to adopt a *laissez-faire* attitude with regard to any form of initiative which would require sanctions or discipline. An elder when complaining about unwanted visitors claimed the elected leaders would never do anything because of the fear of compromising their popularity. A former chief mentioned that his way of initiating something in council was to talk informally ahead of time to a person who if he agreed would raise it in council. The chief explained that if he initiated something himself he would not likely succeed in getting it approved. A certain amount of confidence appeared to be held in the postmaster and ferryman because of his ability to contact the local Member of Parliament and the Member of the Provincial Parliament. Although band members had no federal vote (1958) it was felt that their man might gain sympathy and perhaps concessions from the government members.

An equally important client-patron attitude was expressed regarding personal contact with the local Indian superintendent. One or two persons said he was "O.K." as they could drop in and talk with him in his office. Some others expressed much the same attitude towards the provincial game warden who supervised fishing regulations and towards the police. It would appear therefore that at least in some quarters the important political relations were of a client-patron nature with individual administrative officers rather than through the internal elective and legislative process.

Social Sanctions—Sanctions might be considered as of two types, external and internal. The first would consist of supervisory controls exercised by the Indian superintendent as general administrator including band council meetings, government school teacher in the form of educational discipline and instruction which extends into the area of values and moral behaviour; the clergyman whose advice would be in the same direction; police supervision including occasional visits from RCMP representatives to attend dances and generally control potentially illegal behaviour; the game warden exercising jurisdiction over fishing regulations; senior Indian Affairs Branch officials with welfare workers who admonish the people to raise their moral and health standards; and finally in the event of police court proceedings the supervision of the magistrate and court social workers who "treat us like children". In general therefore the characteristic external sanction is one of paternalistic control superimposed on the band population by non-Indian persons, in addition to personal contact by administrators toward a few individual persons.

Internal sanctions would consist of indigenous informal controls on the individual by fellow band members. In this area there appear to be few sanctions which are operative. Several times during fieldwork persons spoke in a derogatory way against another to the ethnographer. They would complain that they could do nothing and the chief and councillors were either away from the reserve or did not want to question anyone's behaviour for fear of losing popularity. There appeared to be few occasions except random meeting in the shops or meeting for the ferry when adult peers would meet socially or otherwise at which time the use of gossip and discussion could become operative as sanctions to individual behaviour.

II PRESENT DAY INDIAN CONTACT SOCIETIES

In order to analyze some of the problems in present day Indian contact[12] societies a number of factors should first be dealt with. First, there is the concept of culture. In the face of rapid changes in technology and their consequent behavioural adjustments, if culture is to be used then some way of assigning values to various degrees of change in traditional forms must be evolved. Hawthorn, Belshaw and Jamieson say, "we have arrived at the conclusion that no customary actions, elements of belief or attitude, knowledge or techniques, have been transmitted from earlier generations to the present without major alteration. In other cases, the social inheritance has undergone radical alteration, even inversion" (1958:39).[13] Ethnographic data from Pine Tree (Part I of this paper) support this view. The late G. Gordon Brown solved the problem by ignoring culture as a concept. He said, "I do not necessarily expect the concurrence of fellow anthropologists in thus slighting one of our most sacred terms but have personally found it expedient to think without it" (G. G. Brown, 1951). A more meaningful way to analyze present day Indian contact society is perhaps in terms of social interaction, social sanctions and social organization rather than by accounting for cultural phenomena.[14]

A factor of some importance within the context of traditional ethnic

[12]By this is meant those societies which have had long term association with the national economy and way of life, e.g., Type B.

[13]See also James 1961:721. "Where such aboriginal traits apparently survive without corresponding cultural causation they will be found to be functions of new cultural conditions and as such, are not the same thing as their primitive antecedents."

[14]Hawthorn et al. speaks of "customary ethnic relationships in a community" (61). Aberle et al., speaks of functional prerequisites to a society. Leighton speaks of sharing physical space, frequency of interaction and membership in communities (310). Talcott Parsons says, " ... the conception of a social system must be differentiated from the encyclopedic conception of culture which both groups (Malinowski and the 'culture and personality' school, e.g., Kardiner and Mead) on the whole share, leaving a more restricted conception of 'cultural tradition' " (68). Edmund Leach says, "British social anthropologists have increasingly tended to think of their special field as the study of the behaviour of small groups operating within a defined structural-cultural matrix. The concept of the corporation with its associated hereditable estate—its 'bundle of rights' over things and people—is tending to become central to our analysis" (136).

society is the proportion of persons who were apparently socially unacceptable. In 19th century Kiowa society a leader would refer to this type of
person as "my weaklings". They were of a different status in society, being
capable of lying, stealing, and ignoring the prestige system of war prow-
ess.[15] In essence they were lower-class persons whose sanction system was
different from that of full status warriors and hunters. These persons, who
were outside the norms of the traditional status system would probably be
part and parcel of the hereditable background of the modern society. By
this I mean that present day society is made up of both the descendants of
the high status and the low status persons, and consequently a discussion
of present society must take into account these people, who were closely
integrated into the status system as well as those who were less interested
and perhaps less successful.

This phenomenon of lower status or unacceptable persons being part
of society is seen even in subsistence level societies. Among the Northern
Ojibwa of Pekangekum, Ontario, the difference in value of fur trapped
during the 1954–55 season by household units (containing approximately
two trappers) was from $1,720 to $300 or even lower (Dunning 1959:
38–9). Some camps were composed of trappers who trapped almost nothing. They are part of the social system, but obviously either not participating or are unable to participate fully in the status system.

A further aspect of present-day Indian society is the relatively long
history of contact. Eighteenth and nineteenth century writers have mentioned the impact of the European socio-economic system on the hunting
and collecting people. Hearne described the phenomenon of the acculturated Indian around Fort Prince of Wales (Churchill) as the "Southern Indians" who appeared to him to be qualitatively different from the remote
peoples, the "Northern Indians".[16]

Although the Indian groups were doubtless different, the northern
being Chipewyan and the southern being Cree, what Hearne describes is
their conduct *vis-a-vis* the whites. Surely Hearne's comment about the
Southern Indians being ". . . the most debauched wretches under the Sun",

---

[15]J. Richardson, 1940. See also B. Mishkin, "Rank and Warfare Among the Plains
Indians," American Ethnological Society, Monograph 3, 1940.

[16]"Much does it redound to the honour of the Northern Indian women when I af-
firm, that they are the mildest and most virtuous females I have seen in any part of
North America; though some think this is more owing to habit, custom and the fear
of their husbands, than from real inclination. It is undoubtedly well known that none
can manage a Northern Indian woman so well as a Northern Indian man; and when
any of them have been permitted to remain at the Fort, they have, for the sake of gain,
been easily prevailed on to deviate from that character; and a few have, by degrees,
become as abandoned as the Southern Indians, who are remarkable throughout all
their tribes for being the most debauched wretches under the Sun. So far from laying
any restraint on their sensual appetites, as long as youth and inclination last, they give
themselves up to all manner of even incestuous debauchery; and that in so beastly a
manner when they are intoxicated; a state to which they are peculiarly addicted, that
the brute creation are not less regardless of decency. I know that some few Europeans,
who have had little opportunity of seeing them, and of enquiring into their manners,

should refer only to those persons who had adjusted at the lowest level to living around the trading post.[17]

With regard to the Indians around Fort Garry at the beginning of the nineteenth century, Coues said the traders referred to some of them as "Bungees", meaning them to be nothing more than beggars (1897).

In consequence therefore of these two phenomena, a differentiated traditional society as well as a differential in the degree of acculturation or adjustment of individual persons or groups in the modern world, assumptions about society deriving from a so-called homogeneous aboriginal unit are inadequate. The presently constituted grouping at Pine Tree may be in part the result of the above factors, which make for a heterogeneous social unit. Moreover the incidence of emigration of certain persons, as well as the inclusion from time to time of non-Indian persons further differentiates the group. Social analysis of this unit therefore must take into account these various factors.

A further disadvantage in viewing the Indian population unit as a unit of culture lies in the implicit assumption that the national socio-economic system is internally differentiated in a horizontal (e.g., various ethnic groups including Indians and Eskimo etc.) rather than a vertical (individual) way. This would tend to reify the Indian population into a unified entity when perhaps it is merely a segment of the larger society. This view of the Indian populations as cultural entities is implicit in government policy which has differentiated persons descended in the paternal line from Indian persons as persons who have a special legal status of Indianness. We have seen from Part I of this paper that in terms of linguistic knowledge, kinship obligation-relations, marriage and the family, mythology and magico-medical therapeutic practices, the population isolate is by no means unified within the boundaries of traditional Ojibwa norms.

If however we think in terms of social interaction and structural-cultural systems, a rather different view of the population emerges. According to Aberle et al. society is "a group of human beings sharing a self-sufficient system of action which is capable of existing longer than the life-

have been very lavish in their praise; but every one who has had much intercourse with them, and penetration and industry enough to study their dispositions, will agree, that no accomplishments whatever in a man, is sufficient to conciliate the affections, or preserve the chastity of a Southern Indian woman.

"The Northern Indian women are in general so far from being like those I have above described, that it is very uncommon to hear of their being guilty of incontinency, not even those who are confined to the sixth or even eighth part of a man.

"It is true, that were I to form my opinion of those women from the behaviour of such as I have been more particularly acquainted with, I should have little reason to say much in their favour; but impartiality will not permit me to make a few of the worst characters a standard for the general conduct of all of them. Indeed it is but reasonable to think that travellers and interlopers will be always served with the worst commodities, though perhaps they pay the best price for what they have." (80–83)

[17]It is possible too that some of the great differences in behaviour of the Cree and Chipewyan is partially accounted for in the nature of their economic pursuits. E. E. Rich has most insightfully demonstrated the Cree occupation as middlemen in the fur trade. (1960:35–53).

span of an individual, the group being recruited at least in part by the sexual reproduction of the members". And further, the authors list the functional prerequisites to a society as: (a) provision for adequate relationship to the environment and for sexual recruitment, (b) role differentiation and role assignment, (c) communication, (d) shared cognitive orientation, (e) a shared, articulated set of goals, (f) the normative regulation of means, (g) the regulation of affective expression, (h) socialization, (i) the effective control of disruptive forms of "behaviour" (1950).

From this view (in terms of social prerequisites) our ethnographic sample, the Pine Tree community does not qualify as a society. The sample comes much closer to Leighton's concept of the "Collection". He says:

> In the Collection there is by definition no sociocultural integration. Instead there are numbers of individuals occupying the same geographical area having nonpatterned encounters with each other. Such unity as exists is based on sharing physical space, on frequency of interaction (even if unpatterned), and on the absence of current membership in any of the communities that may lie adjacent to the collection. The boundaries, in short, are largely boundaries of exclusion.
>
> In terms of the unit, the Collection is posited as nonfunctional. While as individuals the people may be able to wrest a living from their environment and thus achieve participation in a process of energy exchange and biological survival, the Collection itself has no patterns of procuring food, shelter, and protection against disease. What persons do in these regards are separate acts without mutual linkage. There can be procreation, but with the care of children completely individualistic both maternal and infant mortality rates would be high.
>
> Since the Collection by definition lacks patterns for these primary activities, those other patterns based upon the particular style in terms of which the primary activities proceed are also absent. There is, in short, no culture so far as the Collection is concerned.
>
> The main point it is desired to make is probably self-evident—namely, that in a Collection there are circumstances conducive to psychiatric disorder. Children born in a Collection would not have a sociocultural environment in which they could develop basic urges, unconscious processes, cognition, and affect into coherent sets of sentiments, and hence there would be defect in personality formation.
>
> The one postulated need that might find frequent channels of expression is hostility. The strong would be literally able to get away with murder.
>
> The position of spontaneity is equivocal. In some respects the situation would be conducive to this trend in personality since there would be no conventional barriers to any form of originality of expression. On the other hand, there would not be a cultural heritage to provide inducements and guide lines for the definition of objects. There might be opportunity enough for the expression of spontaneous physical activity, but little for progressive and developmental spontaneity of thought. (310–11)[18]

[18]"It is patent that neither the Model nor the Collection can occur in nature. They have been posited in order to represent what might be called absolute social integration and absolute social disintegration. Now, while the extremes depicted in the two

If it appears logical to conclude that this population isolate is neither a cultural unit nor a social entity, then how can it be conceptualized? The most fruitful approach might be to consider it as a part or sub-system of the national socio-economic or structural-cultural system. My hypothesis therefore is that much of the behaviour of the Indians in the contact situation though judged or pre-judged by others to be Indian behaviour, is in fact normal behaviour of the class (in the national socio-economic system) in which the actors are.

With respect to the Puerto Rican immigrants to New York City, Fitzpatrick points out this problem. He says: "there is a danger in identifying as prejudice something which is part of the routine of living in the modern city"; and "it is important not to confuse prejudice against the Puerto Ricans with certain kinds of difficulties which are simply part of the problem of urban living for poor (*i.e.*, lower-class) people whether they are Puerto Rican or not" (1960:45). It would seem in the above situation that non-Puerto Ricans tend to identify the behaviour of Puerto Ricans as Puerto Rican rather than as lower-class American behaviour. Something of the same confusion exists in the Indian situation.

I propose to look at Pine Tree specifically for evidence of this hypothesis of part-membership in Canadian society rather than as an ethnic entity. We have seen how the population fails to organize itself in terms of traditional cultural or social norms. It remains to examine its participation in the total socio-economic system.

A general view of the economic situation suggests one of marginal labour. The few who have successfully integrated into the national economic system either live away permanently or spend most of their time away from the reserve. The remainder, except for the person who operates the ferry and mail service, are engaged in casual unskilled or semi-skilled jobs of short duration. The summer tourist season accounts for some of this work, as well as a minimum of tourist business on the reserve for two families. Tourist ice fishing in winter provides a little income for two or three families. This apparently casual attitude toward work is further exemplified by a similar attitude toward gardening and animal or poultry raising. In the midst of a good garden area with no shortage of land, with the exception of two small garden plots and the leading economic person running a number of head of cattle, foodstuffs are all purchased out of the grocery and butcher shops. Nor is the situation with respect to tourist accommodation any more businesslike. The only charges for services and hospitality rendered are symbolized by one person's comment about the tourists; "they drop a lot". Parenthetically this person's wife epitomized her reactions to the kind of hospitality required, *i.e.* drunken parties, by saying: "I hate them; there is only one who pays his way".

constructs do not exist, community units occur which approach the Model and others occur which approach the Collection in general character. It is suggested that such communities can be compared and contrasted to each other in this dimension." (312). Excerpted from Chapter IX of "My Name is Legion": *Foundations for a Theory of Man's Response to Culture* by Alexander H. Leighton, M.D. © 1959 by Basic Books Inc., Publishers, New York.

Moreover we have seen in Section I the amounts of relief payments together with parliamentary and band fund appropriations for housing (during 1956–57), all of which accord with the general economic pattern of a marginal economy and one which is completely dependent upon the national economy.

Regarding the state of Indian education, several writers have commented on the general picture. Renaud discusses residential schools which include an element of non-English speaking entrants. He suggests that the students are academically considerably behind non-Indian students. He further points out that in the higher grades the age retardation claims many Indian students as drop-outs (1958:18–19). Speaking for the American Indian school children, Boyce presents much the same picture. He says,

> Up through the second or third grade the medians of academic achievement for Indian children of every tribe compare quite favourably with published medians on standardized tests. Thereafter, the medians of Indian children fall increasingly below the published norms. By the end of the elementary grades the characteristic pattern is for Indian medians to be several grades or more below published norms. An increasing number of Indian pupils withdraw from school as they advance in grade, while those who hang on become increasingly over-age for grade. In the United States only four out of ten Indian children who commence high school succeed in graduating. Many more never enter high schools. (*1960:3–4*)

The Pine Tree Ojibwa shows less age retardation than the above statements suggest to be normal. This is seen by comparing median ages by grades for our Ojibwa society and the Province of Ontario figures.

Median Ages 1958

	Grades 1, 2, 3	Grades 4, 5, 6	Grade 7
Ontario	8.1 years	11.1	13.1
Ojibwa Pine tree	8.4 years	10.7	14.

In the past ten years Pine Tree Ojibwa has had fully qualified teachers. Their qualifications were as follows: five teachers, all of whom had senior matriculation (Grade XIII) and four of whom had first class teaching certificates (the fifth had a second class certificate). It should be noted too that these children have not suffered from the handicap of a foreign language as have many of the northern Indians. Considering therefore the familiarity with the English idiom and the recent continuity of qualified teachers at the school, it is perhaps not surprising that median ages are equivalent to those of the province as a whole. The significant factor in the school figures however is the large drop out in the later years. For this society 81% of the total school enrolment consists of children from seven to twelve years inclusive; whereas for the province this age group represents only 52.8% of the total.

In seeking reasons for this failure of most of the older children to carry on their education, it should be noted that high school services are offered in the local town, about four miles distant from the island. Arrangements are made with the help of the Indian superintendent for boarding the children in private homes in town during the school week. These facilities, although not convenient for the Indian children, are not in themselves sufficient to account for the low incidence of high school registrations.

It seems fruitful to view the apparent difference in academic achievement between Indian and non-Indian students not as a cultural difference so much as one of socio-economic differences. Knoblock and Pasamanick, in dealing with 300 Baltimore children, half of whom were Negro, suggest this factor. The authors are quoted as saying that during the early years of life:

> The general developmental quotient rose for the white children, while it fell for the Negro youngsters; language ability rose in the whites and fell in the non-whites.
>
> Failure in these areas is quite understandable among the non-white groups, usually of the lower socio-economic background, ... There is less motivation to learning in most of these non-white homes in the study, because there is more of a deterrent to it. There is more sickness, more working mothers, lower nutrition and less, if any, stimulus to intellectual achievement. The Negro children in the study just did not have the motivation to achievement in all phases of their physical and intellectual development. (*H. Knoblock and B. Pasamanick, paper read to the American Orthophysical Association, February, 1960, Chicago; reported in* New York Times, *February 28, 1960.)*

From this viewpoint of socio-economic factors the situation at our community of study becomes more meaningful. Teenage boys who had left school reported that they would not return at the next session. "You don't learn anything." "One guy went to (the town) school and got his matric. It didn't do him any good. He couldn't get a job." "I've got a job fixed up, working with a carpenter." Moreover the example of older men on the island who work as casual labourers does not serve as an incentive to secondary school education. With regard to female students, I was informed that there were three or four at high school in the town last year (1957). They all became pregnant however and had to leave school.

Within the context of the island as a community there appears to be little reason to struggle on towards higher education. The few persons who become successful usually leave the community and as they tend to identify with the outside world, they are socially lost to the community.[19] The real example of adult behaviour comes from the remainder who have stayed on in a subsidized and marginal economy. This is not conducive to academic achievement.

[19]In a recent speech (1960) on the C.B.C. network, Chief Genevieve Monkman of the Chilliwack, B.C. Band stated clearly one view of the problem besetting a modern acculturated Indian population. They were emotional ones which included poor environment and home backgrounds. The educated persons left the community and, failing to return, left the uneducated on their own. Chief Monkman sought any measures which would help self-confidence in her band.

The Pine Tree people have been associated over a long period of time with the social and economic systems of Southern Ontario, as well as with two levels of government. Judging therefore from their low level of economic success and educational achievements they as a group do not appear to have become part of the society of their immediate rural environment. Neither do they appear to have maintained a viable entity as an Indian group—judging from their minimal knowledge and use of language, kinship and genealogies and supernatural beliefs. Moreover their spotty or minimal level of social interaction and sanctions within the community would appear to deny the emergence of a midway adjustment to *Indianness* or *pan-Indianism*.

It appears that this legally defined group is not an identifiable group either as ethnically Ojibwa in the modern world or even as a society organized around more general Indian values.

Furthermore, judging from their extremely marginal economic status, it is therefore my hypothesis that this grouping is more closely identifiable with lower-class behavioural patterns of the national society, whose identity otherwise is merely based on a permanent legal attachment (registered with Indian Affairs Branch, Ottawa) to Indian band land.[20]

FACTORS MAKING FOR PERMANENCE OF THE SITUATION

There appear to be three major factors which make for permanence of the depressed rural conditions of the reserve Indian (the analysis and hypothesis deal only with the southern acculturated areas).
1. The structure of the Indian band living on reserve land is set first and foremost by the Indian Act which says in part: " 'band' means a body of Indians (1) for whose use and benefit in common, lands, the legal title to which is vested in her Majesty, have been set apart before or after the coming into force of this Act, (2) for whose use and benefit in common, monies are held by Her Majesty, or (3) declared by the Governor in Council to be

[20]Bernard James makes this point for the Wisconsin Ojibwa as follows:

"I am suggesting that as far as the loss of Ojibwa culture traits is concerned, the village has become deculturated and that its minimal appropriation of new cultural traits has produced a *'poor White' type of subculture* in which the conservative-progressive distinction actually operates as a socioeconomic class line. A 'poor' family tends to be considered 'Indian' in cultural orientation regardless of the loss of Ojibwa cultural habits or techniques." From "Social Psychological Dimensions of Ojibwa Acculturation." Reproduced by permission of the American Anthropoligical Association from the *American Anthropologist* 63:728, 1961.

Gordon Hirabayashi and C. L. French make the same point in a paper read at the Canadian Economics and Political Science Association annual meetings, Montreal, June, 1961:

"We hypothesized that a main factor in the Metis' present situation stems, not from a lack of acculturation, which in this area at least seems quite far advanced, but from *acculturation into the lower classes of Euro-Canadian society* so that they are able to function only in a manner not markedly different from lower class persons throughout North America, regardless of race or ethnic status. It would appear that the acceptance of disease and other unpleasant life situations which these people show might indicate an internalization of a lower class set of norms and values which would include poor self image, feelings of unworthiness and general apathy toward the environment." "Poverty, Poor Acculturation and Apathy: Factors in the Social Status of Some Alberta Metis", p. 2. (italics mine).

a band for the purposes of this Act; . . ." (Indian Act, 2-a, p. 1, 1952). In areas where the Indian population is completely exposed and has been for several generations to the rural and urban parts of the national society and thus having the opportunity for participation in the educational, economic and social life of the larger society; and where the Indian population does participate to a considerable extent in the latter, then the legal structure of the reserve system poses an obvious anomaly.[21] The system requires common inheritance of land in perpetuity, and maintains the composition of the band through inheritance in the paternal line by means of a registered band list.[22] Thus a person's social and economic membership and participation in a band although to an extent a matter of his own choice,[23] becomes at least in part a result of government fiat. The role of government therefore in maintaining the band as an entity or society is not to be minimised.[24]

One of the few exceptions to this picture of an externally imposed system on an Indian group appears to be the Fox Indians of Iowa. These people purchased some land in Iowa and consequently became ordinary citizens to the extent that they were subject to state taxation.

> In the middle fifties, the Fox, dissatisfied with their Kansas home (a reservation provided by the federal government in 1842) and with

[21]Fitzgerald speaks of the United States Indian groups as follows:
"This anomalous political status (considering the tribes as domestic dependent nations), seldom understood by the Indians themselves, arbitrarily maintained by the Federal Government but contradicted increasingly over the years by the actual facts of their situation, has worked along with their physical isolation on their reservations to retard their development and their integration into our national life." (1956:19)
With regard to the United States Indian tribes, Fitzgerald says: "The 185 Indian tribes, or 'domestic dependent nations' in a very real sense are not a part of the American Government. They are actually an anomaly in the American political system. They are like a grat that flourished on a tree while the part that was grafted still had some life-carrying sap in itself, but which because there was no way for the graft to take, has long since become a dry, useless appendage or may be in the process of becoming so." (1956:15)
[22]Section 11-e of the new Indian Act allows for the inclusion of illegitimate children of female Indian status persons. In fiscal 1959 there were 148 children and in 1960, 115 whose inclusion as band members was protested by Indian status band members.
[23]The Governor in Council through the advice of his Minister has discretionary power to declare an Indian person enfranchised—Section 108-1 (a), (b), (c). The main criterion is whether in the opinion of the minister the Indian person is " . . . capable of assuming the duties and responsibilities of citizenship". In fiscal 1960 the Branch approved applications for enfranchisement of 1,123 persons while refusing applications for 63 Indians which involved 148 persons.
[24]The Indian Advisory Committee of the Ontario Department of Public Works brief to the Joint Commons-Senate Committee on Indian Affairs calls for " . . . granting Indians outright possession of their land. As it is now, said Mr. Moses (a member of the Indian Advisory Committee), the regulations treat Indians like children." *(Canadian Press* dispatch, 19.5.60)
The American equivalent of this is state jurisdiction rather than the Federal administration. Hoebel says about this kind of different treatment for Indians: "On some reservations chaos prevails where order should rule. It could improve matters for such people and their neighbours to have the local state move in with its laws and its officers." (1956:14)
Fitzgerald comments: "Where tribes have little or no communally held tribal property and are already well along the road to acculturation there may be much more good than harm in eliminating the *fiction* of the tribe as a separate political entity." (1956:17, my italics.)

the government's policy, moved back to Iowa where they bought a little land on the Iowa River. Unrecognized by the government, they barely existed by their little agriculture and by begging until, in 1866, the government sent an agent and resumed annuity payments. Since that time, living on their reservation near Tama, Iowa, they have increased their lands and their population and are now well established.

The Fox today, on their reservation where they own and administer the land communally, are still a going concern (the whole community pays taxes to the state of Iowa). Their culture has changed in many respects, but replacements rather than losses have constituted the chief process of change, and the society and its individuals seem integrated almost as well today as they were at any time in the past. *(Tax: 243–245)*

For the Canadian Indian band (Type B), the consequences of this permanent and secure legal and political position might be a negative incentive to most of the persons who desire the benefits (as they see them) of increased economic participation in the outside world. It is thus easier to remain secure at a subsistence level than to risk entering the competitive social and economic environment. The reserve and registration system provide this minimal but complete security.

2. The administrative system makes for permanence of the system. The Indian Act provides for a line organization. Considerable discretionary powers devolve upon the Governor in Council. In practice his agent, the Indian Superintendent, is responsible for many administrative decisions concerning persons on the reserve. His reports provide the Minister with information for purposes of advising the Governor in Council. The Indian superintendent's position is made easier by means of a chief and councillors in the band through whom he works. Regarding this type of rank differential in the band, Hawthorn *et al.* say:

> Some special difficulties... arise where, traditional forms of government and rank distinctions were minimal in the culture, and where the later, administrative or mission-inspired pattern of an appointed or elected chief has failed to bring for him from the community meaningful recognition and opportunities for leadership. *(35–36)*

And with regard to the paternalistic principle Hawthorn says:

> The barriers set up in opposition to paternalistic policies are likely to be higher and more formidable when misunderstanding increases because the White official sees only the proferred benefit, and the Indian sees only the dominating position of the White official. Our recommendations... for placing more power and responsibility in the hands of the Indians themselves were devised, at least partly, in order to circumvent the effects of this misunderstanding. *(61)*[25]

The imperatives of the 19th century pioneer areas which gave rise to a paternalistic form of Indian administration have disappeared. But the administrative structure, though modified and improved, has remained. The Indian Act serves to differentiate the Indians from their nearby neighbours.

---

[25]This position has been recognized by the Joint Senate and Commons Committee in their report of August, 1961, in which they recommend both an increase in the duties and responsibilities of the chief and band as well as making those responsibilities explicit.

Police, welfare and government administration are different for the Indians.

From the Indian person's point of view it would appear that the only way to achieve results with the administration is by means of personal client-patron relations. One person commented on the aimiability of the superintendent because one could always call on him when in town. Moreover the prestige of the ferry man was enhanced by the fact that he claimed to maintain relations with the local M.P. and M.P.P. Some persons spoke warmly about their contact and conversations with the regional supervisor of Indian Affairs on his occasional visits. This was the way to get concessions from government, rather than through the elective system of chief and councillors. The position of chief appeared to be given (by means of elections) to a person who would not oppose anything or anyone on the reserve. But the idea of electing a chief to represent the interests of the band to government seemed essentially irrelevant.

From the point of view of the administration a major difficulty of the system (a federal government bureaucracy encysted in the democratic milieu of the national society) appears to be that of exerting influence or imposing sanctions on the welfare recipients. For example in 1959 the Sussex County Council (England) ruled that recipients of Council houses were required to keep a garden as a condition of remaining in a subsidized house. If this kind of "arbitrary" action were to be taken by the superintendent's administration there might be sharp reaction on the grounds that government was interfering with the Indians' internal affairs.

3. Most of the recent increases in welfare benefits have been made by the Federal Government (see Part I), the same government which administers the Indians and to whom the Indians look for help. To the members of Ojibwa Pine Tree the Provincial Government has little contact with them. There is a provincial game and fisheries person, but his contact has been rather a negative one, limiting or prohibiting fishing in their traditional waters. In consequence the latter government has little meaning to them, whereas the Federal Government's role as Indian administrator is emphasized by the new welfare benefits.[26]

---

[26]As welfare benefits increase, an apparently inescapable result seems to be that of greater dependency of the recipients on the system. And this is anathema to any expression or development of initiative. Boek and Boek comment on this phenomenon for the City of Winnipeg: "One of the women interviewed said that welfare would not let her family live in a poor area that they were used to. This may help the family improve its social position, and it may also be beneficial for children. However, the more comfortable quarters purchased for them without their own personal effort might lead a family to see welfare as a better way to live than to work for an income." (1959:85)

To emphasize the implications of this policy of welfare it might be noted that the three main areas of welfare benefits offer more income than a reasonable wage in the unskilled labour field, *e.g.*, Manitoba minimum wage, 1960, 66c per hour; a more realistic wage might be $1.00 which would be approximately $170 per month. A family with three small children would draw the following from welfare agencies:

City of Winnipeg relief	$178.68
Province of Manitoba, Mother's Allowance	$193.00
Dept. of Veterans Affairs; total disability pension	$247.00

Regarding Indian societies, the welfare benefits administered by the Federal Government are not likely to decrease with time. More probably they will increase and if so it would seem likely that the peoples' sense of dependency upon the Federal administration will correspondingly increase.

In general the legal, political and administrative systems appear to the members of the community to be vastly different from the systems which structure and govern the lives of other Canadians. This fundamentally different structure plays an important role in the "separateness" and "differentness" which the Indians feel.

Moreover it is my hypothesis that for the Pine Tree Ojibwa this governmental recognition and control is the essential basis of community for the people, rather than any internal organization or indigenous expression of ethnic unity. If this is valid then the collectivity of persons recognized by Government as Indians in Pine Tree is an artificial one. These persons who appear to have lost the essence of their traditional culture and who themselves would have been lost in the larger population but for government protection, might be termed *Indian Status Persons* rather than *Indians*. This might be in contradistinction to Indians who have either integrated and become operative citizens of Canada but recognizing their Indian ancestry, or members of those isolated groupings who view themselves as independent trappers, hunters and fishermen.

The *Indian Status Person* is the person who lives and depends on government grants in various forms to support his marginal subsistence level of living. Occasional wage labour increases his income, but the solid, one might almost say overwhelming basis for security appears to be not the group of interrelated families sharing a common history, culture and residence, but the land itself with the implication of a paternal government in the form of the agent who will not see him starve on the land.[27]

---

[27]James comments for the Wisconsin Ojibwa as follows: "If it is correct to conclude that native cultures have been replaced by reservation subcultures of a 'poor-White' type, and an essential functional requirement for their existence, as we know them, is an extreme socio-economic status differential, prescriptions that attempt to perpetuate this 'Indian way of life' may be both unwise and inhumane". From "Social Psychological Dimensions of Ojibwa Acculturation." Reproduced by permission of the American Anthropolical Association from the *American Anthropologist* 63:744, 1961.

References

ABERLE, D. F. ET AL. "The Functional Prerequisites of a Society." In *Ethics* 60 (1960): 100–11.

BARNETT, M. L. AND D. A. BAERREIS. "Some Problems Involved in the Changing Status of the American Indian." In *The Indian in Modern America*, edited by D. A. Baerreis. State Historical Society of Wisconsin, 50–70, 1956.

BOEK, W. E. AND J. K. BOEK. "The People of Indian Ancestry in Greater Winnipeg. Appendix 1: A Study of the Population of Indian Ancestry Living in Manitoba." Manitoba Department of Agriculture and Immigration, 132; 1959.

BOYCE, G. A. "New Goals for People of Indian Heritage." Sixth Annual Conference on Indians and Metis, 1960. The Welfare Council of Greater Winnipeg, pp. 27–28.

BROWN, G. G. "Culture, Society and Personality: A Restatement." *American Journal of Psychiatry* (1951)108: 173–75.

COUES. E. ED. *Manuscript Journals of Alexander Henry and David Thompson.* Vol. 1. New York: Harper, 1897.

DUNNING, R. W. *Social and Economic Change Among the Northern Ojibwa.* Toronto: University of Toronto Press. 217; 1959.

———. "Ethnic Relations and the Marginal Man in Canada." In *Human Organization* 18 (1959) 3: 117–22.

———. "Rules of Residence and Ecology Among the Northern Ojibwa." *American Anthropologist* 61 (1959): 806–16.

FITZGERALD, K. Introduction to *The Indian in Modern America.* Edited by D. A. Baerreis. Wisconsin State Historical Society, 1956.

FITZPATRICK, J. P. "The Adjustment of Puerto Ricans to New York City." *Journal of Intergroup Relations* (1960): 43–51.

HAWTHORN, H. B. ET AL. *The Indians of British Columbia.* © 1958 University of Toronto Press, p. 499.

HEARNE, SAMUEL. *A Journey to the Northern Ocean.* Edited by R. Glover. Toronto: Macmillan of Canada, 1958.

HOEBEL, E. A. "To End Their Status." In *The Indian in Modern America*, edited by D. A. Baerreis. State Historical Society of Wisconsin 1–15; 1956.

LEACH, E. R. "The Epistemological Background to Malinowski's Empiricism." In *Man and Culture*, edited by Raymond Firth, 119–37. London: Humanities Press, 1957.

LEIGHTON, A. H. "My Name is Legion." The Stirling County Study of Psychiatric Disorder and Sociocultural Environment, 1959. New York: Basic Books 1:42.

PARSONS, T. "Malinowski and the Theory of Social Systems." In *Man and Culture*, edited by Raymond Firth, 53–70. London, 1957.

RENAUD, A. "Indian Education Today." In *Anthropologica* (1958) N6: 1–49.

RICH, E. E. "Trade Habits and Motivation Among the Indians of North America." *Canadian Journal of Economics and Political Science* 26 (1960) 1: 35–53.

RICHARDSON, J. "Law and Status Among the Kiowa Indians." American Ethnological Society, Monograph 1, 1940.

TAX, SOL. "The Social Organization of the Fox Indians." In *Social Anthropology of North American Tribes*, edited by Fred Eggan; 243–82. Chicago: University of Chicago Press, enlarged edition, 1955.

3

Urban Indians

INTRODUCTION

THERE ARE NUMEROUS PROBLEMS in determining the number of Indians who have migrated to Canadian urban centers. However, one factor seems to be clear, the dominant group has so far sought to ignore them. The Hawthorn Report mentions urban Indians once. In a report that was supposed to give a comprehensive picture of Canadian Indians, it certainly fails in this respect. Because of the Indians' high transiency, their inconspicuousness, and the government's traditional lack of concern over keeping adequate statistics on this issue, we are faced with many problems in attempting to present meaningful information on their urbanization. However, some figures are available. Statistics Canada in 1961 claimed that nearly 30,000 Indians were living in urban areas.[1] Of these, nearly 80 per cent were in large urban metropolitan areas. In 1951 about 17 per cent of the registered treaty Indians were living off the

[1] It is important to remember that these data only concern registered Indians. See first chapter for the differences between the "types" of Indians. However, the data we will be assessing include both treaty and non-treaty Indians. Vincent (1970) for example found that in his sample, about 40 per cent were treaty Indians.

87

reserve but by 1961 the rate had increased to well over 30 per cent (Walsh, 1971), suggesting a trend of migration toward large urban centers. In 1971, *The Native People* presented figures for three urban centers. This research showed that nearly 20,000 Indians were living in Winnipeg, 10,000 in Edmonton and 5,000 in Calgary. Other sources of information substantiate this increase in urbanization. These figures of course suggest that the rates of increase between 1951 and 1961 are far lower than those for 1961–70 as Table 7 shows.

The results generally suggest that the heavy influx of Indians to the city between 1951 and 1961 has not receded but has increased. Why has it not been noticed? A review of the literature shows a paucity of data on the trends of urbanization of Indians, their problems and general adjustment to urban life. To date most people are not aware of their entrance to the urban area because of the feeling that they are "transients" and because they do not attempt to infiltrate the city as a united whole. As a result, they tend to be inconspicuous to the white community. The feeling seems to be (as in past dealings with Indians) that if we ignore them, they will go away. However, as the data suggest, this is not happening. Each year greater numbers of Indians are migrating to the cities.

Sociologists and other researchers have found Indians to be inconspicuous in urban areas (Dosman, 1972). Many researchers have suggested that Indians try to pass as whites or as Metis (thus French). They may label themselves Hawaiian or members of another such "acceptable" group to obtain jobs, social services, *etc.* and nullify any stigma that may be attached to them. Interviews with urban Indians revealed that some had not told their husbands (or wives) that they were Indian even though they had been married several years. Children also sometimes did not know that they were Indian or Metis. Statistics Canada generally has Indians under the heading of "other or not stated." This of course obscures any interpretations that could be made about their migration patterns or social characteristics. Their transcience is another reason why they tend to be inconspicuous. Not only do they frequently move in and out of the urban areas, but they also often move within a city. It is not uncommon to find an Indian family moving six to eight times a year, although the average seems to be about three times. Another reason which helps to make them inconspicuous is the fact that the urban Indian is usually first generation. Because of this, Indians have not had time to develop well established ethnic enclaves, such as Jews, Italians and Japanese.

DECISION TO MIGRATE

What makes Indians decide to migrate to the city? Generally it is an economic reason. They seek improvements in their occupations, social welfare or living conditions.[2] As Deprez and Sigurdson (1970) point out: "the

---

[2]Children are a very important "spin off" factor in the number of Indians migrating. About a third of the Indians migrating from the reserves are children either who leave with their parents or are taken away by agencies such as Children's Aid (Denton, 1972).

economic base on the reserve, as it presently stands, is incapable of supporting the existing native population, thus outmigration is essential." This sets the stage. The reserve Indian foresees no immediate change in his socioeconomic status by remaining on the reserve. However, this in itself is an inadequate explanation. Other factors have combined with the low economic productivity on the reserve to foster this high outmigration.

The high birth rate is another reason. Currently the annual natural rate of increase for Indians (3.3 per cent) is about twice as high as the national rate. Coupled with this is the slowly decreasing mortality rate. In 1956 the infant mortality rate was 96 per 1,000 live births. In 1965 this had dropped by half—48 per 1,000 live births (still twice the national average). The result is that more and more people are attempting to live on the same land area. But the young Indians, aged 18 to 25, are leaving the reserve to try to live in the city. It indicates how many are leaving when one realizes that over half of the present Indian population are aged 20 or younger.

Vincent (1970) found that in his Winnipeg study over half of the urban Indians were younger than 30. He also found that 60 per cent were married and 30 per cent single. However, those married were not necessarily living with their spouse at the time. In addition to their youth, most Indians going to the city are better educated than their reserve counterparts, and their expectations are much higher. Over half of the respondents in Atwell's (1969) study had completed grade 5 and an additional third had at least a grade 9 education. This may be a low educational attainment by general population standards but it is higher than "average" for Indians. While data by Davis (1965) on the same subject do not show educational attainment to be as high for urban Indians in northern Saskatchewan, he does show the same trend.

These young Indians, knowing they have had more education than those around them, feel they are more capable of competing in the larger social system. They are more exposed to the values of the dominant society and have relatively high aspirations and motivation. They feel they can "make it." The decision to migrate is made using the older Indian group for comparison in attempting to ascertain their chances of success in the urban area. We can therefore easily see why they believe they will be able to compete successfully.

Before continuing the discussion about the reasons for migration, we must diverge briefly to see what the norms and social control mechanisms are on the reserve. As Denton (1972) and others have shown, there are strong norms encouraging work and independence (which today means earning money). Thus, from early childhood, children are socialized into work roles and as they grow older, more and more is expected of them (Honignan, 1967). But parent-child conflicts emerge because while independence is encouraged, the young are expected to contribute more and more to the family in money and work.

To a degree, young people are encouraged to support themselves. Thus, the young Indian leaves home to be self-reliant. He has no desire to stay at school because he cannot see the relevance of education. By the age of 15 or 16 most Indians have left school.

However, few are able to become "permanent" city dwellers because of factors such as unavailability of jobs, discrimination, and cultural shock. They remain in the city for a short time (two to five years) then return to the reserve. But some do remain as permanent or marginal residents. We can consider these as three types: (a) middle class, (b) marginal, and (c) chronic unemployed.[3]

While most urban Indians belong to (b) or (c), a small and significant proportion can be labelled middle class or, as Dosman (1972) referred to them, as the "affluent." The most oustanding characteristic in which these differ from the other two groups is that they have steady employment through various government or government-financed agencies.

Those in (b) do not have a steady job. They may have several different jobs in a year but may not be employed all year. The grouping simply implies that they have a job which allows them to maintain a residence and meet minimal living requirements in the city.

Those in (c) are generally without jobs for long periods. If they get work it usually consists of single day jobs. That is, they may unload a truck for a day or lay sod for one or two days and then become unemployed again.

Other attributes which differentiate these three groups are (i) conspicuousness, (ii) mobility, (iii) family stability, and (iv) personal disorganization. The middle class Indians rate high in (i) and (ii) and low in (iii) and (iv).

Why do these people choose a *particular* city when they migrate? We have already discussed two important "push" factors—low economic development and high natural increase rate. Now we can turn to the "pull" factors. There seems to be two but the data appear to suggest that one is more compelling than the other. The first and more important factor is a city's availability of employment. Indians find out about job opportunities in various urban areas through the mass media (TV, radio and newspapers) and informal conversations. Generally they choose the towns or cities where they will have the best chance of obtaining jobs. However, we will discuss later some intervening factors that must be included in trying to analyze how a decision on a city is reached.

Davis (1965) found that in his study of urbanization of Indians in Saskatchewan, well over 40 per cent of the subjects gave "economic opportunities" as their major reason for migrating to the city. Atwell (1969) in her study of urbanization in Alberta, found a slightly higher rate—55 per cent. The data collected by the IAA (1971) and Nagler (1970) corroborate the above findings except for different percentages. Thus younger Indians aged 16–25 first migrate to an area where jobs seem relatively easy to obtain. About these ages they marry and this introduces a new variable. If they marry whites, they generally do not return to the reserve. However, since most marry within their group, they must decide whether to stay in the city or move back to the reserve. We will consider this later. A second "pull" factor in migration is the knowledge of friends and relatives who have "made good." While objectively these people still exist well below

---

[3]All registered Indians must return to the reserve for a short period every year (or maintain a residence on a reserve) if they wish to maintain their legal registered status.

the government poverty line ($3,500 for a family of four), they see them-
selves as better off than they would have been had they stayed on the reserve. This "success" information may be passed back to the reserve when
a native visits the city for recreation, shopping or medical reasons. The impact of this information is particularly strong on young people.

It is also considered important for the young Indian to leave home
and assert his independence. Those who never leave the reserve are considered timid. When these young people come back to the reserve on week-
ends, they pass on much information to other young Indians still on the
reserve, extolling the virtues of the city and the fun to be had there. Obviously there is a selective process in what those listening are told. For example, those who come back don't like to talk about their failures; they
concentrate on their "good times."

While Davis found that about a quarter of his subjects moved to the
urban area because of "relatives and friends," Atwell and Nagler did not
find comparable results. And results found by Snyder (1971) in his research
on urbanization of Indians in the US, directly contradict both. His results
suggest that perceived educational opportunities seem to be a much stronger
"pull" factor. That is, perceived training opportunities are thought to be
one of the major reasons for Indians coming to the city so that when the
training is finished a job can be obtained in the same city. However, in Canada such educational training programs are not well established. An alternative explanation to the seemingly contradictory results by the above research is that when the Indian moves to a *small* city, he utilizes his friends
and relatives in establishing a residence or obtaining a job. However, he
does not do this when he moves into a large urban center.

The above evidence runs counter to previous theories of migration
(concerning international migrants as well as American Indians). (See Waddell and Watson, 1971.) On the whole, it seems that a minimal amount of
contact is made with relatives when the migrant Indian enters the city.
There seems to be an implicit feeling that the relatives will help if they can
but they are not expected to go out of their way, nor does the newcomer
feel antipathy toward the relative if he does not help. However, having a
friend or relative in the city is generally an assurance to the newcomer that
he will at least have a roof over his head for a day or so and that he will
not go hungry.[4] There is also the possibility of help with a job.

It might seem from this that most Indian migration to the city is well
thought out. Perhaps for some individuals these forces result in a decision
to migrate but it should be pointed out that a sizeable number do not make
such purposeful and analytical assessments before deciding to move. This
seems especially true for young men and women. Young women generally
come to the city because their parents move. And it seems common for
young men to drift in. As Davis (1965) points out in interviews with urban
Indians in attempting to ascertain "reasons" for migrating to the city, some
did not display a rational, logical reasoning process suggested by most de-
mographers in their explanations of migration. Responses such as: "I guess

---

[4]Relatives generally include both family of orientation and procreation as well
as kinfolk in both families, *e.g.* uncles, cousins.

I just like staying in town," or "I got used to staying in town, so I stayed," are not uncommon. They do not reflect serious consideration before the decision.

Parents who have had some education seem to make a conscious, rational decision when they choose to migrate to a city. Perceived job opportunities and better educational facilities for their children and for themselves seem to be the deciding factors. According to Atwell and Davis, about 10 to 15 per cent claimed that education was the main factor in their decision to move into an urban area.

There are then two different groups of Indians who migrate into the city. First, there are those who have made a deliberate decision to move (not without many reservations as to the wisdom of doing so) and have attempted to become permanent residents in the city. They continually try to move into the mainstream of the urban way of life. Since these people see urbanization as a way of solving their problems (as well as resolving the problems their children would have faced had they remained on the reserve), they consciously attempt to assimilate into the larger community. As long as they are able to maintain some work continuity they remain in the city. They are generally referred to as the "white oriented" group and they differ from the other "transient" group.

Indians in this second group go to a city to work but as soon as the job is finished, either they leave and return to the reserve or they join the unemployed and move in and out of the city depending on the scarcity of labor. Most seem to vacillate between staying and returning to the reserve for a time. They are caught in a conflict between liking the city for its amenities and desiring the "security" of the reserve where they still retain many of their "rural values." They seem to have resolved the problem by shuffling back and forth between city and reserve. It is curious (and perhaps a way to reduce cognitive dissonance) that most permanent city Indians see themselves as having a "better life here than on the reserve."[5] But objectively it seems to be a toss up as to which is the better life.

The vacillation between staying in the city or returning to the reserve seems to be quite acute for most urban Indians. They are very conscious of this feeling of ambiguity as to which "route" they should choose. On the one hand there is a feeling that "something big is going to happen" on the reserves one day and they will miss it if they are not there. At the same time, they realize that nothing may happen and thus it is to their advantage to remain in the city. As a result, most city Indians still maintain close contact with friends and relatives on the reserve in an attempt to bridge the gap.

Though information is scant, it seems that migration takes place through a series of steps before the Indian reaches the urban center. The first step appears to be a movement from the reserve to a small nearby city.

---

[5]Cognitive dissonance refers to the case in which an individual recognizes that two (or more) of his attitudes and/or aspects of his behavior are in conflict with each other. As a result of this, cognitive dissonance theory predicts that a person will seek to resolve the contradiction.

If he is somewhat successful in obtaining a job, he then moves to a larger city (depending on job opportunities and known "friends"). He continues this process as long as he is marginally successful in obtaining jobs in each place. If he fails to get work he returns to the reserve.

Migration to the city is promoted to a certain extent by the Department of Indian Affairs. In 1957, the IAB became somewhat interested in the urbanization of Indians and began to set up urban placement programs. By 1959 nearly 300 young Indians had taken part in the program and 90 per cent were found jobs. But the important point is that at the inception of the program, there was careful screening and it was not designed to care for or help seasonal migrant Indians. It was directed to the young, relatively highly educated Indian. However, the basic orientation of the program has changed from quality to quantity (Dosman, 1972).

The IAB has now begun a program of family placement which involves moving and settling entire families. Members of families receive transportation to the city and to all accommodation *en route* to their destination, monetary help for accommodation when they arrive, a small personal allowance, tools and clothes. The IAB will make job contacts for those seeking work. Families can also receive up to $3,000 in additional benefits. In all, $5,000 is available in benefits per family. This is supplemented by nonmonetary benefits such as job contacts and training. However, the average claim per family so far has been only about $1,000. An IAB urban housing program was established in 1967 to provide an off reserve housing grant for Indians when they moved to the city. Indians who migrate to the city are offered a $10,000 grant to buy a house. After ten years the grant is written off. Likewise up to $2,500 can be obtained to purchase household appliances and the money is written off after a specified period.

ENTERING THE CITY

Once the Indian enters the city he is confronted with a new way of life. How he reacts to this new social milieu depends on how well he has followed the described series of steps and/or what type of reserve he is from. Hawthorn *et al.* (1967) and others have made important distinctions between types of reserves. Those classified as "isolated" do not have easy access to the larger Canadian society. They lack easy transportation to nearby cities and are relatively untouched by the outside industrialized society with its electricity, newsprint, roads, *etc.* A second type, classified as "transitional," have easy access to the outside world. These have electricity and are accessible by road and rail to nearby cities.

Indians who migrate from the isolated reserves into the city find adjustment much more difficult (and consequently have a higher return rate) than those migrating from the transitional reserves. However, if they have followed the steps discussed earlier, then adjustment is minimal. Employment would then determine whether the individual stayed permanently. For this to happen the work would have to be reasonably stable.

An additional factor which may affect an Indian's decision to remain in the city or leave, seems to be the distance of migration. If the reserve is only a few miles from a large urban area, the decision to remain is not nearly as crucial as for those who have traveled a long way. If things don't work out in the city, a return to the reserve is not particularly costly or psychologically upsetting. The Indian knows that he can continue to visit the city for occasional recreation, shopping or medical purposes and be back at the reserve within a few hours.

When he gets to the city, the newcomer generally looks up friends or acquaintances or seeks the friendship centers, depending on his age. The older migrant would generally look for friends while the younger one would be likely to go to the friendship center. After this, the newcomer is generally on his own. For the older ones, further contacts are made through the taverns or hotels catering for Indians.

To date, the friendship centers have not greatly helped the young Indian to adjust to urban society. Bear Robe (1970), in a comprehensive report on friendship centers across Canada, points out that lack of money is the predominant issue. This shows in the shortage of proper facilities.

In 1970 less than $350,000 was allocated to the country's 37 friendship centers. In looking at the structure and impact of friendship centers we find that they did not emerge out of government foresight but out of Indians' planning. They have been a creation of Indian leaders, not whites. They have not been long established (the first was set up in Winnipeg in 1959). Therefore they have not provided a traditional "transitional" institution for migrating Indians to use. The government neither wants to finance nor establish more centers. For example, there are none in Quebec nor the Maritimes.

As Bear Robe (1970) points out, the federal government disclaims any monetary obligation toward status Indians who move into the city. At the same time, the provincial and municipal governments argue that they are under no obligation to provide social or welfare services to Indians because they are a federal responsibility. As a result, friendship centers are under-supported. Again there is a facade of government action, but so minimal that it really doesn't change the status quo. For example, while the centers can send people to job interviews, (thereby providing a very important function of locating job opportunities), they have little control over whether the person keeps the appointment. If he does, they have no control over the employer's reaction. Likewise for housing. They can locate accommodation and send the Indians to inspect it but they have no control over whether landlords will accept Indians as tenants.

However, the centers do provide a "drop in" place for young and old Indians (once they are temporarily established in the city). For example in 1965 more than 15,000 Indians participated in the Toronto center's program, over 1,000 used the Winnipeg center and in Calgary, nearly 2,000 Indians were given legal advice, small loans and job contacts (Wuttnee, 1971). The centers vary in effectiveness and in attempting to assess their usefulness. Some have been "taken over" by small cliques of Indians and provide very few services for the new arrivals or permanent settlers. Many Indians, commenting on their experiences in different centers, recognize the variations. The result is that in some areas Indians rely very heavily on services provided by the center while in others, they neither go nor recommend anyone else to go.

However, friendship centers have an unanticipated latent function. They provide the migrant Indian with an "enclave" in which he can emerse himself and thereby partially isolate himself at the social level from the larger white urban society. This satisfies the newcomer (who doesn't know how to fit into white society) and the white society (it keeps the Indian in his place). It would be wrong to convey the notion that these organizations are totally effective. Some Indians go to them but a substantial number do not try to use their services. One reason has already been suggested. An additional factor is that when Indians were asked where the friendship (or Metis) center was, fewer than 20 per cent could vaguely identify the area. Fewer than 5 per cent knew the actual address.

The initial contacts of migrant Indians are then almost totally of their "own kind." Further social interaction is also limited to other Indians. The only interaction between whites and Indians takes place at work. As pointed out previously, strong contacts are maintained with relatives and friends on the reserve.

Just as the Indian had to adapt to the pattern of social life on the reserve, so he has to adjust to urban life. The traditional values of natives clash with white urban values, as Table 35 illustrates.

Table 35. Cultural Differences Between Whites and Natives

White	Indian-Eskimo
Man dominates, exploits and controls nature	In harmony with nature
Future-oriented	Past and present oriented
Doing and activity oriented	Being-in-becoming
Individualistic	Collaborative (tribal)
Capitalistic (commercial)	Communistic in the non-political sense (sharing)
Nationalistic	
Human nature evil but perfectable	Communal

The Indian values noted here are seen in the attitude to life on the reserve; it is "easy" and everyone knows everyone else. The contrasting urban society is seen as rigid. Everything from the houses to the job to the income is fixed. The urban society compels people to become aggressive, competitive and to fight if necessary. This is counter to the values of Indian migrants entering the city. This conflict in values maintains ethnic social boundaries and restricts Indian participation in the labor force. Thus, to date, Indian orientations have been a serious liability to new arrivals in urban centers. If the Indian is to stay he must attempt to readjust. So far these attempts have been unsuccessful. Some adjustments he has made have been nullified by the white society's reaction. Even though the native may be willing to adopt some of the white society's values he may still not be accepted and may suffer discrimination. Vincent (1970) found that about 10 per cent of his subjects claimed they had been discriminated against. This corroborates the findings of Davis (1965).[6]

I do not think that this low rate of reported discrimination is a true indication. In a case of discrimination, the person doing it becomes more powerful than his victim and thus able to direct his life. The situation is extremely uncomfortable and ego deflating for the victim. As a result, people tend to dismiss the objective act of discrimination or provide a "motive" for the discriminator to nullify its impact, *e.g.*: "He didn't really mean what he said; he was just having a bad day."

Indians in the city usually mix socially with each other. This applies to the affluent as well as to the chronic unemployed. About two-thirds of the migrant Indians acknowledge that most of their social contacts in the city are strictly with other Indians. Few of their social activities involve whites. Most Indians feel that they will be rejected by whites so they avoid the possibility. They feel that whites are dishonest, violent, and generally "no good." Most Indian social activities in the city take place through Indian organizations, a church group or in taverns.

We will discuss Indian organizations later, but it should be noted that while most Indians have information about them, very few, if any, are members. Vincent (1970) found that a large proportion of natives felt they would join if contacted by the organization. However, most Indians migrating to the city had very little information concerning the agencies or organizations which might have helped them to cope with urban society. Church-sponsored activities are important in providing recreational and social activities. Since most Indians are Roman Catholic or Anglican, and these churches provide buildings, *etc.* for recreational activities, many young Indians participate. While the activities are not strictly religious, they are not overlooked by church officials as an attempt to influence young people's attitudes. But perhaps the most important religious organization for supporting urban Indians is the Salvation Army.

While the effectiveness of their program varies from city to city, they do try to help Indians. Dosman (1972) notes that in Saskatoon, the Salvationists estimated that about half of their clientele were Indians. The length of time that Indians are allowed to remain at Salvation Army hostels varies from three to five days a month but it does provide a base for operations. Unfortunately the time limit for using the Salvation Army facilities is too short to allow for job hunting. Also, if an employer discovers that an ap-

---

[6]Davis discusses further the "low rate" of perceived discrimination by natives.

plicant is living at the Salvation Army hostel he may be considered a social outcast and rejected.

The third center for Indian social activities, the tavern, is perhaps the most widely used because it is always available. This results in a self-reinforcing cycle. The tavern provides a common meeting place where Indians can stay for long periods and then plan what to do next. There is also a minimal amount of social control by the white society.

PARTICIPATION IN WHITE SOCIETY

Our primary concern in this section is the impact of the large urban centers upon Indian labor force participation. The suggestion that the urban Indian is better off than his reserve counterpart implies that only one criterion—income—is being considered. Agreed, most urban Indians make more money per capita per year than their reserve counterparts, but it does not necessarily mean that they are "better off." Other factors such as free rent, free access to hunting and trapping on the reserve, and lower rates for electricity and food must be considered. This also does not include the "cost" of personal disorganization to the Indian. Being "better off," it is suggested, is a relative subjective term, and can only be evaluated by the individual.[7] However, let us look at the objective picture of labor participation in the urban area.

According to the IAA (1971) and Vincent (1970), the Indian unemployment rate in urban areas is extremely high—68 per cent—compared to 65 per cent for reserves. This suggests that objectively the Indian has a better chance of finding work in the city than on the reserve. But fewer than 10 per cent of those who can find work are able to obtain jobs classified as skilled or better. Most of their jobs are part-time and unskilled.

It is interesting to analyze how such jobs are acquired. Since fewer than a third of the migrants had worked when they first arrived, how did the remainder find employment? The Manpower Department helped an additional 15 per cent to find their first position, but helped only 4 per cent with a subsequent job. The remainder generally found employment by themselves, meaning short term, low status jobs.

The above research also found that the 20–30 age group had the highest rate of unemployment for urban Indians. Nearly 80 per cent of this group were females and 21 per cent males. It should be remembered that these represent the best educated group of Indians. Thirty-five per cent of Vincent's (1970) subjects earned less than $3,000 per year and 50 per cent earned less than $4,000.

In the light of this information, it should not be surprising to find a high degree of alienation and frustration among the young urban Indians who see no future on the reserve, migrate to the city with relatively high

---

[7]While the urban Indian may have a higher "per capita" income per year than his reserve counterpart, other factors must be considered for a comparison. Such things as free rent, free utilities, lower cost of food, no taxes, *etc.* on the reserve offset much of the higher "per capita" income of the urban Indian.

aspirations, and then find themselves without jobs. It should also be no surprise to the white society when protest movements emerge.

It has been suggested by researchers in the United States (and the suggestion has public support) that Indians live in ghettos. The research upon which this report is based did not find this to be the case. On the contrary, all the research seems to suggest that Indian ghettos do not exist. The IAA report as well as Dosman's study clearly demonstrate that the stereotype of a "ghetto" in such areas as Saskatoon and Edmonton simply does not exist. Most whites seeing large numbers of Indians congregating within "poor" areas of the city (during the day for conversation and at night to drink at specific taverns) conclude that this must be the Indian ghetto.

When Indians move to the city they naturally go to the poorer sections of town with the cheapest rents. At this level, we would have to agree that some "ghettoization" has taken place. However, no concentration of Indians has been found in any of the major metropolitan areas throughout Canada. Low cost seems to be the prerequisite for housing when the Indian first comes to the city.

Some ghettoization does take place on the basis of SES and "tribal" affiliations. That is, Indians are attracted to urban areas where rents are fairly low and large houses are available. When such a house is rented, most of the families and/or individuals in it belong to the same "tribe." This is to be expected since they speak the same language (dialect) and share similar cultural outlooks, kin, *etc.* But this does not mean that all Indians migrating to an urban area follow such patterns. In fact, as suggested before, we generally find independent, spacially isolated family units. The average size of an Indian household is slightly bigger than the national average of 3.8 people. Currently Indians have 4.4 people per household. Vincent (1970) found similar results in his Winnipeg survey.

This picture of isolated families suggests, of course, that little daily communication is possible for the urban Indian unless he goes out. He must go to areas designated as "Indian hangouts" to interact with other Indians.

What is the composition of the households? The stereotype is that they are mostly one-parent families but statistics show this to be false. Latest figures from Statistics Canada show 39 per cent are two-parent families with an additional 11 per cent including extended kin. Thirty-two per cent are one-parent families. Existing records and studies suggest that urbanization has produced this large number of one-parent families. However, the IAA found that nearly all such families were like that when they arrived in the city. Therefore, urbanization seems to have a minimal effect on family disruption.

THE DECISION TO LEAVE

In attempting to predict the "return rate" to the reserve several problems confront the researcher. At what point may we claim that the Indian is a "permanent" member of the urban community? Existing data show that well over 80 per cent of those who go to the city return to the reserve within five years. However, they may go back to the city and then leave

again. Presently, fewer than 10,000 Indians (treaty and non-treaty) could be designated as permanent residents (ten years or longer) of large urban areas. Of these, most have one or more of the following characteristics:
- high educational attainment (university or equivalent) and subsequent stable occupation
- left the reserve as children
- enfranchised and/or married to a white.

Females who have married whites have no alternative but to remain in the city because with such a marriage they lose their Indian status and are ineligible to live on the reserve. These women (and their children), while not legally Indians, seem to make up the bulk of the permanent Indian urban population. The second largest group are those who have gone through the enfranchisement process of legally renouncing their Indian status. They too have no legal right to live on the reserve. The third group, quite small, consists of highly educated (or highly skilled) Indians who find that they can compete in and integrate into the white urban society and feel no need to return to the reserve. Perhaps they are the most invisible of all urban Indians. They have had to undergo major changes in their value orientation to "make it" in white society. They do not want to associate with other Indians in any way and generally take the attitude: "If I could make it, so could you." They do not seem to participate in any of the usual Indian social activities. Atwell, for example, shows that a sizeable number of Indians who have "made it" have an unlisted phone number or have the number under another name. They isolate themselves from Indians leaving the reserve in case they might wish to contact them and possibly take up temporary residence. Most of them do not want to be known as Indians and try to pass as members of acceptable ethnic groups (or, if it is possible, as whites).

To find out what leads up to the Indian's decision to leave the city we must try to identify the advantages and disadvantages he sees in the two ways of life. Again, research on this subject suggests that Indians do very little systematic "thinking through" (over a lengthy period) before they decide to move back to the reserve. There seems to be a feeling that the decision can be weighed more thoroughly once they are there. Getting layed off, getting a ticket, hearing rumors about "activities on the reserve," *etc.* have been some reasons why Indians returned to the reserve after they had established semi-permanent residence in the city. While such events would seem irrelevant to whites making a decision about moving, they become crucial turning points for Indians because of the psychological strain they suffer in the city (Wax and Thomas, 1961).

Ablon (1965) has attempted to isolate the advantages and disadvantages of the city to the urban Indian. Table 36 lists the advantages and disadvantages for the reserve and urban area.

An additional problem, which Indians seem to find almost insurmountable when they enter the urban center, involves communications. The problem arises through the specialization of white society and the Indian is struck by the lack of total communication he is used to. In white society, we do not find it unusual only to speak to other people within a general framework, *i.e.*, on a broad level. It is assumed that some people's activ-

Table 36. Reserve and City—Advantages and Disadvantages

Reserve Advantages	City Advantages

Family and friends
"Security"
Free rent
Commodities
Open land
Slow pace of life
	Employment
	Household, medical and shopping
	  conveniences
	Educational opportunities
	  (for adults and children)
	Diversions

Disadvantages	Disadvantages
No conveniences Dependent relatives Bad social conditions	No family/friends near High cost of living Crowded city life Fast pace of life Structured life styles Discrimination

ities are entirely too specialized for others to understand. There is a premise that one cannot understand large portions of other people's behavior and social environment. One does not pretend to understand the jargon of lawyers, doctors, physicists, or even sociologists. However, this does not happen in Indian culture. Admittedly, there were shamans who were able to do things that were unknown to the average Indian, but most people had a clear idea what they were doing. Everyone else in a particular tribe clearly understood each other in the everyday communicative processes.

Conclusion

Urbanization of Indians is proceeding very fast. Unfortunately federal, provincial, municipal and private agencies have not attempted to prepare for this heavy influx. A result is that while federal and provincial governmental agencies are establishing programs to encourage migration to the city, municipal governments are not prepared to extend or continue this help and there is continual conflict between them.

Indians moving into the city find many conveniences that they have never experienced on the reserve. But they also find that they are more exposed to alien ways of thought as well as direct discrimination. For example, one of the most important, immediated differences that confronts the Indian moving into the city is the nearly complete compartmentalization of whites' activities. Whites play roles which are to a great extent mutually exclusive and independent of each other. A second cultural shock is the importance of time and punctuality to whites and their subsequent regulation of behavior. These two factors together produce a high degree of marginal existence in the city and transiency. Most Indians move into the city, but because they are unable to cope with middle class industrialized culture (and discrimination) they return to the reserve. Thus, while the number of Indians going to the city is increasing there is no corresponding rise in the number of stable, permanent families remaining there.

4

For Every North American Indian that Begins to Disappear I Also Begin to Disappear

WILFRED PELLETIER

As AN INDIAN it has been very difficult for me to begin thinking about my place in society. It's very difficult because I have been told since early childhood by white teachers and clergymen and community development officers that my background is one where people are stupid. Because learning has been equated with literacy, I have been urged to discard and suppress everything my people have learned during the thousands of generations that they lived on this continent. That is pretty difficult for me to do, because it involves rejecting myself, and I can't do that.

The Europeans who came to this continent automatically assumed that everybody that was different from them was inferior. Now, some four hundred years later, the dominant society still operates on that assumption. But I cannot forget that originally we had a very different relationship to this land and that we had evolved a society which was much more closely integrated with nature, a society where the order that existed was organic rather than mechanical. Take, for instance, the economy on this continent at the arrival of Columbus. It seems that the whole of North America and South America had total unemployment at that time. We didn't have "jobs," we lived a way of life that sustained us. We were related to something called "survival." We knew how to live off the land without destroying it. We also knew how to survive spiritually, in harmony with our fellow men and the land and the forests and the waters that surrounded us.

Most Indians have been forced to give up their life because both the economy and the ecology have been transformed by the European settlers. If they don't want to integrate with the technological society today, they can choose to spend their days in inactivity on the reserves, holding on to their social order even after it has lost its economic relevance.

There are, to be sure, still some small groups of Indians who have refused to accept these choices and have made heroic efforts to get back to the original relationship with nature. I know of a group of Indians who have gone back to the hills of Alberta, but there is so much interference that they can't really get back into that environmental flow again. Somebody else has to make sure that they survive. The authorities told them that they had to have a school and forced a school upon them. Then they were told that they had to have teachers, so these were also forced upon them. The province sent somebody down who told them that they couldn't survive without welfare, so they gave them welfare. Yet the people in these isolated camps who have risked leaving the relative comfort of the reserve to survive in the hills and woods have experienced a spiritual transformation. Lots of them used to be heavy drinkers, but they have stopped completely. Periodically people from these communities go up to the hills to meditate and fast for a couple of weeks. In one of these communities there is a little boy, seven years old, who is regarded as a prophet. He tells the people what to do and they follow him. Perhaps he'll grow out of this in another year or so and somebody else might take over as a prophet. People there feel confident that the right leaders will emerge without any explicit process to select them.

Yet communities of these kind, even if they manage to survive in a few instances, cannot be the answer for most Indians. We have experienced a profound physical and spiritual dislocation which has had a disturbing effect on all of us: we have had our land taken away from us and have been made strangers in our own homeland. Our way of life is continuously being assaulted from every direction. Even if I as an individual Indian might be able to hold on to my identity, I am undermined by the collective fate of my people. Every time a North American Indian begins to disappear, I also begin to disappear, because I cannot be an Indian, if that identity is taken away from all the rest of the people, my people. When those values begin to change and I don't have anything to offer, except the kind of values you have, then I am lost, too. And that is what is happening to our people.

HOW TO SURVIVE IN AN ALIEN ENVIRONMENT

The first step towards surviving in an alien environment is to feel proud of who you are. Being surrounded by an aggressive and confident majority has made me somewhat defensive: I have spent a lot of years trying to convince myself, after being told all my life that I was no good, because I was an Indian, that I am really alright. That I am a human being like everyone else and that maybe we Indians did have something to contribute to society, something that was sadly missing in the dominant culture.

In trying to do this, I have thought a lot about the Indian way of experiencing the world and the ways in which it is in conflict with white society. Every Indian kid is exposed to these contradictory ways as soon as he begins school. When he has to leave the reserve and go and look for work in the city, he can feel the tension between these cultures in his bones. He is caught in the middle, and often he finds the conflict just overwhelming. I don't know the statistics, but I know from talking to a lot of people that the number of Indian kids landing in mental hospitals is very high. Some avoid the hospitals by staying drunk a great deal of the time. And then there are those who find that nothing will take away their pain except doing away with themselves. We have the highest suicide rate of any ethnic group in the country.

WHITE EDUCATION FOR INDIANS

Being educated in white schools was a painful experience for me like for most Indian kids. I have therefore given a lot of thought to the Indian way of learning. I believe that it has a lot to do with our difficulties in your schools.

I grew up in a community where kids were allowed to discover everything for themselves, by personal observation rather than formal instruction. Nobody said to us "this is a desk." We learned that that was a desk by other people using the word, calling it "a desk." We began to use that word, too, but we related to that desk in our own way, not because somebody told us that was a desk and that's what you do with it, you write at it, or that is a table and you eat off a table, and this is a chair and you sit on a chair. We probably used chairs in many different ways, like most kids, but we also knew that you could sit on that chair. We made the same discoveries that other people had made centuries before us, but they belonged to us, they didn't belong to some despot or expert, someone who tells you, I've got the answers, so you quit being curious, quit exploring. That didn't happen to me until I went to school. From then on it was a matter of suppression.

I don't much like looking back at what happened to me at school. It seems to me that the only thing I enjoyed was playing hooky and running away from school. One of the difficult things I had to cope with at school was something called "time." The teacher would talk about wasting "time." I didn't know what that meant, I didn't know how you could waste "time." And then she would say you could make it up, you could make up "time." She'd read us a story in school and then she'd say we've lost all that "time," so now we have to hurry and make it up. I couldn't figure out what that meant, either. There were all kinds of things about time that really bewildered me. I did not understand what all this clock watching was about, because in our community we ate when we were hungry and slept when we felt tired. We did not do things on any kind of schedule, yet that never presented a problem. The things that were necessary always got done.

I discovered gradually that white people lived in two kinds of time, the past and the future. Indians, on the other hand, live in an eternal present. Our history only ran back to the oldest member of the community, so there was no way we could live in the past or in the future, we could only live in the here and now. When we become like you people, dealing with the past, trying to live some kind of a future that doesn't exist, then we'll have taken ourselves completely out of the present. That's what happens to me when I switch from our language to English. After I have been out in white society for a while, speaking English, I find myself having a really difficult time when I go back to an Indian community. I don't know how long it takes me to readjust, and I don't realize when it happens, I just find myself flowing in that community again, forgetting about that abstract time outside.

White educators always complain that Indian kids have difficulties with abstractions. I, too, had that problem. It is hard for us Indians to make sense of the segmented approach to learning taught in the schools to study "chemistry" or "math" or "French" without relating them to each other and to some larger whole. We Indians approach things the opposite way. We start with the whole and examine every part in relationship to that whole. This is because our way of life was total, nothing was outside it, everything was within. So we didn't begin to explore in the same way you people began to explore; we looked for answers within ourselves, but always related it to the natural order that we saw ourselves part of.

This affected our politics as well as our education. I can remember as a boy, when we sat in council, we came to unanimous decisions. Everyone agreed, and if one person objected we didn't suppress that person. What we did was ask ourselves a question: "Is it possible that we don't see this thing the same way as the other person? Let's explore ourselves." I see white people attempting to use the same method, but they cannot make it work. For what they do, if one person disagrees, they begin jumping on that person trying to change that person's mind and to suppress him. They say, you're holding up the works, there is only one person who disagrees, so you must be wrong, because the majority cannot be wrong. I don't think that it works out that way, because it is quite possible for the majority to be wrong. I look around at the majority culture around me and at all the suffering it has caused both in this country and abroad, and I am very sure that something is wrong.

ATTITUDE TOWARDS NATURE

Because of our holistic world view, our attitude towards nature is very different from white society. We see ourselves as part of nature, we relate to it spiritually. As children, when we got up in the morning, we thanked the Great Spirit for letting us see another day. We spent a lot of time help- ing our parents gather food in the forests and lakes, hunting, picking ber- ries, fishing. We had a great deal of reverence towards nature, but we also felt intimate with it: we looked into the water and it was like blood in our veins. The white man, on the other hand, always sees himself apart from nature, above it in some ways, but also threatened by it. His impulse is always to try to master it, never to flow with it.

Let me tell you a story—a personal experience I recently had—which illustrates the two attitudes towards nature: It was summer and I was on top of a mountain in the interior of British Columbia. It was grassland, rolling hills with clumps of poplar and pine as far as the eye could see. I was with a friend of mine. We stood in a little hollow, a sort of pocket of green grass and clover, kept that way, perhaps, by an underground spring or even the drainage of land. All around us the hills were brown, the grass burned out and dried by the sun.

We stood there in the hot sun, looking all around, and my friend said: "Wilfred, try to imagine that we have been appointed by some Board, 'The Board in Charge of Everything', and our job is to improve this place. What improvements would you suggest?" We stood there and we examined every- thing with a very critical eye, and I thought to myself: "Well, we might take that big cloud over there in the south and move it a little further to the east." But then I decided against that. Then I thought: "Maybe we could put a few more birds in the sky," and I was just going to suggest that, when I noticed an old board, a plank lying at my feet. It had been there a long time. It was grey and weathered and one end was warped. It had sunk into the ground and the grass had grown up all around it. But it had been moved, perhaps by a cow who had stepped on it. Anyhow, it was pushed over at one end so you could see a thin wedge of bare ground where it had been lying for so long. On the other side it was lying on the grass, holding that grass down so it couldn't grow. And I thought: "Ah . . . this is something we can improve. I can move that board back off that grass, which is getting choked out, and then the grass can grow again."

So I took hold of one end of that board and lifted it up a little bit, to move it over. And under it, right there under the end of it was a spider. And that spider was looking me right in the eye and I was looking back at it. And it was stunned, the spider was in shock. Somebody had just lifted the whole damn roof off its world. Then I lifted the board higher and under- neath it was a whole insect community. A thousand ants were scrambling to move their eggs to safety. Woodlice were digging to get down into the ground. Earthworms coiled themselves up like snakes. The ground under that board was a network of insect paths, and the underside of the board was grooved out, too, to form the upper half of tunnels. Well, I set that board back down very gently. And I tried to put it exactly where it had been before I lifted it up.

I apologized to those insects and thanked them for teaching me a great lesson. You see, the first thing I realized was that my decision to move that board back to where it "belonged" was based on good intentions. I wanted to help the grass grow. I was making an improvement. Another thing was that when my eye fell on that board, I lost sight of the total environment. I made a special case out of that board. And my attention was so focussed on only one part of the situation, that bent-over grass, that I had no awareness at all of that whole community underneath. It was invisible to me.

That is what happens to Indian communities over and over again. Whites look at those communities from the outside, just like I looked at that board. They begin to feel sorry for all those poor Indians and they want to help them. They have really good intentions, but they don't see people, they only see Indians. A special category different from what human beings are supposed to be. The organic life in that community, the *organization* of it, is invisible to them, just as the life under the board was invisible to me. So they tear the roof off that community to satisfy their curiosity, to see how it functions, because they assume that there is no organization.

When the adults in our communities wanted to teach us something, they always did it indirectly, through stories like that. They also encouraged us to listen and to observe and to learn from nature.

Nobody ever tried to teach us a lesson by frustrating us or "challenging" us. We therefore didn't grow up angry and aggressive as many white kids do. I thought of that the other night when I was visiting some friends. There was a little boy there, an Indian child around nine years old. There were also two other boys, one was eight and the other was four. The nine year old boy played all night and nobody knew he was in the room, nobody heard him, he played in silence. The two other boys were not Indian. They fought a great deal of the time and made a lot of noise. There were guns going and every movement they made had to have a sound with it.

That evening made me think about my own childhood games and about the stories we used to hear about going hunting or about war parties. When the adults talked about war parties going out to steal horses, they always stressed the silence that was necessary for success. You had to be very, very still, because people on the other side were always listening. If they heard a bird or an unusual noise they could tell right away that there was someone there. We grew up to really know what was going on in that silent way. You can well imagine how hard it is for people brought up that way to get used to the aggressive ways of city people. These are people who don't talk, who don't make noise, who don't shove themselves out in front or push their way in.

PUSHED ASIDE IN THE CITY

So what happens to us is that we continuously find ourselves pushed aside when we move into the city. I remember going to a PTA meeting together with some Indian friends in a large white community. They were serving a big lunch and we were fairly close to the beginning of the line-up because we happened to be talking near the table where the food was served. What happened was that we ended up at the end of the line. I don't know how we got there, but people just moved right in and we found ourselves going back, back, back, until finally we were right out of the hall, at the far end of the auditorium and we were standing there talking. Now we got pushed there, we didn't move back there. People got in front of us, so we backed up. It wasn't until later that I realized that there was something that made us do that. We were not pushy, we didn't barge in in front of any-body.

This happens to Indian kids all the time when they first come to the city and they get on a bus or a streetcar. They want to get off at a certain stop, but what happens is that people get on and shove them not only through that street car but right out the door. Sometimes they go two blocks and they find themselves outside. Some kids I know have ended up walking ten blocks coming home from school or work. These kind of experiences can be very frustrating yet Indians don't know what to do about it. Eventually somewhere along the line they become discouraged and the respect they have for other people diminishes. I don't think that they really see the change in themselves, but it happens to them somehow. Their behaviour begins to change and they become bitter, but not bitter enough to take any kind of action. What they do instead is they end up quitting their jobs or moving out of their homes. They are constantly on the move in the city. Very few of these people settle down and stay in one place, unless they buy a house. I can remember from way back in the early sixties how we tried to keep a list of people who belonged to the North American Indian club that we had at that time. We would phone two hundred people to invite them to a party and we would get twenty, because everyone else had moved. There is just no use trying to keep a list of Indian people in the city.

There are other frustrations, too, for Indian kids coming to the city. Many of them come down here to take courses that somebody has advised them to take. Before long they discover that these courses are meaningless, because there are no jobs available. It never fails to surprise me that there are all these courses, some run by the government and others by private schools and no jobs in most of the fields they teach. Boys are often told to take welding and they get out and discover that most welding jobs are done by machine. Nobody needs them. Girls take hairdressing courses and when they graduate they are lucky to get a job shampooing hair for the next two years, because the diploma is meaningless and it is only experience that counts. They soon learn that jobs are very hard to come by and they have to find a different way of surviving. They try the Unemployment Insurance Office, but usually with little success. And finally the only thing left to do is to go on Welfare. That used to be quite humiliating for them, but things have changed lately, with the large number of Hippies that go on Welfare. I am told that the Welfare office is a much more cheerful place these days with the Hippies sitting there and laughing and joking and not feeling at all embarrassed about having to apply for Welfare. Their spirit affects everybody, even some of the social workers in the office.

Indians use all institutions in a different way than white people, even those created specially to serve them by other Indians. We have an Indian Centre in town called the Canadian Indian Centre, where a lot of the young people end up once in a while trying to get involved or find something they can grasp onto that is meaningful to them. There was a time when we had two or three dance clubs and everyone was trying to entertain these kids in different ways. I used to be a program director and I would ask how many people would want to see the Grey Cup Game, last year's game, we will show it on a film, and about sixty kids would put their hands up. They are all going to come. So we get the film and it ends up that the only people who show up are the four of us who are organizing the thing. We are sitting there with twelve cases of Coke and a whole lot of sandwiches and nobody shows up. The same thing happens when we organize a dance. Nobody comes into the auditorium where the dance is being held, but there is a steady stream of kids coming and going, maybe two hundred kids during the evening. They look in the door and see that there is nobody there yet. So they hang around in the hallway and talk to each other and then they leave. Then another two or three will come and see that nobody is there and away they go, meeting others on the stairs, talking for a while, and maybe they all leave together. Sometimes the place gets filled up just about midnight, when it is time to close up, and you see people leaving in small groups.

The point is that the kids are using the place, but not in a way that we had planned for them. They use it to gather together with people they like and to meet new people, perhaps, but they don't want to commit themselves to any scheduled program. It is very much like a Pow Wow for them. If you go to a Pow Wow you will find that people are putting up their tents, all in a circle and sharing the same tent pegs and food. Two or three people who have never met before will get together to build a fire. A woman will build a fireplace and she will bring over the twigs and you will see somebody else coming out and starting to dry their meat, preparing to stay for three or four days. They find a way of being comfortable together, with no activities planned ahead of time. The Pow Wow goes on, but nobody tells you that you have to dance or dress up or not dress up, for that matter. You can spend three days just visiting other teepees, learning about medicine, listening to legends and stories or trading something you got or maybe sharing some experience you have about farming or something else.

We often do things for different reasons than white people. A while back, I used to have a dance group, and any time we went to perform anywhere we were invited, the first question that I was asked by the group was: "Are they going to feed us?" And I'd say: "No, but they're paying us two hundred dollars to go there." And they'd say: "Is there any other place we could go this weekend?" "We can go to Orillia, but they're not going to pay us any money." "Are they going to feed us?" "Yes." "O.K. then, that's where we're going to go." Money had no meaning to them and it wasn't just the food, but rather something to do with being with people. I don't know how to explain it, but that's where I too wanted to go, where we could meet people and maybe all enjoy ourselves over a meal.

Indians see a meal much more like a ceremony. A few nights ago I spent an evening eating Moose Steaks with some Indian people and some white friends. There was some booze there, too, but people were only interested in the food and that's what they all talked about. Eating together is tremendously important and it probably goes way back to a time when we used to share all our food and game and that created a community. Kids really miss those communal meals in the city and they go home every other weekend, if possible. They'll go back home and when they get there, they'll have such a good time that they decide to stay an extra day. They will miss work on Monday and sometimes they will miss Monday and Tuesday. After two or three months the boss will say, you're unreliable and we can't depend on you, you're not a responsible person. So he finds himself on the street going to the Welfare office.

ATTITUDE TOWARDS WORK

Our attitude towards work is very different, too. It is often said that Indians have such a hard time surviving in the white society, because they are lazy, they have bad work habits and they cannot be depended upon. Again it is a question of Indians looking at work in an entirely different way than the white man. Indians can work very hard if the work is meaningful to them. But they can't just go to work and get a paycheck for doing something if they don't know why they are doing it.

It was very difficult to survive in this country when you didn't have any tools except maybe a bow and an arrow. What made it even harder was that there were other people around whom you didn't know, who talked a different language and who were of a different tribe and sometimes quite hostile. Indians were used to working very hard, but they also functioned by the season. They would work hard during the summer and the fall gathering food, and then they might relax for a couple of months when the cold weather came. But they never saw any virtue in work *per se*. Take a couple of Indian hunters, if they had a strong hunch that deer were coming out around four o'clock in the afternoon, they would not start hunting early in the morning. Rather they would have a good time all day and visit their friends and then they would go hunting at four. I know that many white people frown on this attitude.

If at all possible, Indians will make work into a communal experience. If they can be part of a work team rather than work in the isolation typical of modern factories, they can be amazingly productive. This is a true story and it happened in Longlac, Ontario: There is a saw mill there and they have men working there three shifts a day. There were a number of Indian people working at the mill. A community development officer went up there from Orillia and spent some time there, wanting to find out how the Indians were getting on. He went to see one of the managers of the plant and he was told that they had a lot of trouble with their Indian workers. The Indians were missing a lot of work. The manager was really disgusted, he wanted to know how to get these Indians to work. He said that every fall, as soon as the duck season comes they have no Indians at the plant, they all take off and go hunting.

The community development officer suggested that he put them all on one shift, let them run a shift. "What about the boss?" said the manager. "They don't need a boss, you'll see," said the organizer. It took six months to get the manager to try it. They set a quota for this shift for the end of the year, we'll say a million board feet. Those plants never stop, if you want to go out and have a smoke, then you have to get somebody to come and relieve you. The equipment is not in very good shape; the conveyer belts keep breaking down and the saws are often dull and then there are fights over who was supposed to sharpen them. When the Indians took over the shift various things happened. They had no foreman and when they wanted to smoke, they shut down the plant and all had a smoke together. They also shifted around so nobody would get too tired: if a guy was using his left hand, after a while he would switch with a guy who was using his right hand. On October the first they had a million board feet produced and they all went hunting. The belts didn't break down at all during that time, and the saws were always left sharpened for the next shift. They did not have one serious problem during all that time and you know what happened? The manager gave them a quota of a million and a half for the next year. That was the end of the productive Indian in that plant.

Indians always discover, sooner or later, like these fellows in the plant, that they are in a "can't win" situation in white society. Even if some of them are lucky enough to be able to function for a while straddling both worlds, sooner or later somebody will come along and change the rules and they are back to base one. When the power is all on the other side, you finally have no choice but to either withdraw or assimilate. But the question is: assimilate to what? It seems ironical that Indians have to face this choice at a time when a great number of young white people are dropping out from society and attempting to live like Indians. I don't believe that the Indian can or will assimilate. But he might well decide to join in some way or another these young people in trying to nudge society into another direction. There was this great orator in United States called Clyde Warrior who used to say that civilization is just a passing phase like the hoola hoop and the skateboard, and that if we just wait long enough it will disappear. The Indian has always been a patient man.

5

Indian Organizations

ATTEMPTS TO RE-ESTABLISH IDENTITY

THE FORMAL ORGANIZATIONS of today have not had a long tradition in the culture of Canadian Indians. The first (Native Brotherhood of BC) was established in 1931. Members were almost entirely from the northwest coast of BC which limited the scope of the activities. By 1936 a second organization, the Pacific Coast Native Fishermen's Association, was founded. Although there was some conflict between the two groups, in 1942 they merged, adopting the original name, the Native Brotherhood of BC. The brotherhood was Protestant and a year later a rival Catholic organization, of the North American Indian Brotherhood, was also established in BC. The two groups did not clash overtly but there was much "under the table" conflict and consequently neither accomplished much. Most of their time and energies were directed at "out doing" or "getting at" the other. The dominant group capitalized on the differences between the two, using the "divide and conquer" technique. Each time a hearing was set which called for briefs to be submitted by Indians, seemingly contradictory recommendations were prepared, so the dominant group ignored the requests of both, claiming that they didn't know what to do. Instead, they did nothing. Later these two groups met with Eastern Canadian Indians and agreed to form a new national organization—the Brotherhood of Canadian Indians. This new organization had no religious bias and consisted solely of *non-treaty Indians.*[1]

In 1946 these non-treaty Indians attempted to form a coalition with the treaty Indians from Saskatchewan to set up a national organization. Their first contact proved fruitless, partly because of interference by the CCF (Cooperative Commonwealth Federation) government. Later contacts were more successful but a definite division remained and still persists between non-treaty and treaty Indians and the Metis. Lately the National Indian Brotherhood (for treaty Indians) has had considerably more impact than the Metis Federation (for non-treaty organizations) because it is organized on a provincial basis—thereby reducing intertribal differences and producing greater uniformity among the governing bodies. Perhaps even more importantly, this group is given substantial funds by the federal government. (The IAA received $970,000 in 1971.)

While the BC Indians have the longest history of attempts at organizing, other Western Canadian Indians have also formed organizations since the thirties. The Saskatchewan Indians have been organizing since the end of the Second World War. In 1944 the Saskatchewan Indian Association was formed, followed a year later by the Protective Association for Indians and Their Treaties. By 1946 these two organizations had resolved their differences and merged to form the Union of Saskatchewan Indians. Again, another organization sprang up in opposition to the union—the Queen Victoria Treaty Protective Association. It took over ten years for these two groups to reconcile their differences and merge into the Federation of Saskatchewan Indians. Another organization, still a viable force, was established in 1970—the Saskatchewan Native Alliance. The Indian Association of Alberta was established in 1939 and has remained the only really active organization within the province. Others such as the Catholic Indian League (1962) emerged but died out quickly.

While the formal structure of the IAA had its beginnings in 1939, it really started in 1919 with the establishment of the League of Indians of Canada. These early organizational attempts were conceived in the East but attempts to formalize were generated in the West. However, whenever Indian leaders attempted to organize, the RCMP and/or Indian agent would arrive and stop further organization.

In 1920, leaders of various tribes got together in Manitoba and as a result of the meeting, established the League of Indians of Western Canada. Further meetings in Saskatchewan (Big Iroquois meetings) and Alberta took place in the early twenties in an attempt to organize Indians. By 1930, a serious rift had emerged between the Alberta and Saskatchewan Indians and the league was subdivided along provincial lines. The Alberta league then changed its name in 1939 (with some organizational changes) to the

---

[1]Not to be confused with non-status Indians. These were Indians who never signed a treaty with the federal government.

IAA. It is important to realize that until 1939, the federal and provincial governments did not recognize the existence or legitimacy of the league and thus refused to act upon recommendations sent to Ottawa by the organization.

Organizations in Eastern Canada do not have the long and torrid history of those in Western Canada. Even though over a quarter of the Indians live in Ontario, they have not seriously attempted to build provincial or national organizations. Analysis of the situation reveals that the independence and aggressiveness of the Iroquois on the Six Nations Reserve have given them a unique position among Indians in Canada. In addition, because of their simultaneous relationship to the US and Canada and the legal status they have attained from both countries, they have not felt the need to organize provincially or link up with other national organizations. Other Indians in the East, *e.g.,* in Quebec, are considered non-treaty and as such are only nominally recognized by the dominant group as a legal entity.

The National Indian Brotherhood (like most Indian organizations) was relatively inactive until the federal government's White Paper on Indian Affairs, presented in 1969. As Patterson (1972) notes, Indian organizations seem to be crisis oriented. When a situation likely to produce a crisis arises, an Indian organization with all its bureaucratic machinery comes into existence. However, when the crisis is over (or is solved), the organization simply declines and/or disappears. During the fifties and sixties hundreds of local and provincial Indian organizations, from women's groups to youth corps, emerged and died within a year.

The NIB was set up in 1968 and has been extremely active in promoting Indian activities as well as providing leadership for natives. The National Indian Council, composed of middle class, urban Indians, dissolved in 1970. Internal divisions were largely responsible for its disbandment. In their attempt to form the organization they had included registered, non-registered and Metis within one framework. Conflict emerged between the three factions and after several years of failure to achieve any of its goals, the organization decided to disband.

Since the late sixties, the federal government has nominally recognized (in a legal sense) the Metis as a distinct cultural group. Provincial governments have recognized them for many years. In fact in Alberta there are several Metis colonies, occupying over 14,000 acres of land. In addition to recognition, the federal government now provides funds for the Metis Federation, Metis Friendship Centers and the Native Indian Council. Though the amount is much smaller than for status Indians, it does suggest that some changes are taking place. However, since these organizations are very recent, the impact on the Indians (in their confrontations with the larger white society) cannot be ascertained.

Indians belonging to the League of Nations—Pan Am Indians, are generally considered the most "radical." The league is a very loose intertribal organization. Even splinter groups such as the National Alliance for Red Power (NARP) have emerged from it. For further discussion of this, see Jack (1970), who was a NARP founder. More and more militant youths are joining the league or one of its splinter groups. The members rally under the central issue of the treaties. They argue that Indian tribes must be viewed as nations. Any litigation between the Indians and the Canadian government cannot be solved in Ottawa, they say, but rather at the United Nations. The militance of these groups (exemplified by peaceful and violent demonstrations at the Canadian–US border in Ontario during the past decade) is continuing to grow.

Waubageshig said in his discussion of the possibility of violence in Canada:

> Violence in our communities, both on and off the reservation, is occurring at this very moment . . . If this does not stop . . . then there is going to be a very angry young Indian population which will say, 'what the hell!' I have nothing to lose. And we may have political violence. If no one listens to what these young people are saying and nothing is done, then violence will erupt. *(1970:167)*

While people like Waubageshig are "politically" militant today, the more moderate politically oriented Indian is beginning to evaluate more positively their behavior—quite different than their response ten years ago. Today, the NIB has formally stated that if issues between the federal government and Indians cannot be worked out to their satisfaction, they will appeal to the United Nations. The Indians are not officially recognized as a nation, but they are approaching various UN member nations to plead their case. The public knows only that the NIB has so far made "contacts" with non-white nations (particularly the "yellow people"). Since 1970 the notion of Red Power has been used increasingly by these political activists, as Lurie reports:

> In many Canadian reserve towns the white population is relatively small but dominates business and commercial interests. All across Canada there have been hostile, even violent 'incidents'—so far without fatalities—and many more are threatened. *(1971:466)*

One further organization should be mentioned although it also is quite new—the Indian-Eskimo Association. It has now changed its name to the Canadian Association in support of Native People and moved its headquarters to Ottawa. It was felt that being in the political center of Canada would be more beneficial than remaining in Toronto. This organization was started by whites (who still dominate its structure and direction) for Indians and Eskimos in the NWT. It was initiated before the NIB was actively concerned with northern natives. To date, its main function has been to provide a legal service, but it also disseminates information through newspapers and conferences. The importance of the association in the future will depend on whether natives can assume control.

The formal native organizations have been discussed at length because it is felt that they present an "adaptive" strategy for Indians to maintain their identity. However, before looking more closely at the strategy, three additional factors that reinforce tribal or Indian identity should be discussed. The first two are considered variants of the pow-wow. The tribal pow-wow is a local activity promoting local customs and languages. The young are encouraged to learn from their elders. It is hoped that eventually these pow-wows will build community solidarity. The second type of pow-wow (pan-Indianism) is a planned intertribal affair usually held on "neutral" ground. There is dancing and social interaction but they go beyond this. Healers also attend and perform their rituals and there are serious discussions about the fate of the Indian and his resources. The third Ecumenical Conference was such a pow-wow. It was held at the Stoney Reserve in Alberta in 1972 when cultural awakening had reached a peak.

A third type of activity may be unique to Canada—a prophet religion whose leader is Chief Smallboy of Alberta. Smallboy and his group have returned to the mountains and are attempting to re-establish their former culture. They also have set up a school consisting of two mobile classrooms and 44 students. However, the federal government is refusing to allow his camp to be permanent and in 1972 revoked his permit to remain on a federal forest reserve. The important theoretical point is that cultural revitalization movements such as this are generally found when colonized people begin to reject their subjugation. Again, this can be viewed as a nativistic movement; its impact is too recent to analyze fully. However, several other "camps" have been established by other prophets who are beginning to attract small followings.

When it was suggested previously that these organizations and movements were helping the Indian to retain his culture and identity, the term of reference was to a pan-Indian movement.[2] What does the term mean? There are several values and beliefs central to the Canadian Indian culture which override local band differences. We shall briefly allude to them to see the long range goal of these movements.

There are two different types of pan-Indianism—religious and reform. Religious pan-Indianism has developed in rural areas (in reaction to governmental harassment). Its theme is man living in harmony with nature. Man is viewed simply as one element of nature, which is always to be respected. Reform pan-Indianism is largely an urban phenomenon. It aims not only to promote the traditional values of Indian culture but also to facilitate Indian involvement in the business and professional life of the larger society. Its proponents feel that Indian culture should be retained and that it should continue to contribute to the cultural mosaic of Canadian society (Hertzberg, 1971).

There are several interesting points about pan-Indian movements. Their emergence coincided with the conservation movement in North America. And the founders were marginal in a sense. The leaders have extensive contacts with the dominant society but they all belong to Indian tribes. They are "part-white," bilingual, have good educations and "typical" white occupations. The last point about these movements is that they have been supported by whites and there is little evidence to suggest that this will be stopped. But though these reform movements initially receive

---

[2] The term "pan-Indianism" is not used by Indians but was invented and is used now by social scientists.

help from whites, when the movements become militant and demand real social-structural changes, the whites are placed in the embarrassing position of having to reject their claims.

ATTRIBUTES OF PAN-INDIANISM

In decision making, Indians feel that preceding discussion must not be inhibited by "rules." They also believe that the decision must be reached by consensus, not voting. There have been many examples ir the past when the IAB and the Indians have conferred over an issue, only to see the Ottawa officials tire of the seemingly meaningless dialogue and decide that Indians are incapable of making a decision. So they make it for them. To the Indians, all the procedures involved in a dialogue are important in themselves. They place a high value on oratory, for example.

The validity of the consensus approach to group decisions has been questioned by non-Indians. They find that after consensus has been reached (and a decision made), many Indians talk afterwards as though they were really not in favor of the decision. These outside observers claim that the consensus approach is really a "put on." Such an analysis reflects a rather shallow understanding of Indian culture.

Indian humor—the style of presenting "jokes" and the topics—is another aspect of pan-Indianism. Humor and its presentation are important in Indian culture. But Indians do not make jokes as white society knows them. Instead, they tell stories or anecdotes. A group of BC Indians found the following story extremely humorous:

> In a white community several Indians lived nearby. One day an old Indian's horse died. Since it was winter, he pulled it near a creek which provided the town with water. Since spring was nearing, the community was concerned with the dead horse polluting their drinking water. A member of the white community was delegated to talk to the old Indian and ask him to move it. He agreed and three days later the delegate from the community saw the old Indian's son move the horse five feet. It of course did not solve the problem. The result was that the white delegate moved the horse. Several weeks later, a second horse of the old Indian also died. He pulled this dead horse onto a hill near a Catholic church. Each day the priest would ask the old man to move it and he would agree but things always kept coming up which prevented him from moving the horse. Each week the stench grew greater so that after church services one Sunday, the priest and several white men moved it two miles out of town.

Funny? Not to whites. Yet this story is told amidst broad smiles and gales of laughter. The "joke" is that an old Indian was able to get white men to do his job.

Other more widely recognized cultural traits basic to pan-Indianism include emphasis on sharing and absence of emotional attachment to personal possessions. Status can be achieved by sharing worldly goods (exemplified in the historical potlatches) and not to do so is interpreted as self-ishness. Other characteristics of the culture have not received much attention from anthropologists, *e.g.*, the way Indians do not try to control the behavior of others and the way they respect each other. The contrast between these attitudes and white society's conception of "respect" and control over others clearly spells problems for the Indian attempting to understand and join in Canadian life. Lurie (1971) also pointed out that "withdrawal" from situations defined as "anxiety producing" was another common element of Indian culture.

The final point about pan-Indianism involves the conception of the reserve. Some Indians and whites see the reserve either as a prison or as a physical and psychological refuge, but members of pan-Indian movements regard the reserve as a viable community. Agreed, they are poverty stricken, isolated and lack essential services, but they are viewed as communities that can continue their existence.

The formal and pan-Indian organizations as well as the local pow-wows are contributing to Indian nationalism, providing the Indian with a sense of identity. There seems to be a feeling of despair and disillusionment among Indians that they cannot be accepted into the larger white society. This feeling seems to be most pronounced among the Indian leaders and the younger generation. These are angry people; angry at the way the white world treats them when they attempt to integrate and angry at the government's attempts to abolish their reserves.

How have these organizations and social movements helped the Indian? Until today, Indian response to the larger white society has been called an "articulatory movement" (Lurie, 1971). However, with the growth of the various organizations and "ideological" movements, Indians are becoming more politically, socially, and economically aware. The formal organizations have given Indians an opportunity to hold discussions with the federal government. At present the government argues that it doesn't know whom these various organizations represent. But it won't be long before it finds out. These organizations may be asking for different things but collectively their demands approximate what has been stated in the *Red Paper*. However, the government has found that if it feigns inability to see through the Indians' confusion (again notice how it is regarded as the Indians' problem) it can move politically the way it wishes and can convince the white population that Indians really don't know what they want.

The formal organizations are also providing Indians with leadership (one of the main characteristics of an articulatory movement is a lack of identifiable leadership). Though the leaders and spokesmen are unlike those in white society, they are capable enough and are becoming a viable force in the Canadian political structure. People such as George Munroe, Harold Cardinal and David Courchene are perhaps most widely known.

Indians have traditionally lacked the leadership necessary to gain political and economic goals in the larger white society. The formal organizations are working like an umbrella, allowing leaders to emerge while holding the different cultural and linguistic groups together.

However, the IAB, because of its overriding power, is still able to render these individual organizations relatively ineffectual. As Dosman (1972) explained, when natives organized in Saskatoon the Indian and Metis Development Society, which was completely independent of the IAB, it did everything in its power to discredit the society and eventually bring about its demise. But perhaps the most notable example was the IAB's reaction to the Indian Association of Alberta (IAA), led by Cardinal, when it became evident that he was moving away from standard IAB policies. Indian Affairs charged the IAA with improperly spending the money allocated to it by the IAB and with not accounting for nearly half of its expenditures. Most Canadians are aware of the incident but few know of the subsequent events. First, documents produced by the IAA showed that the association spent the money the way it was forced to, with written approval from the IAB and the Secretary of State Department. Second, documents were produced which showed that both federal departments requested sizeable portions of the IAA grant to be spent on programs for which money was not originally allocated. But perhaps more importantly, the IAA was denied a hearing at the standing committee on Indian Affairs, during which it could have made public that all money was accounted for and spent in accordance with the initial terms of the IAB.

Cardinal, who was president of the IAA, said that because "personalities" were becoming the issue, he would resign. However, a year later he was re-elected president. From the time of the charge against the IAA until Cardinal resigned, all money designated for the association was cut off. Within weeks of Cardinal's resignation, the remainder of the grant was paid to the IAA as well as additional money not requested. While the resignation of controversial leaders and subsequent loosening of the purse strings may solve problems in the short term, such actions by the IAB unwittingly contribute to the pan-Indianism movement as well as to other social movements. However, the field of control over Indian organizations extends beyond money to include information which is essential for effective planning and operations. Other techniques of control involve co-opting of leaders and defining an organization as radical to reduce the chances of other private groups financing it.

The conflict over residential schools (perpetuated by the IAB) was perhaps one of the first local issues that gave impetus to a resurgence of pan-Indianism. This led to intertribal political organizations through which the Indians sought control of their own schools. While they may not have been totally effective, the tables on Indian education show that there have been rather substantial shifts.

One additional factor that has contributed to a heightened Indian identity is the mass media which is becoming an invaluable aid. Newspapers such as the *Akwasasne Notes*, *Tawaw*, and the *Indian News* carry both news and information about positions.

These urban-based periodicals aim to develop political awareness, identity, and eventually action on issues. In an analysis of three major Indian papers (*The Calumet*, *The Native People* and *The Drum*), Price (1972) found that in the north, the newspaper favored an assimilationist position and in the east, the policy was more integrationist. However, the newspaper for western Indians reflected a basic liberationist or separatist ideology. Several themes were repeated in all three papers. For example, almost all articles in these three papers argued that the "Indian problem" was really a "white problem." Other topics included the superiority of traditional Indian culture, inability of whites to understand Indians, and the necessity of Indians to develop their own resources. Some papers are bilingual, which means they achieve maximum coverage. Price includes a list of all Canadian and US Indian papers.

In the north, Indian radio programs in native tongue not only disseminate information but also provide "speaker's platform." However, the government still censors the programs before they are aired. An example of the dominant group's unwillingness to allow natives to use mass media was the CBC's rejection of an Indian proposal which would have given native broadcasters some access to the new satellite system being introduced in the north. At present, all programs are white controlled and originate in the south.

Beyond providing the Indian with a sense of identity and attempting to salvage part of his culture, the organizations are producing the Red Power advocates of today. Red Power is only in its seminal stages and it is not wished to convey the notion here that all Indians advocate it. Quite the contrary, most Indians (like their white counterparts) are very apathetic in their commitments to gain social change. The "activists" are in two camps—the traditionalists and the Red Power advocates.

The first group seeks the integration of Indians into the system, though they want to remain a distinct ethnic group in the economic, political and social activities of the country. The second, more militant group, sees integration as irrelevant. They consider a major task is to build Indian institutions (economic, political, *etc.*) which they will plan, own, and control. This militant group can be further subdivided into those who are locally oriented in their behavior (concerned only about issues which directly affect their local reserve or community) and those who are more concerned about changing the larger Canadian system. To date, most of the militant organizations have chosen to act on local issues, which suggests that their impact on the total system has so far been minimal.

What is Red Power? Some of its major idealogical themes have been derived from the Black Power movement but there are some important differences. In general, Red Power advocates self community support, self community direction, and community ownership. Indians wish to create, develop and carry out their own ideas and programs (political, economic, social, *etc.*). Red Power also attempts to improve the Indian's image on a personal level and change the stereotyped Indian traits of laziness and drunkenness to something better in the eyes of the white society. They want the stereotype to change from a "negative" to "positive" image. At present it is commonly thought that they are too apathetic and unwilling to go out and become involved with the larger society. This kind of attitude reflects lack of understanding and people who think this way fail to realize that one of the most potent forces of colonialism is the way it "breaks the spirit" and subsequent resistance of a minority group after the arrival of the dominant group. Subjection is continued by withholding of medical facilities, and by not providing education or permitting involvement in the labor force, *etc.* Somehow the dominant group expects these people to rise above all of this (within a few years) and become an immediate success.

When Indians begin to establish Red Power groups in an attempt to retain some of their culture and realistically place themselves in a position where they might begin to integrate into the larger system, they are again criticized by the white man on other grounds, *e.g.*, militancy. No matter what the Indians do they will be criticized so the most sensible solution for them is to progress with their own plans and forget the whites' continual bickering.

Broadly, Red Power is an answer to the Indians' dilemma of neither being able to separate from the rest of the nation (although the Six Nations community is attempting to do so and this may explain their lack of "militancy") nor integrate (Franklin, 1969). While Red Power has so far failed to present a clear cut program, the most important focus seems to be on control of reserves. Its advocates are attempting to unite a number of other militant and moderate groups into a network across Canada.

This can be best seen in the Indian reaction to the educational process. Red Power activists have made an impact on various reserves. In the past few years there has been a great shift in the Indian attitude to education. Education is not seen solely as an "integrative" goal but rather as a community experience. Indians are demanding their own school boards and attempting to control curriculum development and hiring of teachers.

The reader finishing this section may agree with what has been said or think that Red Power is not really a viable force in Canada today, nor likely to become one. Agreed, it will never win mass support. In doing my research I did not find more than 3–5 per cent of Indians who could be considered Red Power advocates in either the "local" or "cosmopolitan" sense. But people who disregard the movement should be cautioned about the naivety of their view. In all previous research dealing with riots, revolutions, urban guerrilla warfare, *etc.*, only a small percentage of the total population have ever been shown to take part in violent activities. The small group actively participating in violence need "support"—and it must range from moral support to technical information. At present, Indians seem willing to give moral support to various Red Power activists. It is only a matter of time before they can begin to provide other types of support. Thus, it is not crucial that only a small number of Red Power advocates might engage in violence. This should not be taken as evidence that Red Power will succumb to external forces. Its supporters have shaken off the old white liberal humanist idea that violence is the "worst sin." If one is attempting to combat racism and achieve self determination (to destroy the colonistic relationship that has emerged), then violence is almost inevitable. Few whites are able to see this way (let alone agree), but militant Indians are beginning to do so.

Until 1969, little was spent on the formal Indian organizations. However, during the 1969–70 fiscal year nearly $1.5 million was allocated to the various organizations across Canada. The funds came from the DIA,

DREE, and the Secretary of State Department. Again, this provides valuable ammunition for the "anti-Indian" in claiming that the "taxpayers' " money is being wasted. What the critics fail to realize is that: (*i*) these organizations have been in existence only a short time, so the worth of their goals cannot be evaluated; (*ii*) the organizations have no formal power so any decisions they may reach are always subject to federal government approval.

CHANGING RELATIONS BETWEEN WHITES AND INDIANS

Two very different courses are open to Canadian Indians today. On the one hand, the Indian is under strong pressure to aspire after goals which are currently held by white Canadians. Some want Indians to leave the reserve and take an active part in the larger Canadian society. The 1969 white paper perhaps best indicated the government position and reflected the basic sentiments of the larger white population. It contended that if Canadian Indians were to become fully integrated into Canadian society, they must change radically—not whites. It argued that the separate legal status of Indians has kept them from fully participating in the larger society. The white paper proposed the following changes:
● Repeal the Indian Act to enable Indians to control their lands and acquire title to them.
● Have the provincial governments assume responsibility for Indians as they have for other citizens in their provinces.
● Make substantial funds available for Indian economic development as an interim measure.
● Phase out the Department of Indian Affairs and Northern Development which deals with Indian affairs.
● Appoint a commissioner to consult with the Indians and to study and recommend acceptable procedures for the adjudication of claims.
(*Indian Policy*, 1969:6).

The dominant group has estimated that these changes would take about five years. Such a policy is not new to Canada; previous governments have tried it before, *e.g.*, in 1963, Bill C–130 (providing for the disposition of Indian claims) was introduced.

Supporters of this strategy argue that the creation of reserves and subsequently the Indian Act precluded Indians from participating in the development of Canadian society. They feel that Indians have been legally and administratively discriminated against and therefore have not been given an equal chance of success. Not only the federal government has taken this position. Others, including Wuttunee (1972), who has been "de-Indianized," have consistently advocated this position which, it should be noted, agrees essentially with the "myth of equality" attitude discussed previously.

The opposing course concerns the issue of "control of one's destiny" and the "right to maintain one's ethnic identity." Critics of the white paper feel that Indians should remain a legal, administratively and socially separate group. The Hawthorn Report called for the retention of Indians as a unique ethnic group and even went as far as recommending that they be given the status of "citizen plus"—one equivalent to that which the English gave themselves after they defeated the French and claimed to be the "charter group." The report considered that the treaties set a legal bind between Indians and whites which must be maintained. The white paper is seen as a disguised program of extermination (Cardinal, 1969).

Indians have submitted three major briefs in response to the 1969 white paper. They are the *Brown Paper* of BC Indians, the *Red Paper* (or Citizen Plus) of Alberta Indians and the Manitoba Indians' *Wahbung*. All three have attempted to do two things—present arguments against implementation of the white paper and present their own positions and recommendations.

It is unfortunate (but not unusual) to hear people say that all Indians do is criticize the government for its white paper; that they have never made constructive proposals of their own. The above briefs and the many more specific proposals by Indians are an obvious answer to these critics. A detailed reading of the Indian briefs reveals that they have taken positions and made concrete proposals for strategies to handle the "problem."

Critics of the white paper say that its proposals do not match the desires of the natives themselves. They argue with adequate justification that when the minister of Indian Affairs suggests that the white paper is a response to Indian recommendations, either he is acting on behalf of other "economic interest groups" or he had an entirely different interpretation of what was said at the few meetings between Indians and whites. Both are plausible explanations, but the point is that Indians say they were not consulted for the drafting of the white paper. The counter argument to the government line is that Indians must be allowed to remain a distinct ethnic group, free to control their own affairs without interference by provincial or federal government. They want things affecting Indians to be turned over to Indians through the establishment of inter-provincial Indian organizations and through restructuring present Indian social institutions. In other words, political organizations have to be created by Indians, for Indians and controlled by Indians for the betterment of Indians.

Let us turn to the recommendations in the Indian briefs which followed the white paper. Since each brief is in itself a book, we can only attempt to summarize the major recommendations. The *Red Paper* has received most recognition and is the most specific in its proposals concerning education and economic development.

The *Red Paper* argues that the Indian Act must be reviewed and amended, but not repealed. This recommendation is echoed by the other briefs. *Wahbung* is most explicit in its recommendations for changes to the act. It covers topics such as wills, health and elections of chiefs and councils. The briefs also argue for immediate recognition of the treaties (and aboriginal rights) and the establishment of a commission to study the meaning of the treaties and the government's obligations. The *Brown Paper* and *Wahbung* do not make specific recommendations on Indian claims. They recommend a claims commission established by consultation with Indians and able to make binding judgments. The *Red Paper* is quite explicit in its rejection of a claims commissioner. It argues for a full time minister of Indian affairs and the creation of a permanent standing committee of the House of Commons and Senate which would deal *only* with registered Indians.

The Manitoba Indian Brotherhood (*Wahbung*) recommends that a joint committee of the brotherhood and the Department of Indian Affairs (regional office) be established with equal representation between Indians and whites to handle Indian affairs. From this, several boards and commissions covering local government, economic development, welfare, education and police would be established. These boards would assume representation of both the department and Indians. *Wahbung* also recommends that a cabinet committee be established consisting of Indian leaders. When policy decisions were made by cabinet, the committee could provide more and better information for more realistic and meaningful policies concerning Indians.

The IAB is discussed in all the briefs. They reject the proposal to abolish it, arguing that it should change to "a smaller structure" attuned to Indians' local and regional needs. However, only the *Brown Paper* states that IAB personnel should be exclusively Indian. If the IAB is to become smaller and more locally oriented, this obviously implies a need for more local control. Again, all three argue that local tribal councils must be given more decision-making powers so that they can take the initiative in social, political and economic development. All the briefs agree that while potential resources abound on the reserve, few have been tapped.

The *Brown Paper* concentrates on the land issue. Since treaties have never been negotiated with BC Indians, this is still the paramount issue for them. The other two briefs also allude to the issue but they do not discuss it in detail.

The last two issues in the briefs deal with economic and educational development. The *Brown Paper* is the least comprehensive in its treatment of these topics, while the *Red Paper* is very explicit.

The *Red Paper* deals with two major areas. On the economic issue, it proposes the Alberta Indian Development System (AIDS)—a program to bring about changes in socio-economic status through community economic development. This would be achieved by arranging for Indians to do work needed in the community and by developing jobs related to industries. The AIDS would be controlled by a dual corporate structure of Indian and white leaders. Indians would be responsible for setting the goals and priorities of all projects and non-natives would advise and assist in the development. A capital fund of $50 million would be needed, $30 million of which would come from the federal government, $10 million from the provincial government and $8.7 million from private industry. Alberta Indians would begin with an initial investment of $1.3 million.

The second major proposal in the *Red Paper* centers on education and discusses an Indian Education Center (IEC) which has now been approved in principle by the federal government. Finance is now being directed toward the construction and staffing of the center. The IEC was proposed in conjunction with the AIDS and was also introduced to ensure the survival of Indian culture and the future development of Indian communities. The center was proposed for the heart of Alberta so that all tribes could have equal access to it. The program will allow Indian children to learn how to develop ways of successfully applying Indian culture to the larger Canadian society. It should also enable them to use modern skills and behavior for vocational success. In essence, the IEC proposal argues that it should be run for Indians by Indians to assure them a secure place in the larger Canadian society.

Other issues covered in the briefs include Indian control over finances on the reserve, taxation, reconciliation of all injustices, housing and health services. The most important point to be made about these reports is that though the proposals were basically developed independently, there are very few (if any) contradictions. However, the proposals reflect a bias of each group's special needs. BC Indians are concerned with land, therefore they focus their proposal on treaties, aboriginal rights and the land issue. There are similar biases in the other two briefs. But all agree on most major issues such as economic development, education and the act itself. Opponents of the white paper argue that if it was accepted, all outstanding legal suits against the government (specifically the land issue) would be redundant. And they contend that when the government claims it will "make substantial funds available for Indian economic development" the amount and use of the funds do not meet with Indian needs.

Where do most Canadians stand on the question? The majority of white Canadians seem to favor the white paper proposals while Indians obviously are against them. It is encouraging to find that young whites seem to be divided. Frideres (1972) found in a recent survey that over a third of white university students argued that Indians should have control over their own affairs. In fact, these students believed that if Indians were ever to edge into the mainstream of Canadian life, the only reasonable way (in a political and economic sense) was through control of their affairs. Federal and provincial governments do not want this.

Reserve Termination

Some evidence is available which we can use to evaluate the case for retaining or phasing out reserves. In the US between 1953 and 1960, over 60 reserves were terminated. However, it was found that by 1960 the results were so disastrous that the scheme was halted. We will look briefly now at a specific case when the Klamath Indian reservation of Oregon was terminated in 1954. The phasing out took three to four years and before it was completed, the Indians had a thriving business derived from forest products on the reserve. The average income for each person (from this resource) was about $800 a year which meant that the average family income (from this source only) was $3,000–$4,000. In addition, many Indians worked at other jobs on and off the reserve, which raised the average income per family to nearly $6,000. This placed them—on the 1954 standard of living—in about the 90th percentile of the US population. By 1958, when the termination was complete, many Klamaths were on welfare and had suffered extreme social disorganization. Family stability had decayed sharply, crime against people and property had risen acutely and the stable social network of the community had broken. By 1960, nearly a third of the Klamath Indians were on welfare or in mental or penal institutions throughout Oregon. The evidence seems overwhelming. How could a self-sustaining group so deteriorate? The answer is clear—termination on white man's terms. It should also be pointed out that theoretically the Klamaths should have succeeded in their transition. As Spencer and Jennings (1965) noted, they were quite "individualistic" (much more so than other Indian tribes), and thus similar in this very important cultural aspect to the larger white society. However, the results (for a group with cultural attributes similar to the dominant group) should make others have second thoughts about quick termination of reserves. Other instances of termination in the US have produced similar results. When those who want reserves phased out set forth their program, they conveniently ignore the consequences that have beset these Indians.

Indian-White Legal Changes

Here we will examine some recent changes in the relationship between whites and Indians on legal and non-legal grounds. First, let us look at federal developments and then review provincial changes.

Friendship centers have already been discussed but they need to be mentioned here as an agent of change. They were created with the notion that they would provide services to Indians entering the city and thus reduce the problems of adjustment to urban life. We have seen that the impact has varied considerably.

Three major federal programs have been:
1. The setting up of a joint committee of the Senate and the House of Commons to investigate the administration of Indian Affairs and make recommendations (1959).
2. Training for Indian chiefs and councillors in band council management and community leadership (1961).
3. Training in community development for staff of the IAB (1965). (Melling, 1966:387)

All three were conceived and are controlled and financed by the federal government. Nearly $10 million has been spent on these programs but their impact has been minimal and the actual changes in Indian social status (or relationships with whites) nearly non-existent. While changes are being made on paper, corresponding changes in the behavior of the federal government have not taken place.

The two most important federal innovations has been the introduction of the Technical and Vocational Training Assistance Act (1961) and the Agricultural Rehabilitation and Development Act (1961). Part of the finance for these projects comes from the federal government. Both projects are sponsored by the Department of Regional Economic Expansion. The first act greatly increased the amount of aid that the federal government would provide to the provinces. The ARDA scheme, while initially a federal program, has now set up a federal/provincial committee and may take appropriate action without waiting for full formal approval of the federal government. A third organization set up by the Prairie Farm Rehabilitation Act, is quite similar to the ARDA, These examples show that the government is willing to invest millions of dollars in programs dealing with agriculture rather than other types of economic endeavors, even though an overwhelming number of briefs have been submitted by white and Indian organizations pointing out the non-viability of such programs. Under the Technical and Vocational Training scheme mentioned above, only one program (5), for the training of unemployed Indians and Metis youth, has been actively pursued. The aim is to train young Indians and re-train adults. While the first two have been considerably more effective than the federal schemes, realistically, the social status of Indians has changed little. The main reason seems to be that these programs are always related to agricultural enterprises or at best, semi-skilled jobs.

Traditionally Indians, because of their culture, have been much more tolerant than whites of people with different outlooks. And since the white man has had the necessary power to coerce changes in the native people, he has done so. However, the pan-Indianism movements have developed through the natives' wish to keep their cultural elements.

In the past decade, many other changes in the relationship between whites and Indians have occurred. In the field of civil rights, the Regina *v* Drybones case (1967) was a landmark. Drybones, an Indian from the NWT, was charged with violating the Indian Act which prohibited an Indian from being intoxicated off the reserve. But he was acquitted because the Act was interpreted as being discriminatory. There was an appeal but the judgment was upheld by the Supreme Court of Canada. This of course invalidates part of the Indian Act. Further tests cases are planned. In 1973, over $200,000 went toward legal guidance for Indians and two pilot projects have been established.

Indian Intermarriage

Under the Indian Act, if an Indian woman marries a white man, she and her offspring lose all legal Indian status. However, if an Indian man marries a white woman, she—and theoretically any offspring—become Indian, though the status of children is subject to some dispute.

In another test case in 1972, Jeanette Corbiere Lavelle, an Objibwa, had her Indian status re-instated after she had forfeited it through marriage. But the decision was appealed and in 1973 the Supreme Court ruled against Mrs. Lavelle and she lost her Indian status. As pointed out earlier, well over 4,000 Indian women lost their status between 1958 and 1968. Mrs. Lavelle argued that the Indian Act discriminated against her as a woman under the Canadian Bill of Rights.[3] An additional ambiguity arising out of the case is that her child's status is still undetermined. Since Mrs. Lavelle lost her status when she married a white, under the terms of the

[3]For a partial text of the federal court judgment, see: *The Northian*, 1972:52–3.

Indian Act, so did her child. A court decision is pending on the child's status.

Most well known Indian leaders such as Cardinal, Issac (Chief of the Six Nations Reserve) and Kahn-Tinetactorn argue against this ruling. The husband and any offspring in a marriage between a white man and an Indian woman have no property rights on the reserve but they may live there. Several issues still remain unresolved. What about the offspring from this type of mixed marriage? Do they take on Indian status? (When an Indian man marries a white woman, not only does his wife become Indian, but so do the children.) These Indian leaders feel that white men who marry Indian women will be allowed to assume Indian status and thereby acquire property, eventually taking over the reserve. While one can agree that the Indian Act is sexist, giving the male and his spouse certain rights while depriving Indian women of them, the claims of a "white takeover" seem naive. In the US Indians also have a roll and once a person is listed, he or she can marry anyone of any race and reside on the reserve. The spouse retains his/her ethnic classification but the offspring must apply for Indian status. The results show that their reserves have not been taken over by whites.

A second point of confusion in this question is that Indians are attempting to differentiate between legal, ethnic and racial boundaries. They are suggesting that they are not ethnically, but racially different from whites. Thus, they argue, if one is biologically white, one can never take on Indian culture. Even if a non-Indian took on Indian culture (the total way of life of Indians), he still would not be considered Indian since he would not "look like an Indian." This runs counter to the Indian argument that the reserve is the center of their culture and language. This question makes Indians more concerned about who looks like an Indian than maintaining their culture. As a result of the Lavell decision, serious internal divisions among Indian groups will emerge. Already in several women's organizations, lines of battle have been drawn and there will be further fragmentation unless the differences can be resolved.

The precedents established by the two cases brought a varied response from both the Indian and white population. In the Drybones case, most people agreed with the decision although some Indians disagreed. But in the Lavell case, there was widespread Indian criticism, though some agreed with the decision.

The Treaties

Several other decisions involving legal precedents are pending and may change the relationship between whites and Indians. They are important and deserve mention. One concerns the land argument and another, the medical issue.

The issue of native land claims has been far more contentious in Canada than in most nations, including the United States. The French, who did not recognize native land rights, did not make treaties with the Indians but the British did. The first recorded was made in 1725 with the Maritime Indians. Several others followed but their legality has been ignored and downgraded. In effect, they have not been regarded by the courts as treaties. As well as the treaties various other agreements were worked out between Indians and whites, perhaps the most noticeable being the 1763 Proclamation which, it has been argued, gave various aboriginal rights to natives. But it has been consistently rejected as a precedent by courts.

By 1798, four additional treaties had been signed between Indians and whites in Upper Canada. The provisions of these early treaties were simply that Indians would surrender all rights and privileges of a specified land area in return for cash or goods.

No more treaties were signed until the 1814 Treaty of Ghent. Between 1814 and 1850, when the Robinson Superior and Huron Treaty were signed, whites made many smaller treaties and agreements with Indians. The provisions of these two treaties in 1850 were the result of several recommendations of a royal commission and they became the blueprint for all future treaties. After reviewing a substantial number of cases throughout the legal history of Canada, my conclusion is that Indians not only have a moral right for compensation of their lands, but also a legal right. The first reference to the rights of Indians in Canadian legal history was made in the Articles of Capitulation signed in Montreal in 1761, which states:

> The savages or Indian allies of his most Christian majesty shall be maintained in the lands they inhabit if they so choose to reside there. They shall not be molested on any pretence whatsoever, for having carried arms and served his most Christian majesty.

After a decade of considering the "Indian land problem," the British set forth the Royal Proclamation of 1763. Though it included other issues, the most important aspect was a new policy on "Indian affairs." The proclamation stated that lands not within Quebec or the territory of the Hudson's Bay Company were for the use of "nations or tribes of Indians with whom we are connected." It reads:

> And whereas, it is just and reasonable, and essential to our interest and security of our colonies, that the several nations or tribes of Indians with whom we are connected, and live under protection, should not be molested or disturbed in the possession of such parts of our Dominions and territories as, not having been ceded to or purchased by us, are reserved to them or any of them, as their hunting grounds.

These lands then were for the sole use of Indians. Whites previously settled in these areas or about to settle were to be removed. In addition, only the Crown could purchase these lands if the Indians wished to sell. The proclamation of 1763 has the force of a statute and has not been repealed.

As pointed out by Mickenberg (1971), the proclamation assumed that before its declaration, the Crown had to obtain Indian lands by cession or purchase. Clearly then, the proclamation recognizes the pre-existing land rights of natives. The issue today is whether the proclamation extends to natives who have not signed treaties with Britain, specifically in Quebec,

BC and the NWT. To date, the courts have answered with a resounding no. In 1971, the courts ruled against the BC Indians in their fight for compensation. The decision is under appeal, but the future does not look bright. It is contended (with many legal experts) that the law of aboriginal rights for natives not covered by the Proclamation is covered in the law of nations, now incorporated into the common law of Canada. Evidence for this claim can be found in court rulings on issues such as Indian hunting rights. In addition, some Dominion Land Acts as well as the 1943 Memorandum of British Columbia support this claim.

The land dispute arose following the completion of the railway to British Columbia. It became evident to many whites and Indians that settlers were on their way and competition for land was emerging. Organizations, protests, court cases, *etc.* have been fueled by the issue there since. An Indian claims commission similar to that set up in the US over 20 years ago was suggested by the Indians but has not come about. Compensation for lands "taken away" from Indians is still being evaluated by the courts. Considering the history of the dispute it will probably be many years before a decision is reached. Mickenberg states:

> While Canadian Indians may thus fairly state a substantive claim for compensation for the unconsented deprivation of their aboriginal rights, the procedural impediments to such a claim appear to be formidable. Without legislative intervention, procedural rules such as statutes of limitations and Crown immunity would seem fatal to any action except one for a declaratory judgment. *(1971:154)*

However, some land claims have been partially solved. In 1964 the Indians of Six Nations (Caughwanaga Reserve) received some compensation for land expropriated in 1934. Then in 1973, after nearly 20 years of legal battles, the federal government gave further compensation of nearly 800 acres of land and an additional $1.5 million.

The claims commission[4] sought by Canadian Indians would help to modernize the treaties. award compensation to natives who are registered but not "treaty," examine the existing boundaries of the reserves, and hear other claims. Indians point out that during the Diefenbaker regime, the Tories promised a "claims commission" but have since given this up as part of the party platform.

The land issue is very important to Indians and whites alike. Should the courts (or a claims commission) award compensation for the lands held by Indians, major areas of Vancouver, Winnipeg, Montreal and Toronto would be owned by Indians. Whether the payment would be monetary or actual land ownership would be left to the courts. Another element of the treaties related to the land issue and currently under scrutiny concerns "treaty payments." In 1971, five western bands submitted a bill to the fed-

---

[4]There is a claims commissioner already. But Indians argue that since he is white and has no formal decision-making power (he can only make recommendations), a commission at least half made up of Indians must be established. This commission would have power to make decisions about various Indian claims once they were evaluated.

eral government for nearly $200,00 in back payments related to Treaty 7. They contended that the government made provisions in the treaty signed in 1877 that they be given $400 a year for ammunition and when this was no longer necessary that the money be spent "otherwise for their benefit." The claims commissioner recommended payment to the Indians but the government's initial response was negative. However, in April 1973, $250,000 was paid to the Indians to settle the issue.

Under the Indian Act, Indians living and working on the reserve have some immunity to taxes (Shumiatcher, 1971). They are exempt from income and property taxes but still have to pay provincial taxes and other forms, such as sales tax. If they make money off the reserve, or money on the reserve by leasing houses to whites, they must pay tax on it. The central issue emerging out of this immunity is whether provinces have the right to place a "hospital and medical" tax on Indians. Indians argue that treaties 6, 7 and 8 made provision for a "medicine chest" for the use of Indians, therefore they do not have to pay this tax. The courts have to decide the amount of the "medicine chest." In the case of Regina *v* Swimmer (1971) the Saskatchewan court of appeal held that a medicine chest was not equivalent to medical services and rejected the claim. The decision is being appealed.

The federal government pays for medicare and hospitalization for registered indigent Indians who live on the reserve, but does not pay for those who work. At present, the director general of medical services has yet to issue a policy statement. Thus, since there are no uniform regulations, native treatment will vary according to the attitude of regional and zone medical and administrative officials, *i.e.*, if they feel Indians "deserve" medical care, they receive good payments.

While "medicine chests" are not explicitly mentioned in treaties 1, 2 and 5, the fact that they were placed on reserves covered by these treaties immediately after they were signed has indicated that the Indian claim to free medical services is justified (*Wahbung*, 1971). Indians claim that the medicine chest (the term used in the period to describe available medical services) must also be interpreted today as medical services. This, of course, would include eye and dental care, public health and hospital services as well as drugs and medicare itself.

Recently conflict has emerged over the 1794 Jay Treaty which provided that Indians could cross the US-Canada border freely and transport personal goods across duty free. Without officially commenting on this treaty, the Ontario government has allowed local communities in the area to stop the free flow of Indian goods across the border. Again, a legal decision is being sought and the Six Nations people want the United Nations to adjudicate.

Other issues concerning hunting and fishing rights, mineral rights, and control over reserves have arisen lately. Indians claim that the Royal Proclamation and many court cases indicate that hunting and fishing rights are basic aboriginal entitlements, but other court cases suggest some ambiguity to the claim. The remaining issues have also gone before the courts but with contradictory results, sometimes in favor of the Indians, sometimes the whites.

Conclusion

Supporters of the white paper proposals in essence advocate cultural genocide that would take about five years to complete. They seek the removal of the "citizen plus" or special status of Indians. Their argument is that Indians cannot become integrated (really meaning assimilated) into the larger white society unless this status is removed. It is interesting that this seems to run counter to the position of British Canadians, who claim to be the "charter group" of Canada, and of French Canadians, the official second component of Canadian society.

A close analysis of the situation shows that the Indians are becoming a potential threat to the existing dominant group and one solution is to do away with them as a distinct group. The Anglo-white population has learned too well from its current experiences with the French Canadians what problems will confront them in future if they do not destroy the Indian cultural group. Little consideration is given to the problems this would bring to the natives. However, pragmatically this is a good strategy for the dominant group. If the native population could be legally done away with, the money now spent on them could be diverted to other areas with a quicker pay off. Removal of the Indians' legal status would not, however, automatically result in a lessening of discriminatory actions against them. We would find the Indian population in the same economic position as it is now, yet without any group identification—a classic case of "marginal man." But in this case the marginality would not be wiped out within a generation because the stigma is not only cultural but also physiological. Since miscegenation between Indians and whites is not common in Canada, the marginal Indian would remain for many decades. (In 1961 the endogamous rate of Indian marriages—Indians marrying Indians—was one of the highest in Canada. In fact, it increased from 91 per cent in 1951 to over 93 per cent in 1961.)

Anyone favoring termination of the legal status of Indians implicitly adopts the "myth of equality" position previously discussed. This position advocates that since it is agreed everybody is equal, there should be no discrimination. While it is politically feasible to stop the "pro" discrimination (in the sense that economic incentives, education advantages, *etc.* can be stopped), this is a much easier policy to adopt than attempting to stop the "con" discrimination against Indians. For this reason—political expediency—and for other reasons stated previously, ways to stop the negative discrimination are not pursued.

In a nation that espouses "cultural pluralism" as a desirable goal, the action proposed in the white paper seems incongruous. The naive assumption seems to be that by removing the Indians' special status the problem will be solved. The author's conclusion is that the existing organizations developed by Indians will continue to grow as a political economic voice for them. If these organizations are allowed to control the reserves and the money attached to them, they will become formidable foes within the decade. It seems that this is what the dominant group is reacting to, rather than desiring Indians to be able to "integrate into the larger society," since we know this to be unfeasible already. The harsh reaction by the minister of Indian affairs to the Indian Association of Alberta over budgets and education is a good example of what Indian organizations can expect if they are allowed to continue.

It may be argued that well over $1 million a year has been spent on these organizations, with little to show for it. But these people have never held leadership positions before and must develop the necessary skills that most whites take for granted. Also, their impact as a group is only at the "paper level." The organization may recommend some economic enterprise but IAB approval is needed before money can be spent. Thirdly, conflict between Indian organizations and the IAB is rampant. The IAB has its long range plans and specific "slots" for allocating finance. Even though the local (provincial) organization may clearly see that an allotment is not realistic, it is not allowed to make changes. For example, if the IAB says that $10,000 is to be spent on project x, then no amount of counter argument by the local organization can divert some of this money into another project. When conflict arises, it is always blamed on the local organization.

Tremendous amounts of money are given annually to the Department of Indian Affairs to "help" the Indian. Yet as we have seen above, very little of this goes into meaningful programs that can activate long range social change. For example, in 1971–72 the Department of Indian Affairs gave about $1.2 million to Indian associations for "service contracts." A close look at the breakdown of these funds shows that less than $20,000 was allocated to "economic development" projects. If we look at the total budget of the Department of Indian Affairs, we find that a sizeable amount (43 per cent) is eaten up in salaries and staff support for its white bureaucrats. This money never reaches the reserve. If the salaries alone were given to Indian people residing on the reserve, a sizeable capital base would be established to foster further economic development. Politics is vital to the existence of any group of people. In Canada, the cultural reawakening of the Indians has been preceded and outpaced by their political awakening.

6

The Native Brotherhood of British Columbia

PHILIP DRUCKER

INDIAN ADMINISTRATION IN BC

THE ADMINISTRATIVE ATMOSPHERE in which Indian acculturation developed in British Columbia was a somewhat peculiar one, differing in many respects from that in the rest of Canada. It is interesting to note that, although as the result of factors historically quite distinct, there evolved a set of conditions very similar to those in Alaska. This was particularly true with regard to policy on Indian rights. The topic of Indian lands will be discussed in detail in a later section, but some features of the problem must be sketched in to present the full picture of the evolution of policy in the province.

*From *The Native Brotherhoods: Modern Intertribal Organizations on the Northwest Coast*, by Philip Drucker, 1958. Bureau of American Ethnology, No. 168, Smithsonian Institution, Washington, D.C., pp. 78–103. Reprinted with permission.

In eastern Canada, Indian policy was very similar to that in the United States, for the obvious reason that Canadian and United States policies derived from the same source. Briefly it may be characterized as having the complete assimilation of the Indian as its final goal, that is, through cultural adaption his elimination as a racial entity. The road to this cultural adaption was seen to be though education to white Canadian skills, patterns, and values. To accomplish this thorough transformation, the Indians were segregated on large reservations, or "reserves" as the tracts are called in Canada, where they could be protected from deleterious influences and subjected to intensive education, generally aimed at converting them into tillers of the soil. As part of this process, treaties were invariably made by which the Indians relinquished their aboriginal lands to the Government in exchange for the reserve lands, treaty moneys, and schools and welfare programs guaranteed by the Government. The similarity to United States Indian policy is clear. In British Columbia, however, this administration pattern never went into effect.

During the epoch prior to the establishment of the Crown Colony of Vancouver Island, while Hudson's Bay Company exercised control of the coast, such areas as this Company occupied were taken over through very formal legal transactions. Though some young modern Indians may grumble at the modest prices paid in these arrangements, and though the chiefs who made the "sales" may not have understood all the implications thereof, there is no question but that the Company's servants complied as best they could with Company policy of acquiring such tracts as were needed by means thoroughly correct before English law. Of course the areas thus alienated for trading posts, their gardens, *etc.*, and even the coal mines at Fort Rupert and Nanaimo, were neglible from the regional viewpoint. Sir James Douglas, on establishment of the colony, continued the same course, as far as he could. Title to the lands of lower Vancouver Island not already acquired was to be acquired by purchase, through which native title was extinguished. Douglas, a man who had spent most of his adult life dealing with Indians, and who understood them well, was very honestly concerned for their welfare. His individual opinion was that they would become assimilated most rapidly if left in small groups, scattered among white settlers. Perhaps this was a result of Douglas' familiarity with the basic local group organization of Northwest Coast society. At any rate, he was quite concerned that tracts of adequate size should be set aside for each group.

During Douglas' governorship, he attempted to continue this policy, but ran into difficulties. When the lands in the Cowichan, Chemainus, Salt Spring Island, and other regions of lower Vancouver Island were thrown open for colonization in 1861, Douglas informed the House of Assembly that funds must be provided to extinguish native title to these tracts. The infant colony, which was struggling desperately to keep its head above water financially, did not have the funds, even though Douglas, who like a good Scot did not believe in squandering pence, let alone guineas, estimated that the modest sum of £3,000 would suffice to acquire the many thousands of acres involved. When the colony appealed to the Home Government for aid, the request was brusquely refused. This reply, which infuriated many colonists, stated that the British taxpayer should not be burdened with the colony's internal problems (although it seems that receipts from sales of the lands concerned to white settlers, or a large part of them, were transmitted to England). There was some further fruitless communication over the matter, and eventually the whole thing was dropped. The lands were occupied by whites, the Indians were not paid and were quite annoyed, and there the situation was left.

In the Mainland Colony, Douglas deviated from his policy by making no attempt to extinguish Indian land title. He did, however, order very large reserves laid off in the Fraser River region, some of which were surveyed, and some of which were not. Just why Sir James followed this new procedure is nowhere made clear, but it seems a reasonable guess that the failure to get funds to extinguish Indian title on Vancouver Island led him to try a different solution.

After Douglas' retirement from public life the colony's policy became less liberal (the Colony of Vancouver Island and the Mainland Colony were merged to become the single Colony of British Columbia in 1860). There came to be numerous demands for reducing the size of some of the reserves, on the grounds that the Indians actually made no use of the land. J. W. Trutch, who became Commissioner of Lands and Works in 1866, began to carry out this reduction, and also came to formulate colony Indian policy. In 1867 he specifically denied that the Indians had any right to land beyond that actually required by them, that is, the reserves; in 1870, in an official memorandum, he declared, as a fait accompli, that the concept that the Indian had ever had title to land in fee simple had been completely denied and disproved in British Columbia. In short, he eliminated the principle of aboriginal land right entirely.[1]

At the time of confederation with Canada, in 1871, the conduct of Indian affairs was one of the administrative responsibilities turned over to the Dominion Government. Clause 13 of the "Terms of the Union" states that in Indian matters the Dominion Government was to follow "A policy as liberal as that hitherto pursued by the British Columbia Government after Union." Some writers have objected to this phraseology as shockingly cynical, for British Columbia Indian policy was anything but liberal. Nonetheless, the clause on later occasions served as documentary support of liberal policy in disputes between the Province and the Dominion, and also points up how little was known in eastern Canada about conditions on the coast.

Dominion regulation of Indian affairs brought no changes for some time, despite attempts by the Dominion Government to carry out, as nearly as it could, its policies standardized in the East. There were at this time only 28,437 acres set aside as reserves, of which 5,302 acres were on lower Vancouver Island, and the remainder in the Fraser Valley and southern

---

[1]He appears to have denied that extinguishment of Indian title had ever been deemed necessary in British Columbia, apparently drawing a very fine distinction between Douglas' land purchases for this purpose, which were made under the Hudson's Bay Company regime, and the failure to conclude such arrangements after establishment of the colonies.

interior. The Dominion wanted to set aside additional reserves, and to increase the size of many of those already established; the Province refused to make land available. There was a long period of bickering and conflict. One source of difficulty was the British Columbians' conviction, not altogether unjustified, that the people "back east in Canada" had no understanding of conditions on the coast. Another factor was the growing resentment of the Dominion Government's failure to carry out one of the crucial terms of the agreement: the construction of a railway connecting the Pacific coast with eastern Canada.[2] One must realize the reason for this feeling: even the most ardent proponents of confederation saw that British Columbia had to have easy communication with the East to function as part of the Dominion.

Meanwhile, the Indians in the southern part of the Province were becoming more and more restive, to the point where white alarmists were predicting an Indian uprising. In 1874 a missionary in the Okanagon country wrote a strong condemnation of Indian policy, which received wide publicity in the East. Finally, in 1876, a joint Dominion-Provincial Commission was established to study the Indian question and to solve the reserve problem. In agreeing to establish this Commission, the Dominion surrendered its stand on a number of points, which will be discussed in more detail in connection with the land problem itself. Governor-General Lord Dufferin's vitriolic address at Victoria, condemning Provincial Indian policy, formed another subclimax to this phase of policy formulation.

Meanwhile, another storm was building. As one result of Duncan's successful and well-known missionary work at Metlakatla, there came to be considerable missionary activity on the coast, especially in the north. While none of the missionaries undertook to duplicate Duncan's achievements, many were influenced by his methods. Thus, the Reverend Mr. Doolan built the new town of Kincolith, drawing converts from the pagan villages of the Nass; Laxgalt'sap (later Greenville) and Aiyanch were also new towns, though less far removed, geographically, from the native villages. The missionaries also adopted Duncan's views on the need for complete acculturation—though they did not call it that—to white standards in work habits, economics, dress, and the like, if real and lasting conversion to Christianity were to be attained. Therefore they began to take a deep interest in secular matters, including the already bitterly disputed land question. Eventually, as might be expected, they were subjected to sharp criticism in certain quarters, and were accused of unduly influencing the Indians in nonspiritual affairs—indeed, of stirring up trouble among them. These accusations, if unkind, probably had some basis in fact. The missionaries who came out to devote their lives to the wild tribes of the Northwest were determined men, with the courage of their convictions. They never doubted their ability to make decisions as to what was best for their

[2]The surveys were to have been completed within 2 years after confederation, the railway itself within 10 years. A good number of years passed before even the surveys were completed and the route was selected. Finally in 1883 the Dominion Government reached an agreement with a private syndicate to build the Canadian Pacific Railway, completed in 1886.

flocks. In addition, they had considerable authority in the villages. In 1863 or 1864, Governor Douglas had given Duncan a Magistrate's commission, to aid him in his fight against vendors of liquor to the Indians. The later missionaries were similarly commissioned. The authority to appoint constables in their villages, to order arrests, and to try and punish offenders against the peace was a powerful weapon. None of them were anxious to see the arrival of ordinary civil authority in the form of Indian agents.

A remarkable episode occurred at Metlakatla about 1881 or 1882. Public pressure for designation of Indian agents had finally resulted in the appointment of six. One was detailed to Metlakatla; he went there, along with the Superintendent of Indian Affairs for British Columbia, on a gunboat sent to investigate trouble at that community. The Duncan-Ridley feud was in full flame. After an inconclusive hearing, the agent is reported to have conferred with the Indians by whom he was told, according to Wellcome (1887, pp. 227–228), that they had no interest in "coming under the Indian Act," which was for wild tribes, not advanced people like themselves, and further, they did not want him as their agent. So he humbly went away. It seems incredible that neither he nor the superintendent insisted on recognition of the Government's authority. Most likely they were afraid of getting caught in the crossfire between Duncan and Ridley, both of whom had, of course, strong supporters as well as bitter opponents across Canada and in England.

Many contemporaries, incidentally, deplored the Duncan-Ridley fight, which they alleged was unsettling in the extreme to the Indians. What appears to have been overlooked at the time was that the long, acrimonious, and undignified wrangle focused native attention on the land problem especially. One of the points at issue (to be discussed more fully later on), soon came to be the 2-acre lot in the middle of the village which the Province intended to survey and transfer by deed to the Church Missionary Society for Ridley's use. The Indians' interference with the surveyors, their consequent arrest and imprisonment, and the flood of angry letters pro and con in the Daily Colonist must have made the northern natives more land-problem conscious than ever.

Meanwhile, the Joint Commission on reserves labored as it could, but its accomplishments were limited because of the continued basic difference of view between Province and Dominion. By 1886, according to Shankel (MS), disagreement had reached the point where all cooperation collapsed. Although Provincial officials had originally urged the posting of Indian agents, the Provincial Government refused to make their law-enforcement facilities—constables, courts, and jails—available to Indian agents. The latter were rendered nearly powerless thereby. This appears to be the chief reason why the Department of Indian Affairs was unable to enforce the prohibition on potlatching, which had been incorporated into the Indian Act in one form or another since 1885. (Even later, after tension eased, agents were consistently unable to get convictions on potlatch charges in Provincial courts.) Shankel states also that, in such cases as Indian agents were empowered to try, they refused to turn over the half of each fine collected to the Province, although this was provided for in the

Indian Act itself. In other words, things were at a complete impasse. Nonetheless, a Provincial Commission of Enquiry, set up in 1887 to look into
conditions among the Indians of the "northwest coast" (by which they meant
the northern coasts of British Columbia) concluded that more Indian
agents, and well-qualified ones, should be stationed on the coast. This commission in its findings stated that "complete control" of Indians by missionaries was a mistake. Specific objections were voiced against the missionary
practice of setting up municipal self-government by elective officials in the
villages. Typically, the village councils were allowed (extralegally by the
missionaries) to try and punish minor cases, usually involving violations
of (also extralegal) village ordinances.

Gradually Dominion-Provincial relationships in the area of Indian
affairs improved. Prospects of reaching a final settlement on the land question and other issues helped to relax the tension. When, at long last, a Royal
Commission was appointed to hold formal hearings on the Indian claims,
and rendered a decision (one up-holding the Province's position), the way
was cleared for effective cooperation between local and Federal governments.[3]

As the administrative pattern developed, each Indian agent was responsible for a number of villages and their scattered reserves. Insofar as
practicable, the agencies coincided with linguistic divisions: thus, all the
southern Kwakiutl were and are under one agent; the Niska, coast Tsimshian, and part of the Gitksan under another, and so on. The agencies
were, and still are, quite large. One receives the impression that the agent's
major function was considered to be that of law enforcement. He held a
magistrate's commission, and thus could try minor cases; for more serious
offenses he could bring charges, at which time Provincial police (Royal
Canadian Mounted Police during periods in which the Province contracted
for policing by that organization) made the arrest and the case was tried
before a provincial court. (As stated, there was a period during which
agents got negligible cooperation from the Province, but eventually this
difficulty was overcome.) The agent also kept records on vital statistics
and the like. Education and public health remained in the hands of missionary organizations mainly, the Indian Department assisting through
direct subsidy. The quality of Indian education under this system was highly

[3]All Canadian Federal legislation affecting Indians (but not Eskimos) is incorporated into a single act (except for certain matters relating to enfranchisement, which
are included in the Citizenship Act); a fact that strikes one at first as not only more
orderly but more conducive to consistency of policy than the several thousand scattered and unrelated pieces of legislation affecting Indians in the United States. On the
other hand, tailoring a single piece of legislation, even a long one of many articles,
to cover requirements of groups whose conditions and degree of acculturation differ
as widely as, for instance, those of Abnaki, Iroquois, Babine, and Tsimshian results
in either extreme rigidity of policy and resultant unsuitability to many of the people
subject to the act, or else means that flexibility must be written in by giving considerable power as to extent of application of the law to the administering agency of the
Government—the Department of Indian Affairs. The Canadian Indian Act takes the
latter course, even in its latest revised version; a great deal of discretion is permitted
the Minister of the Department of Citizenship and Immigration, under whose authority the Indian Affairs Branch is now placed.

variable. If the resident missionary in a village was interested in education, and was a competent teacher, the children who attended his school were relatively well taught; were he not qualified, he did the best he could, but education suffered. At residential (boarding) schools, like the one maintained for some years at Metlakatla, that at Alert Bay, and the Catholic school at Clayoquot, teaching was usually more competently done, and was of course accompanied by a more intensive 24-hour-a-day stress on acculturation. The public health work carried on by the medical missionaries was of high quality, but spread very thin; these men labored valiantly but were too few and with too scant facilities to serve the Indian population adequately.

During the depression years of the 1930's, the concept of state (both National and Provincial) responsibility for welfare developed in Canada. I do not know the precise relationship of the growth of this sociopolitical philosophy to comparable developments in England and in the United States, nor is this point pertinent to the present discussion. What is significant is that in the years following World War II legislative enactments providing for such things as pensions for the aged and for the blind, "family allowances" (monthly payments by the State toward the maintenance of minor children), and similar measures were in force, and came to be extended to Indians as well as whites. In addition, more funds were made available to the Indian Department for education programs. The Department took over operation of the day schools, apparently to the relief of the Protestant mission organizations who were wearying of the burden. New schools were built and staffed. Similarly, responsibility for public health among Indians was transferred to the Department of Health, which immediately got a public-health program on a major scale underway.

The same postwar period saw a complete reversal of Provincial Indian policy. It came to be recognized that the Indians of British Columbia, particularly the coast tribes, were well on the way to becoming fellow citizens, and that, sooner or later, the Federal Indian Department would cut back its functions, transferring more and more responsibility for the Indians to the Province, not as "wards" but as Canadian nationals. The Province supplemented Federal funds to bring the level of old-age pensions to that of whites, and it made possible admission of Indian children to Provincial schools (final decision, as I understand, rests with the local school board). When the Indian Department began to equate Indian school curricula and standards with those of Provincial schools, Provincial school inspectors were assigned to visit Indian schools. When the day comes for Indian schools to be taken over by the Province, there will be no violent strain or drastic change, as far as curricula and standards go. Two other steps marking the new Provincial attitude were the giving to Indians the right to enter "beer parlors" and drink beer there (although the right to purchase package goods, either beer or distilled liquors, is still denied them), and the Provincial enfranchising of the Indian. An Indian can now vote in Provincial elections, and can hold office as well—in fact as these data were collected an educated young Niska was serving creditably in the Provincial legislature. Perhaps the most forward-looking step of all was the setting up, in 1950, of an advisory committee consisting of 3 white British Columbians and 3 Indians, with a paid executive secretary, reporting to the Provincial Minister of Labor, to study Indian conditions and problems for the purpose of advising the Provincial government when it assumes the responsibility of governing the native population.

The overall picture of Indian administration in British Columbia is thus one of a relatively long period during which exercise of legal sanctions was the chief work of Indian agents, education and medical care were in hands of missionary organizations who did what they could with their limited budgets (their own funds supplemented by Government subsidies), and general welfare programs were practically nonexistent. Economically, the Indians had to sink or swim in an increasingly industrialized environment, in competition with whites and orientals already well adjusted to an industrial society. The Province during this period meant little to the Indians aside from being the executive agent in enforcing the Dominion's legal sanctions: its police, courts, and jails were the provincial entities with which Indians were most familiar. (As recounted before, in the years following confederation, when Dominion-Province relations were strained, these agencies could be relied on to be lenient; later, they tended to deal quite severely with Indian offenders.) Following World War II, however, both Federal and Provincial attitudes and policies changed tremendously. The amount and quality of educational, public-health, and welfare services were stepped up, to the degree that the Indian is as well cared for in these respects as is the white British Columbian.[4] Similarly, the Provincial government has taken the view that the Indians are well on the way to becoming ordinary members of the community no longer requiring special Federal administration. For that reason it has begun to extend them rights beyond those of "wards" of the Dominion Government, and to plan to incorporate them into the Provincial community.

THE LAND QUESTION

As indicated in the foregoing section, the question of Indian lands and land rights in British Columbia was a focal point in the evolution of administrative policy until the late 1920's, and some aspects of it continue to pose thorny problems today. Here, I shall outline the history of the land question separately, as far as possible, from general administrative matters, and shall sketch Indian reactions to it.[5]

A peculiar aspect of the problem is that in the acrimonious debates over the status of Indian lands, no one appears to have bothered to bring

[4]I do not mean, obviously, that educational and medical facilities in a village of 200 or 300 souls in a place like the Nass River are as good as those in Vancouver or Victoria; they are, however, quite comparable to those in a white community of comparable size and remoteness.

[5]In this section, as well as in the preceding, a great deal of material has been taken from Shankel's MS. (*op. cit.*); I shall not give references to each and every item so used. Data from published sources are documented by page references.

up the matter of Indian concepts of right in real property.[6] It may be that men like Douglas, Sproat, and others who knew a great deal about the Indians, did not regard this as significant, legally speaking. Yet opponents of the concept of aboriginal right repeatedly stated that the Indians had simply roamed randomly over the land, never claiming particular and specific areas. Ethnographic information had made clear, however, that the coast Indians, at least, had very concrete concepts of land ownership. Tracts, whose limits were defined about as precisely as could be done by people with no knowledge of modern surveying, were very definitely considered as property.[7] Title was held, however, not by individuals but by some corporate entity such as a tribe, a clan, a lineage, or an extended family, depending on the formal political and social organization of the group in question. This title was nominally vested in the chief or headman of the owning unit, but evidence is clear that basically all the members of the particular unit shared in the rights. Accentuating the similarity to European usage was the fact that title was regarded as transferable; land could be alienated. Not only could a sort of coterminous usufruct right be given, but a chief, with the consensus of his group, could give any tract—a habitation site, a strip of beach and foreshore with all salvage rights thereon, a fishing place, hunting area, berrying or root-digging ground, *etc.*—to another clan, lineage, *etc.*, who then would have exclusive right to such land. The principal difference between such transfers of title and those customary among whites was that the Indians did not ordinarily make them as sales, that is, in return for wealth goods. They alienated parcels of land most frequently in connection with marriages between important persons of two social units, to cement the bonds between the groups and strengthen both economically and militarily, or for the same basic reasons, on the arrival of some migrating clan or extended family. The frequent formal assertions regarding title to specific lands, made at feasts and pot-latches, were the rather precise counterpart by nonliterate people of written and recorded deeds.

Thus, the coast natives were acutely conscious of land ownership, and had been since time immemorial. The groups of the southern Interior —the Interior Salish and Kutenai—if their aboriginal concepts had been less precise, soon came to be land conscious. They turned quite early to animal husbandry, and by the time of confederation, many of these Indians were successful cattlemen with large herds and fine saddle horses. Range cattle in that region require extensive pastures; every inroad on Indian lands by white ranchmen meant that Indian herds suffered. These people soon became most vociferous in demanding that reserves of adequate size be marked off for them.

In addition, it is clear that it did not take the Indians long to become aware of the technical niceties of establishing ownership under British law.

---

[6]This is highlighted by the fact that Shankel, who seems to have combed every available official document and newspaper, *etc.*, account bearing on the matter, does not mention it either. The major defect of Shankel's otherwise excellent study is his lack of understanding of the ethnographic materials from the area.

[7]See, for example, Drucker, 1951, pp. 20 ff., 247ff.

Shankel quotes (though he does not develop the point) an item in the newspaper British Colonist (Victoria), of July 3, 1865, concerning the Cowichans, who were still waiting, albeit impatiently, for the payment for the lands they had surrendered some years before, during Douglas' governorship (these were the lands for which they were to have been paid with part of the £3,000 which Douglas requested but never obtained). Apparently there was a great deal of bickering over trespass, by people and by livestock, on the reserves; the paper states that the "Cowichans were refusing to fence their (reserved) lands for fear of weakening their title claims to the unenclosed portions." That this maneuver would have done anything for them before a court is dubious, but it indicates that the Indians were trying to defend themselves through legalistic means.

The pros and cons of the concept of aboriginal land rights as expressed by partisans of the Provincial viewpoint and by those adhering to the Dominion position were argued bitterly in the local press in the 1870's and 1880's.[8] There is no clear evidence on the point, but there must have been some educated Indians, such as the Tsimshian Alfred Dudoward and his future wife Kate, both residents in Victoria at the time, who thus came to be informed of the varied opinions on Indian land. Lord Dufferin's bitter denunciation of British Columbia Indian policy, made in 1876 when he, as Governor-General of Canada, toured the Province, spelled out the concept of native land right and the need for extinguishing such title through just and legal methods. And finally, the Duncan-Ridley squabble, as has been remarked, came to revolve about a tract of land.[9] In other words, Indian land and land title was so lively an issue, discussed so much and so bitterly, that the Indians must have become acutely aware of it.

Duncan played another role in the land question, this time helping define Provincial policy. Sir James Douglas had previously requested his

[8]Wellcome, 1887, reproduces a number of "Letters to the Editors" in a series of appendixes, pp. 431–83.

[9]The origin of the controversy was of course quite different: Bishop Ridley wanted to take charge of the mission and village, and Duncan was not willing to share his authority, let alone take second place. Ridley, as authorized representative of the Church Missionary Society, could and did take possession of the mission buildings: the church, the "mission house," and the mission store which were situated on a special tract in the center of the village. At Duncan's insistence, the Metlakatlans protested the land was theirs, part of their village, and had never been given to the Church Missionary Society. Friends of Ridley in the Provisional government, arranged to cut off this tract of about 2 acres, then give a deed to it to the C.M.S. Although apparently Metlakatla Reserve had been laid off at that time, these people maintained that the only existent land right was that of the British Crown, a right which the Province had authority to administer. Duncan and a delegation of Metlakatlans went to Ottawa, to plead for the intercession of the Dominion Government, but got only unfulfilled promises of support. A Provincial surveyor was sent to survey the tract; the Indians, through obstructionist but nonviolent tactics (presumably designed by Duncan) refused to let him work—they obstructed his line of sight, moved or knocked down his stakes, *etc.* This went on for months—the surveyor either had an enormous patience or was being paid at a handsome daily rate. Finally Provincial authorities tired of the situation, arrested a number of Indians and threw them in jail in Victoria. This show of force broke the deadlock, and was the direct cause of the removal to Alaska by Duncan and his congregation.

advice on suitable reserve policy; Duncan had then recommended, among other things, very large reserves, on which entire linguistic divisions should be settled (as opposed to the separate village-by-village reserves of lower Vancouver Island). During one of Duncan's visits to Victoria, he "intervened," to quote the report of the Royal Commission, Provincial authorities perhaps requesting his opinion. They had not become annoyed at him yet; he was regarded as the great authority on "civilizing" the Indians. This time he modified his views. He not only did not stress extent of the reserves, but specified that he considered it unnecessary to have any rule for fixed acreage per capita. (The Dominion had been trying to get the Province to agree to set aside 80 acres for each "average" Indian family of 5.) He brought in a new point, one which has caused difficulties ever since: if a reserve were abandoned, or the Indians decreased in numbers, the abandoned reserve, or in the case of decreasing population, the excess lands, should revert to the Province. This notice that the Province should hold reversionary right to all reserve lands within its borders may have been in the air at the time, but was first expressed as official policy in connection with these Duncan recommendations. From that time on Provincial reversionary right was always claimed, and in 1876, it was conceded by the Dominion Government in the agreement leading to the establishment of the Joint Commission on Indian Lands. This principle of "dual ownership" has complicated sales of excess lands, timber, *etc.* for the Indians' benefit, ever since (Royal Comm., 1916, vol. 1, p. 17), and is currently blocking the mass enfranchisement of the modern Old Metlakatla community, the legal point, yet unresolved, being in essence: if the entire community becomes enfranchised, and thus ceases to exist as an Indian "band," must the entire reserve, including the village lots on which the people's homes are built, revert to the Province?

In 1887, a delegation of chiefs from the Nass and from Port Simpson went to Victoria "to petition for the return of their lands," and a formal treaty guaranteeing their rights to those lands "forever." Apparently the reserves had just been marked out by surveyors. These were no cringing downtrodden natives—they were proud Northwest Coast chiefs. The tenor of their statements was demanding, not pleading.[10] They got nowhere, of course, though their attitude doubtless ruffled some tempers and caused some anxiety—the Nass was frequently used in those days as a route into the interior (miners going into the Cassiar district went up the Nass, then packed over one of the grease trails from Gitlaxtamks to the Skeena, rather than risk the dangerous Skeena Canyon). My Niska informants were of the opinion that the inspiration for the demands for "return of their lands" had come from the Reverend Mr. Green, the missionary who founded Laxgalt'sap (later Greenville). As they recall statements of their elders, Green told them that "even the reserves were not even theirs, but belonged to the 'Government.' " "They began to hold meetings, then, after the Reverend Mr. Green opened their eyes, to discuss the land problem. Finally they de-

---

[10]Report of conferences between the Provincial Government and Indian delegates from Fort Simpson and Nass River, . . . 3d and 8th Feb., 1887 (Victoria).

cided to send the chiefs to Victoria, and to invite the Port Simpson people to accompany them." This appears to have been the first step toward the formation of the "Nishga Land Committee."[11] which finally had drawn up the famous "Nishga Petition" that brought the Indian land problem in the Province to a head. The year 1887 was the same one in which the "Provincial Board of Enquiry into the Conditions of the Indians of the Northwest Coast" (*i.e.*, the north coast of British Columbia) loosed its angry protest against irresponsible stimulation of Indian land claims by missionaries, and, as well, of the missionaries' rousing opposition to the Indian Act and authority of the Indian agents. The Commission specified that Methodist, not Anglican missionaries, were chiefly responsible for such trouble making. Shankel suggests this indicates sectarian bias on the part of the members of the Commission. The fact remains, however, that Laxgalt'sap and Fort Simpson were centers of Methodist missionary effort at that time, and the haughty attitude of the Niska and Tsimshian delegates probably irritated all who heard them.

About this same time the Port Simpson people threatened to follow the example of Duncan's congregation, and move out of Canada to Alaska, if their land situation were not remedied. The value of the threat is hard to assess; many white British Columbians would likely have been delighted to see them go anywhere, as long as they went away. On the other hand, many people were unhappy about the bad publicity resulting from the Metlakatla emigration of 1887. Newspapers in eastern Canada were still editorializing about Provincial treatment of the Indians (especially the Metlakatlans), denouncing it as unjust and brutal. Even in the United States where Indian policy of the day could scarcely be called benevolent, Duncan's partisans were sniping at British Columbia through the press.

For a time nothing was resolved regarding land policy, although the "Joint Commission" (which had been reduced to a committee of one since 1878) apparently continued to study Indian land needs. Provincial surveyors seem to have continued to lay off reserves during this time. Most of the coastal reserves were quite small, including principally villages and campsites, fishing places on streams, graveyards, and the like. The only large area set aside was "Tsimpsean Res. No. 2," divided half and half between the Port Simpson and the Metlakatla bands, which contained in 1916 a total of 44,175 acres, (Royal Comm., 1916, vol. 3, pp. 555, 556, and *passim*) after sale and surrender of the land for Prince Rupert townsite (both bands have other small tracts also). I have not been able to find out just how or when this tract was made a reserve. Tsimshian informants believe that Duncan was responsible for securing the tract. It is possible that he did so in 1874, at the time he "intervened" with his recommendations of no fixed acreage basis for reserves, and the notion of the Province's reversionary right.

The Indians were by no means appeased. The concern over the question led the Niska to continue their meetings and discussions, and apparently in the 1890's (my informants could not recall the exact date), the

---

[11]This spelling of Niska is used here because it appears thus in various official documents.

"Nishga Land Committee" was formed. A Greenville man whose English name was Arthur Calder was said to have been the leader in organizing the group.

Some informants speak of people having been "elected" to the Land Committee, but I gathered that the elections consisted in public recognition of high rank according to ancient standards. Peter Calder, today one of the elderly members of the Greenville community, insisted that the four men of highest rank—four "chiefs"—of each clan, were "elected" to the committee in each village. The village committee elected its own chairman and other officers. There were three village committees, representing Kincolith, Greenville, and Aiyansh—Canyon City (the last-named joined forces because of the small size of the Canyon City village)—and the three together constituted the "Nishga Land Committee."

This organization did more than just meet to discuss their problem. It raised funds (the four representatives of each local clan collected from their claims, to engage an attorney to advise and represent them, and to draw up petitions and other documents. One man who had himself served on the Land Committee assured me that the group had collected and expended many thousands of dollars over the years in its fight for the lands.

Not long after the Land Committee as a formal entity was organized, the Port Simpson people were invited to join. They refused, however. There were probably a variety of reasons, although Niska informants stress one in particular: that the Tsimshian were claiming lands at the mouth of Portland Canal and at the mouth of the Nass up to a place called in English "Red Bluff," and therefore would not subscribe to the claims of the Land Committee, who insisted that all the lands as far seaward as kctdasx ("Squirrel Water" (?)), a stream across the channel from Port Simpson,[12] were formerly Niska property. Some bitterness seems to have resulted from this conflict regarding claims. There were probably other influential factors also: the Tsimshian had their part of the very large reserve, "Tsimpsean Res. No. 2," and may as well have been afraid of jeopardizing their anticipated claims to compensation for the proposed site of the railhead of the Grand Trunk Railway ("Canadian National"). Port Simpson itself was seriously considered for a time as a possible site, it is said, and even after the site of modern Prince Rupert was selected and "cut off" from the southern part of "Tsimpsean Reserve No. 2," the Port Simpson people expected a share of the proceeds from the land sale.

At any rate, the Niska went it alone for a number of years in their struggle. The essence of their demands came to be twofold: first, that they should be given 160 acres per capita, "just like white men," and second,

[12]What this all means is that a good deal of the area concerned was disputed territory anciently. Best evidence, based on clan and tribal traditions, suggests that the Tsimshian claims corresponded reasonably well with the areas principally controlled by them. Kincolith, founded by missionaries Doolan and Tomlinson in 1876, was located on a campsite and fortified position of Chief hai'mas, of the Tsimshian Gitsis tribe. The modern name derives from its ancient one, kng li, "scalp place," because a famous holder of the hai'mas title used to take scalps, not heads, of his enemies, and used to hang them on the bluff just above the modern townsite when he returned from raids.

that they be given just and reasonable compensation for all lands over and above the amount of the per capita grants which had formerly belonged to them. Neither the Province nor the Dominion had much interest in satisfying these demands.

Meanwhile, in the south, other patterns were developing. In 1906 a Squamish chief and two other Indians were sent as a delegation to England to present their grievance directly to the Crown. Their petition is stated to have included four main points:

1. Their land title had never been properly extinguished, as James Douglas had promised it would be.
2. Whites had settled on their lands, against the Indians' wishes.
3. All appeals to the Canadian Government had been in vain.
4. They not only had no vote, but were not even consulted by the Indian agents on matters of grave concern to themselves.

The delegation accomplished nothing, but their approach was the first of a number of attempts by Indians to bypass Canadian authorities and get relief from the Crown. Shankel states that 3 years later, another delegation, "representing 20 Indian tribes," went to England with a similar petition. He does not indicate who the Indians were; they were not northern coast tribes, I am sure, so must have come from Salish villages of the southern coast and/or interior.

At about this same time a new force developed. This was an organization called "Friends of the Indians," consisting principally of white members of congregations of one of the churches which was supporting considerable missionary work along the coast. The "Friends of the Indians" sought through petitions, financial aid, etc., to aid the Indians to get a just settlement of their land claims.

The year 1910 saw a continuation of the efforts for a settlement. The Niska are stated to have subscribed a fund of several hundred dollars which the Land Committee paid to a lawyer for a legal opinion on their claims, and apparently also as a retainer. A number of Salish groups, and the Friends of the Indians also, sent delegations to wait on Sir Wilfred Laurier during his tour of the Province, to present him petitions requesting justice for the Indians. Laurier seems to have heard the petitions sympathetically, and is said to have promised his support. (The then head of the Provincial government, Prime Minister McBride, is reported by Shankel to have declared publicly that the Indian land question was of no importance, and was a new issue stirred up by malicious whites to embarrass his administration.)

It will be noted that up to this time it was principally the Niska and certain coast and interior Salish who were most actively concerned about their lands. However, such groups as the Tsimshian, Gitksan, and Haida were becoming increasingly land conscious. It seems to have been about this time, or a very few years earlier, that the large sum paid for the Prince Rupert townsite was assigned by the Indian Department to the Metlakatlans only (since it had all come out of their "south half" of the large Tsimpsean Reserve No. 2). This created a good deal of bitterness among the Port

Simpson people, who had expected a share, since not only did they share a part of the reserve (even though theirs was the "northern half") with the Metlakatlans, but, also, certain clans represented better at Simpson than at Metlakatla had aboriginal claims to portions of the tract. What the Port Simpson Indians regarded as the tantalizing loss of a share of the per capita distribution and also loss of a part of what was probably the largest Indian trust fund in the Province up to that time, must certainly have driven home the point of the value of lands. Farther south along the coast, most Kwakiutl groups and the Nootkans remained blissfully unaware of the issue. Even a few years later, during the hearings of the Royal Commission on Indian Affairs, at which petitions for enlargements of reserves or additional reserves might be presented, these last-named peoples requested principally small tracts; chiefly fishing and trapping campsites, except for a few scattered individual requests for "200 acres for each adult male" (Royal Comm., 1916, vol. 7, pp. 401–15, vol. 3, pp. 881–84). The Athabascans of the northern interior of the Province likewise seem to have been little interested; the Royal Commission's report does not so state, specifically, but suggests that most requests for additional reserves were made by the agents of the Stikine and other northern agencies.

In 1912 two major events took place, which affected, in opposing ways, the outcome of the land problem. One was the drafting of the famous "Nishga Petition" for the Land Committee by an attorney retained for the purpose. This petition requested both lands allotted on a per capita basis to all Niska, and compensation for the remainder of former holdings. The areas claimed as aboriginal lands were the same as those originally claimed by the Nishga Land Committee and included the disputed tracts on the lower Nass and about the mouth of Portland Canal. This petition was formally adopted by the full Land Committee at Kincolith on January 23, 1913, and transmitted in May or June of that year to the Dominion Government with the request that it be submitted to the Judicial Committee of the Imperial Privy Council. This insistence on a hearing before this committee, which, as I understand, functioned as a sort of court of highest appeal for the Empire, confused the land issue for a number of years. It was apparently a refinement of such attempts as that of the Squamish to present their petitions "to the King," the Indians had at last found out, or had been properly advised, what was the highest ranking judicial body to whom they could appeal. At this time, and many times subsequently, they were advised by legal officers of both Provincial and Dominion agencies that they could not submit a petition directly to the Privy Council; this could only be done through an appeal from the decision of a Canadian court of proper jurisdiction, and with the consent of the Government. The Niska refusal to permit their petition to be brought as a suit before a Federal court or commission, until they were forced to do so, delayed settlement for a long time. The Nishga Land Committee sent delegations to Ottawa to plead for the processing of their petition according to their requests in both 1915 and 1916, but to no avail.

To go back in time briefly, the other signal event of 1912 was the establishment of a "Royal Commission on Indian Affairs in the Province of

British Columbia," the body mentioned a number of times in preceding paragraphs.[13] The Provincial Government, in a memorandum of understanding, approved the establishment of this Commission and agreed to be bound by its findings. In the course of three years (1913, 1914, and 1915), this Commission accomplished the tremendous task of visiting every Indian population center in the Province—and transportation was slow and often laborious in those days, both on the coast and in the interior—and of hearing the representations of almost every band that would appear before it. Some groups, the Skidegate Haida, several Gitksan villages, and a few others, refused to discuss their reserves and needs "lest their claims concerning aboriginal rights be jeopardized" (Royal Comm., 1916, vol. 3, p. 726). The Commission tried beyond all question to be fair, although it was manifestly influenced by the presumption that on the coast where the Indians were primarily fishermen and the land was unsuited for agriculture the land requirements of the natives were small. There is no indication that any of the Indians who did request large tracts attempted to justify their requests on the grounds of interest in developing logging projects. The Commission was empowered to recommend that specific tracts be set aside as reserves where lands requested by the Indians (or the Indian agents) were available—that is, not preempted[14]or under timber lease, and did so in numerous cases. Despite the fears of some Indians, the Commission's work had no bearing at all on the problem of aboriginal rights, however. Its findings were based entirely on the Commissioners' concept of current needs.

The next step in the drama was the formation of an organization known as the "Allied Tribes of British Columbia." A number of Interior Salish groups met at Spence's Bridge, BC, in February 1915, to form an organization for the support of the Nishga Petition, by this time the test case and cause celebre among the Indians of the Province. How much aid and guidance these people had from white friends is mentioned nowhere, but must have been considerable. James Teit, Indian-trader-turned-ethnographer whose reports on the Thompson, Shuswap, and Lillooet form an important section of the AMNH Jesup Expedition series, was the great good friend of the Indians and of the Allied Tribes organization up to his death about 1920. The following year the organization met in Vancouver. Indians from the southern coast were also represented. It was probably at this time that two individuals entered the organization who became major figures in it. Andrew Paull was a young man of Squamish descent, who was quite well educated, and who was, as well, regarded as a leader by his people. Peter R. Kelly, a Haida from Skidegate (living in Nanaimo at that time), had been educated and ordained as a Methodist minister. Both these

[13]This Commission, consisting of two members nominated by the Dominion Government, two by the Province, and a chairman nominated by the aforesaid four members, was empowered to hold hearings on Indian land needs, to approve existing reserves, to extend or reduce their boundaries, to create additional reserves as required and as lands were available.

[14]"Preempting" is a process of acquiring possession and title to land roughly comparable to homesteading in the United States.

men were highly sophisticated, in the sense of combining an understanding of the cultures of their ancestors and that of white Canada.

Paull and Kelly resolved to enlist the coast groups in the Allied Tribes' cause. They visited practically every village in the ensuing years, from Aiyansh and Kispiox to Musquiam, preaching the doctrine of the Allied Tribes as the Indian's only hope. They had considerable success. They were even able to arrange for a sort of gentlemen's agreement between the Niska and the Tsimshian of Port Simpson, according to which both groups agreed not to raise the issue of the conflict in their respective claims until the case for aboriginal land right had been successfully resolved. The Port Simpson people became participating members of the Allied Tribes, supporting the organization solidly. The Niska, ever autonomists, did not actually join, but continued to support their Land Committee while cooperating with and acknowledging the backing of the larger organization. Even the southern Kwakiutl finally desisted from their potlatching long enough to aline themselves with the Allied Tribes. As one would expect, when financial support was needed, they responded promptly and liberally.

The organization of the Allied Tribes was peculiar in certain respects. Its uppermost echelon was organized in a very formal fashion, its local, grassroots level appears to have been most casually organized, in fact, lacked formal organization altogether. At the top, there was a permanent Executive Committee, which elected its officers, such as chairman, *etc.*, from its own members. Kelly and Paull consistently held key positions, such as the chairmanship, secretaryship, and so on, from the time they became active in the work. The Executive Committee worked closely with the organization's attorneys, planning tactics, making representations to Government officials, *etc.* On the village level there was no permanent formal organization. Delegates, usually one or two from each community, were elected to attend meetings held in Vancouver and Victoria, and to act as liaison agents between the Executive Committee and the people. There was a tendency in some villages, especially among southern Kwakiutl, to elect ranking chiefs as village delegates, at first. However, it was soon discovered that facility in English and understanding of white Canadian culture and law were also necessary, for the delegates were expected to call local meetings to explain what had gone on at the conventions, and what the problems were. (The business of the conventions was conducted in English, of course, because of the diversity of the native tongues of the delegates.) Sometimes collections were taken up to pay the expenses of delegates to a convention; occasionally delegates paid their own way. Usually, the notices sent out announcing the date of a meeting requested that delegates collect funds, locally, for the organization: to assist the Nishga Land Committee, to pay for travel by members of the Executive Committee, either on organizing trips through the Province or for a trip to Ottawa to confer with Federal authorities, etc. The local delegates called meetings, explained the need for funds, took up collections, and then took the money to the convention. Over the years considerable sums were raised. Included in the organization's final demands on the Government was the sum of $100,000, requested as reimbursement of expenditures over the years in connection with the case. Some of this had been contributed by the Friends of the Indians (Joint Committee (1927), pp. 37, 69–70).

The report of the Joint Committee (1927) gives, in passing, a good deal of detail regarding the history of the organization. At a meeting in 1916, there were 16 entities or "tribes" represented: from the interior, Okanagon, Lake "or Senjetec," "Thompson River at Courteau," Shuswap, Lillooet, Kutenai, Chilcotin, "Tahlton" (Tahltan), and Kasha (Kaska?); from the coast, Nishga, Tsimshian, Kitikshian (Gitksan), Haida, Bella Coola, Cowishan, "Lower Fraser or Stalo" (Joint Committee (1927), pp. 175–76). The inclusion of the Niska may mean that they had sent representatives on this occassion, or that they were regarded as allied with the organization. The list cited above does not name individual representatives. The Niska insist they never really joined the Allied Tribes. In 1922 there was an important meeting of representatives of a larger number of groups: Haida; Tsimshian (the Niska were not represented, nor, on this occasion were the Gitksan); Bella Coola; a number of Southern Kwakiutl communities, including Fort Rupert, Alert Bay, Kingcome Inlet, Cape Mudge, and Campbell River; a series of Coast Salish—Cowichan, Nanaimo, Naimo, Saanich, "Musquean" (Musquiam), Squamish, and "Lower Fraser tribes;" and a considerable number of people, some claiming to represent linguistic divisions and others single reserves, from the interior —the "Lillooet tribes," Fort Douglas, Pemberton, Kamloops, Smilkameen, Nakamip, Penticton, "Okanagon tribes," Fairview, Nicola Valley, "Merritt Nicola Valley." Some of these groups from the interior never really affiliated themselves with the Allied Tribes; at this particular meeting they simply agreed to work together for the common goal.

The Executive Committee of the Allied Tribes drafted a number of petitions, memorials, and statements during the life of the organization, which they submitted to Provincial and Dominion officials, Members of Parliament, *etc.* Many of these petitions were requests to present their claims directly before the Imperial Privy Council, although their general counsel was specifically, even bluntly, told that such procedure was impossible (Joint Committee (1927) pp. x–xi, 61–64). Why the Executive Committee persisted so long and vainly in this attempt is not clear. Either the Indians' attorney did not inform them of these flat refusals to permit them to bypass Canadian courts entirely, or they were remarkably obtuse.[15] What they were trying to get is much the same as if, in the United States, a party to a legal action should try to have the case heard for the first time in the United States Supreme Court. By their vain persistence, they refused to take advantage of the best opportunity offered them in the history of the land contention for their day in court, with right of appeal to the Privy

[15]The Nishga Petition was actually presented to the Imperial Privy Council apparently through a British law firm, and was studied by the Privy Council, who returned it, in 1918, with a letter making clear that if the claim involved the invasion of a legal right, it should be litigated in Canadian courts, then, if need be, appealed in normal fashion to the Judicial Committee of the Privy Council. This letter also spells out the procedural steps if the Indians' claim was "a complaint of the executive action of the Provincial or the Dominion Government," rather than a matter of law (Joint Committee [1927], p. 61).

Council specifically provided for. Duncan Scott, Deputy Superintendent General of Indian Affairs, submitted a proposal in 1914, providing for a hearing of the Indian claims in the Exchequer Court of Canada, with right of appeal to the Privy Council, subject to the following conditions:

1.   That the Indians agree that, if the final decision substantiated their claims to the lands of the Province, they would immediately surrender such title in return for such benefits, given by the Dominion, in accordance with established Crown usage in satisfying and extinguishing unsurrendered Indian title. (This was of course a logical and obvious provision to prevent the Indians, if they did turn out to have valid title, from simply evicting all non-Indian British Columbians.) The findings of the Royal Commission as to reserves was also to be accepted by the Indians as part of their compensation.

2.   By granting the reserves as finally approved, the Province was to be regarded as having satisfied its obligations to the Indians; other costs would be defrayed by the Dominion.

3.   Both the government of British Columbia and the Indians should be represented by counsel, that for the Indians being nominated and paid by the Dominion.

4.   In the event of a final decision unfavorable to the Indians, "the policy of the Dominion toward the Indians shall be governed by consideration of their interests and future development."

This proposal was adopted by order in council on June 20, 1914, but the Allied Tribes consistently refused to take advantage of it. They would certainly appear to have been ill-advised. Instead they kept on drafting lengthy petitions. One of these, prepared apparently by Kelly and James Teit, entitled "Statement of the Allied Tribes of British Columbia to the Government of British Columbia," seems to have been the first in which they specified all the demands made on behalf of the Indians.[16] The statement states the objections to the McKenna-McBride agreement of 1912, on which the work of the Royal Commission was based. Then the "statement" goes on to spell out the "necessary conditions of equitable settlement." There are 20 points listed, the most important of which are: recognition of aboriginal land rights of the Indians (with such amendments to the land laws as needed to give those rights legal status); rights to "all foreshores whether tidal or inland";[17] increase of reserves based on a "standard" of 160 acres per capita ("standard" meant that in lands of poor quality, suitable only for grazing, trapping, etc., larger tracts should be made available), with compulsory purchase, presumably through condemnation proceedings, by the Dominion where tracts desired and needed by the Indians had been legally acquired by whites; beneficial ownership or reserves vested in the "tribe" (apparently the dialectic division, like Niska,

---

[16]This document was adopted by the Executive Committee late in 1919, and submitted shortly thereafter. A complete copy appears as an exhibit (appendix A) in Joint Committee (1927), pp. 31–38.

[17]Actually there is no such thing as a foreshore, technically speaking, in nontidal waters; some sort of ownership of the streams or lakes, over and above ordinary riparian rights, was apparently meant.

Tsimshian, *etc.*, rather than the band or village); procedures for establishing individual ownership within the reserves, administered by the tribe; greater control of trust funds by the band or tribe; free and unrestricted fishing, hunting, and water rights, including modification of such international agreements as interfered with these (such as the Pelagic Sealing Agreement of 1911, the United States-Canadian treaties regulating the Fraser River fisheries);[18] compensation for inequalities in reserve lands, loss of timber, *etc.*; general compensation for the surrendered portion of the Province through improvements in Indian education, and in Indian health care; removal of restrictions in the Provincial Land Act on preemption of crown lands by Indians; and reimbursement of the costs to the Allied Tribes of prosecuting their claims. It will be noted that cash compensation for surrendered lands was not mentioned. That item did not officially enter the picture until 1923, when a similar list of conditions deemed necessary for settlement of the case was presented to Duncan Scott, Deputy Superintendent General of Indian Affairs, who met with the Allied Tribes' executive Committee in Victoria.[19] At that time he was informed that the precise amount of compensation might be a matter for negotiation, but that the thinking of the Indians was that they would be satisfied with a lump-sum payment about equivalent to the total of 20 years' annuities (or "treaty monies") as paid elsewhere in Canada. Scott, in his report, notes that the current Indian population of British Columbia was recorded at 24,744; the average annuity payments elsewhere in Canada were about $5 per capita. A 20-year total ($100 per capita) would thus come to $2,474,400. Bureaucrats and politicians were not so casual about dealing in millions in those days; Scott appears to have been quite shocked by the magnitude of the demand. Two other new demands were added to the list: the right to cut timber outside the reserves, for fuel, canoe-making, and for basketry materials (presumably collecting of spruce root, red cedar bark, *etc.*, is referred to here); and provision of mothers' and widows' pensions comparable to those provided for white women by the Province.

At this time, the McKenna-McBride agreement had already been adopted by both governments, and despite Indian protests, the Government of British Columbia adopted the report of the Royal Commission on the reserves the same year as the meeting with Scott, mentioned above. This meant of course that the Province agreed to make available lands for all additions to reserves, and additional reserves (and to accept all cutoffs), recommended by the Royal Commission. The Indians had been objecting bitterly since 1916 that though the additions approved by the Commission were roughly twice the sum in acreage than the cutoffs, they were greatly inferior in value, although the Commission's report very specifically states in each case that the reverse is true so far as values are concerned.

[18]These, of course, are based on the fact that Fraser River salmon pass through United States water, offshore, before they reach the Fraser, hence various regulations regarding them are based on international agreement.
[19]Joint Committee (1927). Scott, who testified at the hearing, filed his complete memorandum report on this meeting to his superior as part of the record, where it forms appendix H, pp. 65–71.

Whether the Indians liked it or not, they were unable to prevent the final step from being taken. In 1924, by means of an order in council, the Dominion Government adopted the report. The reserves consequently were of the size, and where, the Royal Commission had decided they should be. The areas and distribution of reserves have remained essentially the same to the present time, except for comparatively minor changes from land sales, and the like.

The final development came about when, in 1926, the chairman of the Allied Tribes submitted a petition to Parliament requesting, among other things, the hearing of the Indian case by H. M. Privy Council. Parliament, however, established a Joint Committee, consisting of a committee from the Senate and one from the House of Commons, authorized to hold hearings and to make recommendations to Parliament which would bring the problem to an end. Presumably this action was taken as the only way to arrive at a solution, since the Indians persisted in their refusal to bring their claims before a Canadian court, even with right of appeal, as provided in the Scott memorandum. The Joint Committee held hearings in Ottawa on March 30 and 31, and April 4, 5, and 6, 1927. Kelly, Paull, and their attorneys were heard, and some interior Indians, as were various officers of the Indian Department, and the Department of Marine and Fisheries. The minutes of evidence make interesting reading. At one point, a diversion was created by some interior Indians, who, with a separate set of attorneys had got into the act uninvited. They contradicted the statement that the Allied Tribes represented all the Indians of British Columbia, and presented a list of complaints completely different from those of the Allied Tribes.[20] If this byplay influenced the thinking of the committee, it can only have been unfavorably. Kelly and Paull made their statements and replied to queries in a straightforward concise fashion that indicated a background of study of the facts and thorough knowledge of them that impressed the committee and won their favorable comment; their general counsel unfortunately antagonized the committee, who nonetheless tried to arrive at a just decision.

The principal findings of the committee were that there was no real basis in fact to the claims of aboriginal right in British Columbia; and that, while no compensation was required to extinguish title, it was true that they received no annuities as other Canadian Indians did. Hence, it was recommended that $100,000 per annum, over and above normal appropriations for education, medical care, *etc.* in British Columbia be provided the Indian Department (the committee found that on a per capita basis approximately the same amount was spent on education, health, welfare, *etc.* for British Columbia Indians as on those of other Provinces), in lieu of "treaty monies." The explicitly stated idea was that this special fund, used for the benefit of all the Indians of the Province, would accomplish more than the $5 dollars or so per capita distribution in the form of annui-

---

[20]Joint Committee (1927), pp. 73 ff. One of the representatives and many of the groups said to be represented were interior Indians who had been present at the 1922 Allied Tribes meeting and had agreed to cooperate with the Allied Tribes.

ties. Another recommendation, unemphasized in the committee's report, but powerfully implemented by Parliament, was that the natives be advised that no further contributions of funds be made to continue presentation of claims now decisively disallowed. Other recommendations called for closer cooperation between the Indian Department and the Department of Marine and Fisheries, with the aim that a liberal interpretation of fisheries regulations be adopted, insofar as Indians fishing for domestic consumption were concernred; suitable working agreements with the Provincial government and the Department of Indian Affairs regarding Indian water rights; Indian rights in the foreshore; and so on. The report of the Joint Committee was approved by both Houses, and legislation was passed to carry its recommendations into effect. The $100,000 "in lieu of annuities" is still appropriated annually. Coast Indians complain that most of it goes for agricultural education and irrigation in the southern interior; the fact is that nowadays it is a drop in the bucket in comparison with departmental expenditures for education, health, and welfare in the Province. The action taken on the recommendation to stop further fund raising to continue the case put the real stopper on the campaign for recognition of aboriginal rights: an amendment was made to the Indian Act making it a serious offense to solicit funds for the purpose of prosecuting an Indian claim against the Government (Indian Act, sec. 141, Joint Comm. (1927)).

With the appearance of the Joint Committee's report and its approval and implementation by Parliament, the Allied Tribes organization, never closely knit at best, fell apart. Most coast Indians, at least, accepted, albeit unwillingly and grudgingly, that the land issue was dead as the proverbial doornail. Only the Niska refused to give up entirely. Their Land Committee continued to meet for years, to thresh out the hopeless questions of ways and means to establish their claims. A Land Committee member with whom I discussed the history of the case in 1953 did admit, however, that the committee had been rather inactive for a number of years.

A summary of the legal bases of the claims is relevant here only as sources of ideas may be revealed. The "aboriginal rights" concept itself, the very heart of the long struggle, was almost certainly not derived from Indian sources. While it was true enough that the coastal groups had clearly defined aboriginal concepts regarding ownership of lands, this meant nothing under Canadian law *unless it could be demonstrated that such right had been recognized and provided for in the organic legislation regarding land law.* The claim for aboriginal rights was based on three documents. The first, chronologically, was a proclamation of George III, 1763, regarding the four "governments, styled Quebec, East Florida, West Florida, and Grenada," to the effect that "the several nations or tribes of Indians with whom we are connected, and who live under our protection, should not be molested or disturbed in the possession of such parts of our dominions and territories, as not having been ceded to us, are reserved to them, or any of them as their hunting grounds..." (Joint Committee (1927) pp. 40–42). (The proclamation goes on to restrict purchases of land, and trade, with the Indians, to duly constituted authorities, *etc.*) The second was an article in the British North America Act, which laid down the provisions for confederation of the eastern provinces, and which governed the confederation of British Columbia to Canada, except where superseded by the Terms of the Union. The article referred to, No. 109, provides that all lands belonging to the Province shall belong to the Province "subject to any trust existing in respect thereof, and to any interest, other than that of the province, in the same" (Joint Committee (1927), pp. 43 and *passim*). The third was an opinion of the Dominion Minister of Justice, in 1875, recommending "disallowance" (veto) by the Governor General of Canada of an act passed by the Legislature of British Columbia "to amend and consolidate the laws affecting Crown lands in British Columbia." The opinion, approved by the Governor General, was based on the fact that the proposed Act made no provision for Indian reserves to prevent them from being preempted. (The opinion, as stated, was approved; the proposed legislation was revised by the legislature of the new Province to provide that settlers could not preempt lands within the boundaries of Indian reserves.)

The whole structure of the claim of aboriginal rights—the concept, the years of effort, the thousands of dollars spent, the time and labor of various persons—was based on the interpretation of these passages, all of doubtful applicability or validity. The Royal Proclamation did not refer to British Columbia, which was *terra incognita* at the time (moreover, the proclamation was subsequently repealed by another). Article 109 of the British North America Act nowhere specifies that Indian title was meant to be included in its provisions for "trusts and interests" prior to those of the Province. The much-quoted opinion of the Minister of Justice first of all was concerned primarily with guaranteeing reserves; second, it was not itself law, but merely an opinion.

The point of this discussion is to stress the fact that the whole basis of the claim was highly legalistic, depending on fine interpretations of meaning and intent of law. It can only have been introduced by persons with some legal training—something no British Columbia Indian of that day had. It is also clear that under the law the Indians had far from a strong case. This must have been highly obvious to any legally trained person.

The inclusion of requests for special concessions concerning fishing and hunting rights probably differed in its source. It seems to have derived from the fact that more and more restrictions and regulations were being put on these activities, for conservation purposes, and also, in connection with hunting for reasons of public safety (restricting hunting in settled areas, *etc.*). Indians, sometimes not understanding the regulations, and at other times disregarding them, were at this period continually running afoul of the law, and being fined or jailed. These demands may represent some real grassroots sentiment, and perhaps the only sentiment so originating in the whole program, that was brought to the attention of the Executive Committee during its members' recruiting tours.

In short, it appears that most of the long campaign to resolve the land problem was inspired by and manipulated by whites, and it was handled according to white techniques.

7

A New Perspective
to an Old Problem:
Macro *vs* Micro

A THEORETICAL MODEL: COLONIALISM

THE NATIVE POPULATION has to become economically developed and subsequently gain control
of its destiny. That is plain. But how that is to
occur is still to be seen. The solutions offered by
the white dominant group have ranged from complete acculturation (through amalgamation) of
native people, (one held tenaciously since the
time of the conquest), to annihilation. The key to
the solution to be offered here is in the manner
of perceiving the problem, *i.e.*, the way the relationship between natives and the dominant
group is viewed will partly determine the answers.
Using a micro model (which concentrates solely
on individual discrimination and prejudice because it is based on individual relationships)
results in a solution centering around individual
advancement, otherwise known as "individual
entrepreneurship." Most sociologists have previously done this.

If on the other hand a macro model is chosen, a different solution will be suggested. This is what will be used here. The model that will be proposed and further developed has already been suggested by Cummings (1969), Patterson (1972) and Carstens (1971). I have drawn heavily on their models, attempting to present the Indian reserve as an internal colony, exploited by the dominant white group in Canada. To extend the analogy, those in the larger white structure (mainly Anglo-Canadian or European Canadian) are seen as the *colonizing* people while the natives are considered the *colonized* people.

.   The colonial analysis has been rejected as misleading by many sociologists who point out that there are significant social-political differences between our domestic patterns and what took place in, for example, Africa or India. While it is agreed that there were some differences, after a careful analysis of the relations between whites and Indians in Canada, it is found that the differences do not obscure the fact that the initial period of Canada's development took on a "colonialistic" perspective in regard to the dominant group's treatment of the Indians and it has since been maintained. Tabb has described conditions in a typical underdeveloped country (parallel to the Indian experience in Canada) as follows:

> ... low per capita income, high birth rate; a small, weak middle class; low rates of increase in labor productivity, capital formation, domestic savings; and a small monitized market. The economy of such a country is heavily dependent on external markets where its few basic exports face an inelastic demand (that is, demand is relatively constant regardless of price, and so expanding total output may not mean higher earnings). The international demonstration effect (the desire to consume the products enjoyed in wealthier nations) works to increase the quantity of foreign goods imported, putting pressure on balance of payments as the value of imports exceeds the value of exports. Much of the small modern sector of the economy is owned by outsiders. Local entrepreneurship is limited, and in the absence of inter-governmental transfers, things might be still worse for the residents of these areas. *(1970:22)*

It is suggested that this is an accurate description of a reserve in Canada today.[1] In conceptualizing the reserve as an internal colony of a larger nation, we will be able to see beyond the individual factors involved in intergroup behaviour. This is not to say that individual acts of discrimination and prejudice do not happen. It is readily acknowledged that they do. But it forces us to utilize a different perspective. What I am suggesting is that ample historical data is available to show us that the previous "individualistic" approach has not been fruitful in attempting to explain the relationship between Indians and whites, nor has it produced any meaningful changes in the Indian's position in our society. Native people are becoming increasingly poverty stricken.

[1]Carstens (1971) uses the analogy of "peasantry" although he agrees that the reserves can be viewed as members of little colonies within the borders of the dominant group.

In my effort to justify using the colonial framework to explain Indian-white relations, let me first delineate the characteristics of colonialism (Blauner, 1969; Kennedy, 1945). The data presented earlier may then be juxtaposed with this material and a decision made on whether the model is appropriate. We can consider the colonization process in seven parts. The first concerns how the dominant group moves into a geographical area. Mostly it is "forced-voluntary" entry, *i.e.* the colonizing group forces its way into an area because it is in its interest. There is ample evidence that this applies in Canada's case. The second step depends on the social and cultural structure of the native group. When colonization occurs, the dominant group has a destructive impact on the natives. In Canada's case, the Euro-Canadians destroyed the existing political, economic, kinship and in most cases religious systems of the natives. Little, if any, consideration was (or is) given to the values and norms of the natives. No further documentation of how this worked in Canada should be needed.

The third and fourth aspects of the colonization process are interrelated, but for analytical purposes can be separated into external political control and native economic dependence. In the standard practice of colonization, the mother country sends out representatives and indirectly rules the newly conquered land. In terms of our model, the IAB (an agency of the federal government) controls every action of the natives. As mentioned earlier, the IAB had authority over natives leaving the reserve until 1940. Another example of social control is that marriages are subject to approval by the IAB district office. Also, as Whiteside (1972) points out, there was, until recently, a restriction on the use of band funds. Members could not use the funds to travel to other reserves in order to develop organizations which could resist the dominant group's control. In some cases the whites have allowed the Indians to create and maintain "puppet" political structures (chiefs and band councils) which give the appearance that Indians are really controlling their own affairs. Thus, if one looks closely at the political organization of reserves today, one finds that "councils" and chiefs still exist, but in name only. They can only make "recommendations," not decisions. Final acceptance or rejection of the council's recommendation is always contingent on the minister's decision.

In the initial stages of colonization, the colonized people generally accept their fate. Only after some time do they reject their powerless state. (Indian leaders on the reserve today are quite different from those who initially signed treaties with the whites. The new Indian no longer accepts his subordinate status but is in a powerless position.) The result is a general feeling of dispiritedness. Under these conditions, controlling the reserve became easy. Communal bonds between individual Indians and between bands were weakened, contributing to the continued failure of Indian organizations. Leadership responsibilities became further divided, accentuating the disorganization. This pattern is corroborated by the number of Indian organizations which have been created and subsequently dissolved.

In the political arena, Indians have been ineffectual too—again, for plenty of reasons. Most importantly, they did not receive the right to vote in provincial elections (Nova Scotia excepted) until after the Second World

War and it was not until 1960 that they received the federal franchise.
Needless to say their ability to make political demands was severely restricted. Any group without a voice in the political structure in which it
acts and reacts has no method of sanctioning the government (or even of
attempting to influence decisions that will affect them). Are Indians using
the vote today? Initially they were skeptical of their new rights and there
has been little participation until lately. Now their outlook is growing more
positive. For example in the 1968 federal election in one riding in Saskatchewan, nearly 90 per cent of the native population who polled, cast their
vote for a self-proclaimed Red Power candidate.

The Indians are economically dependent on the dominant group because the reserves are treated as hinterlands—geographical and social areas
to be exploited. Primary depleting resources (oil, mining, water, forest
products) are exported from the reserves by whites and shipped to the large
industrial centers for processing. This has two important results. It prevents the industries being developed on the reserves and it keeps native
activities on an agricultural level. It has always been the basic aim of the
dominant group to keep the natives oriented toward agriculture. The treaties and the Indian Act itself reveal this. A "two-level" system develops—
the colonizers (whites) who own, direct and profit from the exploitation
and the colonized (Indians) who are the workers. Native participation in
the economic structure is nil or at the level of unskilled, part-time wage
earners. The long-term result is that Indians live at "subsistence" level,
practising agriculture to survive. They also make up a major portion of the
secondary labor pool and profits from raw material production (obtained
through cheap native labor) go to the whites.

To see how close the relationship is between political and economic
control, consider these examples. Section 80 of the Indian Act authorizes
the band council to pass by-laws on, for example, public health or traffic
regulations. However, to date, fewer than two-thirds of the band councils
have permission to do so. This means that unless the minister deems the
band "capable," he can veto any decisions by the band council. Perhaps
a clearer example is section 82 of the act, which allows the band to enact
money by-laws. However, this happens only when the governor-in-council
defines a band as having reached a "high state of development." At present, fewer than 50 bands have been so defined, and of these, most have
concerned themselves only with the construction of waterworks, *e.g.*, sewers,
wells, *etc.* Section 68 of the act allows a band to "control, manage, and expand in whole or in part its revenue moneys." The first band permitted to
do so received authority in 1959 and today we still find fewer than one-
fifth of the bands have been given permission. Section 60 allows the band
"the right to exercise such control and management over lands in the reserve occupied by that band as the governor-in-council considers desirable."
To date, the governor-in-council has only found it desirable for two reserves. Other sections in the act such as 182, 19 and 20 are further examples of the control whites have over Indians.

But perhaps the most important part of the act is in section 35, where
it is explicitly stated that reserve land can be expropriated by the domin-

ant group at any time. This has been done. For example, in 1971 the National Indian Brotherhood announced that the federal government had redrawn treaty maps which stripped titles to a number of land parcels claimed by Indians. The federal government did not refute the accusations. Indians were not consulted before or during the redrawing of the maps. In addition, the NIB uncovered the fact that the government had sent out a classified memo which said all copies of the previous treaty maps were to be destroyed.

A fifth characteristic of colonization is that social services provided for the colonized (the natives) (*e.g.*, health, education) are low standard. Again, the data presented previously should be enough to corroborate this claim.

The last two aspects of the colonization process relate to social interaction between natives and whites. They include racism and the establishment of a color line. Racism is the belief of genetic superiority of one group (whites) and inferiority of another group (Indians). The color line is the establishment and subsequent institutionalization of symbols which allow groups to be quickly and easily identified. In the case of Indians and whites, skin pigmentation and body structure are the indicators most used. Once the symbols are established, they become the basis for determining superiority and inferiority. Interaction then goes on only between members of the same group, *i.e.*, whites interact with whites and Indians with Indians. For example, Indians have the highest endogamy rate (marriage within an ethnic group) in Canada—93.6 per cent.

Why have whites chosen to establish such a relationship with natives? The ultimate consequence of colonization is that the resistance of the colonized people (Indians) is weakened and they are subsequently controlled. This may come about because of religious or economic motives (or a combination of these and others) but the point remains that colonization has practical advantages. These advantages and the profits from treating the natives as the colonized far outweigh the disadvantages and expenses. While Wuttnee (1972) has put the dominant group's "bill" over the past 100 years at $2 billion, he fails to point out that the profits have amounted to $60 billion. For example, the IAB average per capita expenditure per treaty Indian per year is about $530 whereas the federal government spends $740 per non-native. The result is a saving of $210 per Indian per year or a total of $52 million per year (Fidler, 1970).

Before a solution is offered it is important to realize that a "model" is being set up. The world is complex: people, the social structure and the culture change with time. So we must at some point make a "static" recreation of what is going on around us. We construct a "myopia" which we hope will correspond closely to the real world.

And we do this by: (*i*) selecting and incorporating certain variables into our model, (*ii*) discarding or considering other variables as not important, (*iii*) making assumptions about how people behave. If we can use the resulting principles of the model in explanations and predictions, then we can consider that it closely corresponds to the real world and has been successful.

The model may allow us to solve problems. It may then become a "building block" in developing other models of behavior and/or social action programs. On the other hand, if no predictions or explanations follow, we will feel that there is little correspondence between our reconstruction of society and reality and will have to revise or discard the model.

The proposal is that the natives must reject the notion of individual entrepreneurship or individual capitalism. Instead of seeking personal economic development they should aim at "native community development" which entails *community ownership and control* of the economy (Dubois, 1940). The proposal is predicated on the assumption that a "colonialistic" relationship now exists between Indians and whites.

As Hatt (1969) pointed out, in the past, the federal government's development schemes have only allowed natives to "carry out the plan" (not plan the project). In this way, the government has been able to control the schemes. As Hatt pointed out, the emphasis in Indian programs is on experimental or pilot projects. Thus the majority are short-term projects which can be terminated quickly with few problems. Beyond this short-term, experimental bias, Hatt called the focus of these programs "therapeutic." While no doubt these have some value, they do not seriously disrupt the status quo. In the end, these programs can be viewed as effective social control mechanisms. It is suggested then that native people must set up viable economic units within the reserve and control them as a community. This view has been expressed by Deprez and Sigurdson:

> There can be no question that it is imperative for Canada's native population to become involved in more productive economic activities. In strictly economic terms, the continuous dependence of the Indian on government assistance constitutes a serious drain on the financial resources of Canada. Even more significant is the fact that these people comprise a very significant potential labor force and a potential that today is not being utilized. But by far the most important dimension to the employment problem of the Indians is the humanitarian one, because participation in a viable economic activity is essential if the Indian is to maintain his sense of self-respect. *(1969:11)*

Several basic assumptions are fundamental to this position of community development and control. Unfortunately, the dominant group is not willing to accept them at present.

The first assumption is that all people, no matter how lazy they may appear to an outsider, have a wish to better themselves. People have needs which vary from social to physiological and when these are not met, they suffer the results. The second assumption is that the major obstacle for these people to meet their needs and desires is a lack of resources. The resources (money, skill, language, education, *etc.*) that these people have simply do not allow them the opportunity to overcome the obstacles and thereby progress toward their desires. The third assumption is that people will attempt to fulfill their needs and desires when they are given appropriate resources and an opportunity to utilize them. Perhaps one of the greatest problems faced by Indian people is that when they try to solve a problem, they are expected to do so in a manner congruent to white culture. Any procedure foreign to white culture is generally viewed negatively and rejected. The last assumption is that by changing one component of a group's behavior one cannot expect to achieve meaningful, lasting results. In other words, the social behavior of man is intertwined and a change in one component must bear some relation to another. Thus it would be naive and foolish to expect that money could solve everything. Each component of behavior stands in a relationship to another and this must be considered when attempts at change are made (Lagasse, 1962).

The dominant group argues against the creation of industries or more jobs within the reserve. It contends that the reserve is basically a "residential" area and cannot be converted into an industrial or commercial area. For example, recommendation 3 of the Hawthorn Report states:

> The main emphasis on economic development should be on education, vocational training and techniques of mobility to enable Indians to take employment in wage and salaried jobs. Development of locally available resources should be viewed as playing a secondary role for those who do not choose to seek outside employment.

Furthermore, the dominant group is pursuing a program which is forcing the Indian population into existing urban areas. The result is devastating. The most capable and aspiring individuals leave the reserve to be managed by a "residue" of non-skilled, low-aspiring Indians. The reserve is becoming less able to provide the remaining Indians with a minimum life style.

This position is, of course, opposed here. A more realistic alternative is to upgrade existing native industries and create new ones. A program of creating new jobs for Indians would also boost the "profit" for the reserve and ultimately for the individual, and would provide invaluable experience for the Indians placed into leadership positions (for community and business).

It is clear that Euro-Canadians want to push individual entrepreneurship outside the reserve—and it is equally clear that the natives want to increase community development. The natives want more economically viable ventures totally controlled by them, started on the reserve. As Peters says:

> We want access to development resources which means the right to participate in provincial development activity and the right to direct access to all federal departments without intervention of the Department of Indian Affairs. The Indian Affairs Department is playing a "gate keeper" role in opening up these outside resources to Indian communities. There is a tendency for the department to do all it can on its own and turn over what it chooses to the provinces or other federal departments. In this way, the branch ensures its own future, but in so doing, is failing to help the Indians to find their place in the provincial and national community. (1968:6)

HISTORICAL PERSPECTIVE

Before considering the advantages and disadvantages of individual entrepreneurship versus community control development, a sociological-historical perspective of the relationships between Indians and Whites is needed. The natives were initially regarded as savages or beasts. They could therefore be exterminated or ignored. To ignore the natives simply exhibited a minimal amount of tolerance which could be looked on as a manifestation of white man's generosity and burden. The natives were also regarded as lazy, filthy, uninhibited and uncivilized. During the nineteenth and early twentieth centuries, land utilization and technological development were increasing fast. The expansion of civilization that biologically or culturally exterminated the natives (either through conscious or unconscious annihilation) was viewed as a manifestation of Christianity (Pearce, 1965). The new European migrants embodied the Protestant ethic of thriftiness and willingness to work hard. Clearly the natives did not fit this concept of Christianity. They would not be able to comply with God's word. Thus the view was that if God couldn't admire the native then it made good sense for the European Christian Canadian also to reject him (Hunt, 1940).

However, eventually through the proselytizing efforts of the Jesuits and Anglicans (as well as a host of other religious groups), the natives became Christians (Trigger, 1965). The question now to be resolved by the Anglo culture was: How did one still systematically exploit the natives? In other words, these people were now "Christians" and came under the rubric of Christian ethics. Yet prejudice and discrimination were solidly institutionalized in Canadian society. To resolve the problem and continue the "exploitive relationship" the notion of "inherent natural white superiority" was introduced. The claim was that white men dominated other groups of people because of his natural superiority. It followed that since it was the "natural order of things" for natives to be inferior to whites, then it was part of this natural order that Anglo-Canadians should rule and natives be subordinate. This reflects the Social Darwinistic thought in North America at that time.[2] The outlook justified exploitation and allowed and encouraged westward expansion by European Canadians. Just as exploitation had been unnatural by Christian ethic, it now became unthinkable for European Canadians to violate the "laws of nature." As Willhelm points out:

> In the thoughts of the light-skinned people of early America, no white man ever commands because he "chooses" to do so; it is not by his choice, but by the will of God or the act of Nature that he rises to the fore at the

[2]In the middle of the nineteenth century, Charles Darwin published his *Origin of the Species*. His theoretical perspective centered on concepts such as evolution, natural selection and survival of the fittest. It was an easy step for the layman (and the social scientist) to apply these concepts (originally applied only to animals) to man. Thus, the argument went, if one group of individuals attacked another group and won, this could be taken as evidence that they were somehow "better" than the group they had defeated. This was taken as evidence for the "survival of the fittest" phenomenon. Likewise, as a group continued to exploit and make war on other nations, as long as it won, this could be taken as evidence of the "evolutionary process."

expense of inferior races. To rule is really to submit, in the first instance, as an obedient believer of God's command and, in the second instance, as a helpless pawn abiding by Nature's laws governing the races of men. The white races, in the final analysis, never felt superior in an absolute sense since he yielded to Christian Bible and nature's demand for commanding inably inferior races. When the Indian and Negro were in the animalistic state, they were heathens; whites fulfilled obligations to the Almighty in fending racists' feelings against the non-believers and would suffer no sense of loss should they even exterminate the non-white. Indeed, failure to fulfill Christian precepts expose the right to question Christian descent; to be judged by a God on the basis of diligent hard work makes it only proper for man himself to judge others by the identical standard. Consequently, whites merely carried forth their Christian duty to let out extermination and enslavement to non-Christians. *(1969:3–4)*

The next development in racism was the acceptance and endorsement of Social Darwinism by science. Science, particularly biological science, was perhaps the greatest unwitting contributor to racism in North America. Biologists in the late nineteenth century claimed that as a result of discoveries at the time, inferior species could be distinguished from superior species. Racial instincts were accounted for and labelled on various groups to account for their behavior. What the scientists were suggesting was that the genetic make-up of individuals caused social behavior. If this perspective was taken seriously (and it is suggested that it was by Euro-Canadians), then no amount of effort by the natives could compensate for their natural inferiority. In addition it is also suggested that no amount of help by Euro-Canadians could make the natives overcome their intrinsic inferiority. This position was a most notable influence on the dominant group in setting up native reservations. The reserves were to be considered holding pens for worthless people. The implicit political and ideological view held by the Euro-Canadians was that natives should be considered as inferiors—wards of the nation.

No doubt there will be arguments that it wasn't all that "one-sided." Whites did make concessions! Yes, but they were made to coincide with their interests. The concessions were made because whites found themselves in a position where a "concession" would maximize their profit or minimize their loss (Green, 1969). The Riel Rebellion of 1885 (and the subsequent execution of Riel) was perhaps the climax and final extension of the differences between natives and whites. It determined the subsequent direction of Indian-white relations.

However, today Euro-Canadians have a new strategy in their relationship with Indians. It is the "myth of equality" (Willhelm, 1969). The basic premise is that all men are equal no matter what degrees of diversity divide them. This, of course, means that "special privileges" should not be given to various minority groups.[3] One of the latest government reports that

---

[3]Recommendation 7 of the Hawthorn Report says that Indians should be regarded as "citizens plus" because they possess certain additional rights as charter members of the Canadian community.

reflects this new attitude of "equality" is the white paper on reserves, which suggests that all reserves be terminated. This recommendation is predicated on the belief that just as it is illegal to discriminate against Indians it is also illegal to help them attain equality through the unequal practice of giving them greater benefits than members of the dominant group. The implicit notion is that *one law* exists at *one time* and everyone is subject to it. The most noticeable aspect of this perspective is that it ignores any relevant historical events and concludes that no special privileges should be given to Canadian natives. The new laws being introduced in Canada today basically reflect this growing expression of equality. The general argument is that since laws expressing equality of ethnic groups are now "on the books," all historical events and their impact have somehow been resolved. Mills' (1961) suggestions in *The Sociological Imagination* regarding the role of history, should be put into practice. A historical perspective needs to be taken into account when discussing intergroup behavior. This is necessary to be able to understand the relationships between structural components of society and their changing aspects. We need to be aware of such changes that have occurred in the past. It is also argued that knowledge of a nation's history is indispensable for a full understanding of contemporary behavior. The third contention is that a non-historical point of view suggests that the particular society is static. If we want to understand the dynamic changes in a particular social system or social structure we have to ascertain the long-range developments of that nation. Mills (1961) has suggested that the question to be asked is: What are the mechanics by which these trends have occurred? In other words, we must ask how the structure of the society is changing.

FACTORS NECESSARY FOR COMMUNITY CONTROL

Since our initial suggestion is that community control and development is the answer for natives, we should now take a closer look at their economic conditions. The earlier data showed that Indians have the lowest status in Canada. That data also suggested that natives today serve as a kind of secondary labor pool. They become a source of cheap labor when the supply is scarce for the nation as a whole. However, when the labor supply increases, they are the first to be fired. Consequently they provide two very useful services in the Anglo-Canadian dominant structure. They keep labor costs from increasing so prices are kept down (the labor supply is maintained at a fairly constant rate) and they enable white employment to be maintained at a constant level. Buckley, Kew and Hawley (1963) have pointed out that Indians and Metis are hired for mine construction but once that phase is over, few (if any) jobs are offered to them. Outsiders (whites) are brought in to fill the stable, long-term jobs.

Piore (1968) says that every nation has a dual labor market. The primary market consists of jobs that pay well, offer stable, long-term employment with good working conditions and chances of advancement. But in the secondary market, the reverse applies.

The Special Senate Committee Hearing on Poverty (1970) also pointed this out. It cited a large mining firm in northern Manitoba which had employed Indians for years but on a casual basis. Casuals do not get all the fringe benefits of full-time workers. The committee report specifically pointed out that there were natives who had worked at the mine for nearly 20 years but were still on the casual payroll. Nagler, in his study of urban Indians, found similar results.

> There are also seasonal commuters (Indian) who come to the city when employment levels are high. These workers usually stay in cities while employment is available in construction and related industries and then return home during the slack periods to which many of these industries are subject. *(1970:12)*

La Rusic (1965) showed that no Indians working for mining exploration companies have ever been on the full-time payroll and thus given equal working conditions with whites, even though they were highly skilled. Crees who had begun working for wages were still being employed on a casual basis and doing menial activities after 12 years.

Clearly, this remains a very important reason for Euro-Canadians to push the "individual entrepreneurship" position. If natives can establish independent economic enterprises, they can affect the labor supply and eventually the profit made by the larger corporate structure. If they are no longer unemployed, they must be "lured" away with higher wages and better security in the jobs offered by white businesses. Perhaps this resistance is best shown by the case quoted earlier of Vancouver businessmen legally objecting to an Indian high rise apartment block being built near Vancouver.

Admittedly, the present situation for the native is not very bright. But this simply means that it *looks* intolerable; it does not indicate the potential development that can occur. The existing metropolis-satellite relationship can be changed through community development and ownership by natives. We can now turn to the native resources which would need to be used for community development and control. These can be grouped as land, money, natural resources, and population. We will defer discussing a last factor—skills—until later. At this point, it will suffice to acknowledge that Indians have very few technical skills which might be utilized in present economic development.

Land

Today the reserves—about 2,600 of them—consist of roughly 6 million acres of land. (There are also 76 "settlements" comprising a further 14,823 acres.) It is interesting to point out that in areas where westward expansion and subsequent settlement did not take place until the late nineteenth century (particularly Labrador, northern Quebec and Yukon-Northwest Territories), no reserves were established. However, in other provinces the natives still have legally defined lands called reserves. The land on the reserve will be vital if natives are to become economically viable. Possibilities for broadened economic endeavor on or adjacent to Indian reserves vary with the region and even within the region, consequently the assistance required is just as varied. For example, 65 bands with an estimated total population of slightly over 40,000 hold lands strategically located near major expanding urban centers. Considerable opportunity exists for the labor force on these reserves in the nearby cities and there is also undeveloped potential in these lands for urban, commercial, industrial and recreational use.

However, I am not suggesting that natives should become agriculturally oriented simply because they have nearly six million acres of land. This is a major concern of the dominant structure (to develop the Indians' agricultural land), but it is not a viable strategy.[4] Fewer than two million acres are potentially arable and little over one million acres could be used for grazing. The remaining portion would support neither crops nor animals. If the potential arable and grazing land were fully utilized it would still only support a maximum of 4,000 farms. Given that ten people per farm could be sustained this would take care of roughly 40,000 natives. But what happens to the other 200,000? The federal and provincial governments have consistently claimed (in historical tradition) that natives should try to develop their reserve lands for farming. (This is an implicit assumption in all treaties.) This non-viable alternative is a successful social control mechanism of the dominant structure.

There are other issues in the land question that preclude natives from using their property to advance themselves. Section 20 of the Indian Act prohibits Indians from "owning" land on a reserve unless it has been allotted with the "minister's approval." That is, a native who wants to buy land on the reserve first needs the minister's authority. This clearly restricts his mobility. Section 32–article 1 of the act states that sales of products growing on the reserves of certain provinces can only be made to other members of the band and this must have the written approval of the superintendent. Other more, or less, subtle social controls include the Farm Credit Act established by the federal government to help Indian farmers. It gave them long-term credit but also stipulated that a first mortgage had to be made. But since the Crown "owns" the reserve land (which is farmed by the natives) they could not get a first mortgage. The act is therefore quite useless for them.

Natural Resources

Sizeable mineral deposits, including uranium, potash and sulphur still remain on some reserves. For example, the Oak Lake reserve has a potash deposit which could be commercially developed. Many economic feasibility studies have been conducted in the past few years and they all

---

[4]Recommendation 24 of the Hawthorn Report says that "in all but a minority of cases, no attempt should be made to train, encourage and finance any large number of Indians to engage in commercial farming . . ." (p. 15).

NEW PERSPECTIVE TO AN OLD PROBLEM

point out that these resources could be developed by Indians (not exploited by whites as in the past). Resources such as timber, tourist trade, and water are also valuable and untapped. They will be very important within the next few years. Fort Alexander, for instance, has a fair amount of timber that should and can be milled at low cost.

Well over two million pounds of fish were caught commercially by Indians in 1969. Forest products from native reserves in 1967 included 90 million feet of timber, 65,000 cords of pulp wood, one million fence posts and nearly one million Christmas trees (*Canada Year Book*, 1967:205). Oil and gas from reserves in 1965–66 produced revenue of well over $10.5 million. Added to this were nearly $5 million from royalties and rentals for petroleum leases. Mining also has untapped potential. Tourism, which may be regarded as a type of natural resource, has not been utilized much but could (in certain cases) become an important source of revenue for a reserve.

Today as in the past, these natural resources have been developed and controlled by outside white corporations (with official sanction by the IAB). For example, when a reserve is thought to have potential mineral resources, they are explored and developed by oil and mining companies under the provisions of the Indian Act. Oil and gas rights are offered by public tender and are granted to the company offering the highest cash bonus. The possibility of allowing natives themselves to develop these resources is never considered. This is a benefit the dominant group derives from treating Indians as a colonized people.

Population

Mineral rights and lands are not the only abundant resources. As Robertson (1970) observes, the one thing the reserves are good at is production of children. Natives have one of the fastest population growth rates in Canada today. The general Canadian birth rate peaked in 1930 and has steadily decreased since but the birth rate for natives has steadily increased. As mentioned earlier, the birth rate per thousand has increased from 25.5 (1911) to 39.2 (1955) to 41.9 in 1960. We find that while over half of the Indians are younger than 15, less than a quarter of the general population are in this age group. Perhaps the only factor holding down a big increase in the native population is their short life span. As pointed out previously, the life span of an Indian is about half that of a white. However, if the Indian birth rate continues to increase (or remain the same) and the death rate decreases, then there will be a sizeable jump in the proportion of natives. Kahn-tineta Horn suggests that once the natives make up 51 per cent of the population in Canada they will "take it over." The rather naive theory here is that having the majority of population in essence means control. The situation in South Africa, Belgium and Finland reveals that a population majority group does not necessarily hold power and control of a country's political and economic functions. However, if natives made up a sizeable percentage of the total population, it would give them a stronger bargaining position.

Availability of Capital

Though the Hawthorn Report shows that there is a low correlation between the amount of capital per band and economic development, the results are somewhat misleading. The reason is that when a band does increase its per capita income, money is not reinvested in the reserve or in the band. As pointed out previously, few bands are allowed to control their own money. Under federal direction, accumulated finance goes into what is commonly called the "trust fund," government bonds, or one of several welfare projects on reserves. For example, during the 1970 fiscal year, the IAB administered band trust funds totalling $30 million. Money is simply accumulated. Native people "have" money, but they cannot get control of it. For example, an investigation is under way to ascertain how a trust fund of $2.5 million for a western band diminished to less than $500,000 between 1968 and 1972. Native groups or individuals who want money from the IAB generally cannot get it. If money is allocated, it must first go through a series of bureaucratic steps and be approved by the federal government. When natives apply for money there is a substantial time lag and the final terms are never the same as those originally sought. It generally takes from one to five years between a request for a grant or loan and its approval or rejection. In addition, the plan will be modified at each step along the bureaucratic path. The Minister of Indian Affairs and Northern Development, Jean Chretien, pointed out the problems quite vividly in a speech in Toronto.

> First the band council decide that they want to do something constructive and reasonable with a piece of their land as many of them do. They pass a council resolution which they hand over to the Department's Agency office. It is sent from there to the Regional office. The regional people, anticipating that their superiors in Ottawa will ask questions themselves. Back it goes to the Agency and back to the Band. The Band gets another meeting organized. They answer the questions and put the proposal back into the mill. It goes to the Agency, to the Region and it finally reaches the Head office where the lawyers get at it. They ask more questions that the region had not thought of. Back it goes. Eventually all the questions are answered and it comes to me. *(1969:8)*

When a loan or grant is made by the IAB it is never enough. Generally the maximum is $10,000 to be repaid within five years. Less than $500,000 in all was allocated in 1967. This was distributed among 115 grants, so that the average was worth slightly over $4,000. But this was more than the $100 average per grant made in 1965. By 1972 the loan fund had increased to over $3 million (a 189 per cent increase over 1971) but there are still restrictions on amounts and repayments. The Special Senate Committee Hearing on Poverty noted that:

> ... though this fund has been of great assistance to Indians, it is still too small, and, to effect major economic change, more technical and managerial support must be made available. *(89)*

Requests for loans have far exceeded payments allocated by the IAB. At a time when provincial governments are giving millions of dollars to white investors (for example, in Manitoba the development of the Churchill Forest Industry complex) little justification can be found for refusing native loans or making them so small. The point is (and individual white entrepreneurs agree) that very few industrial or economically viable ventures can be established with $10,000 which must be repaid, with interest, in five years. Can the IAB be this ignorant? Hardly so. It simply appears to be another social control mechanism. On one hand the IAB can argue that it is giving Indians money while at the same time aware of the fact that the help is so minimal that it will not significantly affect their position in society.

Let us turn now to the proposed solution—for the natives to become an economically viable group in Canada, able to bargain effectively with the dominant group.

COMMUNITY DEVELOPMENT AND CONTROL

La Violette (1961) says it is crucial to the existence of any ethnic group for it to be able to assert control over its own fate. Essentially it is a struggle for identity. How is the control achieved and maintained? First, the group must be able to have some say in defining its past, and second, it must want political equality and participation. If natives want to control their destiny, community control must be implemented immediately.

Community control is clearly in the hands of the dominant group today. Those in "powerful" positions on the reserve—the RCMP, postal workers, store owners, teachers and federal employees—are all Euro-Canadians. An IAB survey in 1961 found that slightly over 7,000 non-Indians were living on reserves. Of these, nearly 5,000 were self-supporting or children of self-supporting families, e.g., federal employees, merchants, missionaries, etc. As previously mentioned, there are few native teachers or police. Non-Indians in these positions must be removed and replaced with stable, resident natives from the area.

There are many reasons why whites do not want natives to control their own destiny. First, individual entrepreneurship guarantees indirect control of the reserve through the local Indians who are essentially dependent on a larger white business. The control is achieved in two ways: (*i*) by winning the loyalties of the local Indian businessmen who are potentially important leaders in the community, and (*ii*) by reducing the chances of "violence." If Indians see whites in "direct" control of various economic enterprises, there is less chance that they will be violent and destructive. Greater native "ownership" of local business lessens anti-white feelings because the local merchants are Indian. Therefore, by increasing Indian ownership of local businesses, the community becomes more stable, the leadership potential of these Indian businessmen is raised and white domination of the total community economy is made less viable. In addition, discontentment is released through acceptable channels (Tabb, 1970).

Thus the dominant group's general strategy to overcome native poverty (and to end the discontentment and unrest) is to give them "a piece of the action." If the natives adopt the strategy of individual entrepreneurship, their position will not change substantially in the future. It will be argued that full community development must be a prerequisite if natives are to control their destiny.

However, the community development must *not* come from the Anglo "corporate" sector of Canadian society. The federal government must not allow this sector to interfere with (or influence) the development of native communities. Corporations don't want natives to get federal finance. They have so far been successful because of the close relationship in the past between the political and economic elite. If natives were able to get finance for economic development, there would be two important results: (*i*) they would remove a source of income from these companies as a result of them not getting the contract to complete some specific job and thereby reducing their profits; and (*ii*) they would drain off the labor surplus and increase prices.

In addition, if the corporate structure was allowed to initiate economic development on reserves, it would lead to "franchising." Since the individual native lacks substantial capital, corporate structures are willing to advance money to set up franchise businesses. This means that a native is allowed to "run the store" but the larger corporate "mother" makes sure that its product is sold. The mother company provides services and sends staff to ensure proper marketing techniques. In return for setting up the store, providing a loan and initiating "training" for staff, the mother company reaps several benefits. First, it has entrance to the reserve (or a community near the reserve). This accomplishes two neutralizing effects:

● It reduces the costs to whites in that concessions will be minimal and it reduces the chances of a strong native cohesiveness developing.
● Development of the reserve by outsiders from the community allows for external control over the speed and extent of development (Tabb, 1970: 58).

Clearly, the white structure wants to convince the native that individual entrepreneurship is the answer but the result will be continued subordination. Hopefully, natives have begun to reject the notion. In his discussion of the topic, Chance says:

> To accomplish this task, four sets of recommendations are proposed: (*i*) The establishment of economically viable reserves controlled by the Indians with sufficient natural resources to ensure adequate incomes for the residents. The key element in this recommendation is that the natural resources of expanded Indian lands should be firmly placed in the control of the community and its representative leaders. (*ii*) The establishment of an Indian corporation which can receive direct grants and long-term low interest loans, to promote economic development on the reserve, to improve and initiate village services, and in other ways enable Indians to better utilize their natural and economic resources. (*iii*) To undertake a major revamping of the educational system so as to reduce discontin-

uities in learning, sustain positive affective ties with parents, strengthen the student's self-image as Indian, and maintain his self-esteem, as well as prepare himself to be economically and socially competent in dealing with the institutions of the larger Canadian society. (*iv*) The establishment of an Indian social development program, funded by the Federal and/or Provincial governments, which can assist in providing the mechanism for the emergence of new Indian leaders, increase communication with other Indian and non-Indian groups, and promote local and regional community, social and political infra-structure. (*1968:33–35*)

In proposing a model of economic development for natives, it is imperative to realize that a "balanced" approach is being advocated.[5] This approach uses the analogy of a balanced diet and argues that several different industries must be created simultaneously. It is distinct from the "unbalanced" approach, whose advocates claim that a central industry with "high linkage" should be developed on the reserve. That is, any industry which allows new and different industries to be built (in forward and backward linkages) should have preference in subsidizing and government favor. However, this model does not provide any long-range planning. Its supporters feel that once the "key" industry is set up, the social overhead capital will continue to rise without a need for much long-range planning. The author considers that native investment must be diversified over a broad range of industries and economic sectors. Thus, development in a number of industries will allow them to become mutually supporting.

It has been attempted here to show that native people have all the *basic* resources necessary to make the reserve economically viable. A proposal may now be made which would allow natives to control their fate, maintain their identity and integrate them into society. Several easily implemented steps will be explained. These are not necessarily new proposals. Some have been proposed by natives for some time.[6] Groups such as the Manitoba Indian Brotherhood in their publication *Wahbung* and the Indian Association of Alberta (in the *Red Paper*) have put forth similar proposals. However, we will tie all of these together and show in total the revisions that must be made for meaningful social change.

PROPOSALS FOR INDIAN ADVANCEMENT

1. *The full title of reserve lands must be given to natives.* Under the Indian Act, the minister has absolute control over the lands established by

[5]For a more thorough discussion on the relative merits of the "unbalanced" versus the "balanced" approach, see Rosenstein-Rodan, 1943; Nurkse, 1953; Scitovsky, 1954; Hirschman, 1958; Lewis, 1956; Perroux, 1953; Fellner, 1956. The first four authors advocate the balanced approach; the remainder support the unbalanced approach.

[6]Others, such as Walsh and the Native Alliance for Red Power, have also suggested, in addition to some of the factors mentioned, removal of legislative and constitutional bases of discrimination, recognition of the unique contribution of Indian culture to Canadian society, provision by government agencies of services and programs for all Canadians, and higher and more developed social services for natives. (Walsh, 1971: 162–65)

earlier treaties. This control must be taken out of the hands of Ottawa bureaucrats. Indians need reassurance that as they improve their land, large
cities will not encroach further on the reserve boundaries and that as valuable minerals are discovered, ownership of their land will not be jeopardized.

2. *An Indian claims commission must be established with at least
half the membership consisting of Indians.* A bill to establish such a commission was introduced into parliament in 1964 but was killed the following year. However, a white commissioner (Mr. L. Barber) has been appointed. To date, his findings on several Indian claims have pointed toward
compensation. For example, the Blackfoot of Alberta have argued that
they were promised ammunition by the government under Treaty 7, but
never received any. If the government paid compensation it could amount
to between $4 million and $22 million (depending on interest calculations).
Obviously the federal government is in no hurry to establish a commission
which would be inundated with claims, many bigger than this one. The
Prime Minister, Mr. Trudeau, in a speech in 1969, indicated his government's feelings on the treaty issue. He said that aboriginal claims were so
vague and undefined that they were incapable of remedy.

3. *Indians must be compensated for lands taken by Euro-Canadian
settlers.*[7] The most outstanding breaches of compensation involve treaties
such as those in NWT and northern Quebec.[8] In addition, the government has to pay compensation where treaties were not made. As mentioned
previously, fewer than half the natives made treaties with the dominant
group. Treaties were used as a quasi-legal weapon against the natives. By
setting up reserves (through supposedly legal treaties which were accepted
only by other European countries), the dominant group was able to make
prime land available to white settlers and exploit the resources. As Morris
states:

> In consequence of the discovery of minerals, on the shores of lakes Huron
> and Superior, the government of the late Province of Canada, deemed it
> desirable, to extinguish the Indian title, and in order to that end, in the
> year 1850, entrusted the duty to the late Honourable William B. Robin-
> son, who discharged his duties with great tact and judgment, succeeding
> in making two treaties. *(1880:42)*

The Indians were even exploited—subtly perhaps—in regard to the
amount of land they were allowed to keep. For example in Manitoba, 7.45
million acres were given to the HBC, 1.9 million acres to the railroad, 1.4
million acres to the Metis, and fewer than 400,000 acres to the Indians.
When land grants to Indian and white families are compared, we find that
160 acres per person over 18, with later right to an additional 160 acres.

[7]A commission set up to investigate the provisions of Treaty 8 and Treaty 11 recommended in a report submitted in 1959 that money be paid to natives to set up a
reserve system. So far, nothing has been done.
[8]Indian commissioners were paid 10 per cent of money from the sale of Indian
lands.

Another reason why compensation (in land or money) should be made is because of the different conceptualization of land ownership. When the government began to "bargain" with the natives, it was concerned only with the European definition of land ownership, which it knew would be upheld by other European countries. As Nammack (1969) remarks, whites were simply unwilling (in some cases unable) to comprehend the Indian concept of land ownership. Early historians argued that only west coast Indians had notions of land ownership. However, many of the dominant group who interacted with Indians soon became aware that even though Indians had no written records, the idea of land ownership was not foreign to them.

Natives believed that any group who resided on a piece of land and used it (*e.g.*, for cultivation, hunting), retained ownership. Their view of ownership was that land could not be "sold" but rather, people could be "permitted" to use and cultivate it. However, Indians always felt that *they* retained ownership. Thus the argument that Indians need not be compensated for land taken over by whites because it "really wasn't theirs" is naive and false.

A third argument for compensation hinges on the explanations natives were given concerning the amount of land they were to cede. Consider the terms used in the Selkirk Treaty (known as Treaty 1), for example:

> The Indians then inhabiting the region were described as being of the Chippawa, or Saulteux and Illistine or Cree nations. They were made to comprehend the depth of the land they were surrendering, by being told, that it was the greatest distance, at which a horse on the level prairie could be seen or daylight seen under his belly between his legs. The consideration for the surrender, was, the payment of 100 pounds of good merchantable tobacco, to each nation annually.[9] *(Morris, 1880:15)*

The actual areas involved here amounted to about 17,000 square miles.

Finally, compensation should be made because natives were not allowed to choose their land. Only areas inappropriate for white settlers were made reserves. This policy is fully documented in white statements before the signing of treaties. Treaties were offered to Indians on the grounds that if they were not accepted, the territory in question would become crown land anyway.

It is blatantly misleading today to say: "That was all historical; now things have changed." It is false to suggest that historical events have no bearing on the present. Such a view reflects the myth of equality discussed earlier.

4. *The IAB must be turned over to the natives.* They should be allowed to control the agency with little or no outside influence. If this were carried out, the IAB could become just as effective as a lobbying force for the natives as it has been against them in the past. Since the IAB receives

---

[9]In an attempt to test this, I found that using the first technique the distance was about 15 miles. The second technique (light between horse's legs) was considerably less than a mile. Allowing for my poor sight (and keen sight of the Indian) the distance would still fall considerably short of what Morris told the Indians.

well over $200 million a year, it could also be used as a "rallying" point under which "bloc" voting could occur.

The following expenditures for the IAB in 1970–71 reveal that more than 40 per cent of the budget went to community affairs programs—predominantly welfare. Less than 10 per cent went directly into community development. Natives should be allowed to decide where the money should be allotted and how much should be spent. Economic development, the one area which would allow natives to regain social and economic independence, received less than 5 per cent of the budget.

The current projects on some reserves clearly illustrate, as Hatt observed, that Indians are not involved in the actual development. For instance, at the Le Pas reserve, Manitoba, timber land is being leased to a white-controlled industry. In Ontario, where Indians have attempted to develop their mining resources, the government would not give a band money to do so, but gave it to a white corporation. The result is the same —Indians only get to participate in the industry at a marginal level as workers; not owners, planners or directors. Clearly, even the IAB which claims to represent the natives, is committed to a policy of "continued subjugation."

5. *Natives must gain control of the trust fund in Ottawa.* They must have immediate access to it and complete control over spending and choice of projects to be supported. The trust fund is made up of annuities and money accrued from Indian assets. It was established when Upper Canada was settled.

Table 37. Indian Affairs Budget, 1970–71 ($ million)

Education	
Federal schools	23.4
Non-federal schools	36.8
Transportation and maintenance	25.8
Misc. (including administration and adult education)	13.1
Sub total	99.1
Community affairs	
Welfare	42.5
Community government, development and improvement	18.3
Indian housing	17.0
Northern housing	5.8
Other	1.0
Sub total	84.6
Economic development	11.1
Administration	12.8
Indian consultation and negotiation	2.9
Total	$210.5

Most of the money that goes into it comes from land, oil and gas leases and from the sale of natural resources such as timber, chemicals and minerals.

Before 1859, trust fund money was invested in commercial securities, but since then the federal government has assumed responsibility for handling it. Money from the fund has to be used "in the interests of the band." This means that at present, projects suggested by natives have to be approved by the dominant group before any money is released.

Reserves short in skills and money and in indirect competition with white firms are in an extremely difficult position. To date, there have been few federal or provincial plans to make a co-ordinated attack on the problem. One suggestion, by Dunning (1970, 1971), is to establish and develop a capital development grant. This would not be the $50 million grant over five to ten years which the government proposed, but rather a $400 million grant over the same period. Such a grant would make about $90,000 available to each band, none of which would be used for consumer expenses, only for capital development.

However, this proposal may not be enough. Other schemes, such as "forgivable loans" for Indians wishing to set up businesses could be introduced. The group wishing to set up an industry could apply to the government to finance it in the initial stages. Such a method is currently being used by foreign investors in Canada and it could easily be adapted to internal use.

Other suggestions for financial improvements have been made by Heilbrun and Wellisz (1969), who proposed that the federal government could use the International Bank for Reconstruction and Development, the International Finance Corporation and the International Development Authority as models. These organizations make loans to underdeveloped countries and for various projects and provide equity for developments. The advantages of these programs (adapted from international models) would be enormous. First, since they would not be subject to an annual review for continued funds, there would be little fear that the government might decide to withdraw its support at the end of the second or third year. Second, it would allow for the development of projects that progressed slowly (but steadily) in the hope that there might be some cumulative effect. Qualified staff would be attracted because they would not be working under the shadow of the annual review. This would be one of the spin-off benefits.

Tables 38 and 39 show the present commercial and "industrial" development on Indian reserves. There is a notable absence of any primary or heavy industry on the reserve (or even controlled by natives off the reserve). Table 38 also shows that a third of the commercial businesses on the reserve are non-Indian and that the total of nearly 900 commercial businesses employ little more than 1,000 natives, *i.e.* nearly one per business. These figures support the claim made earlier that the "individual entrepreneurship" system is being pushed by the dominant group.

The figures on the industrial development of Indians and Eskimos show that in 1969 they had only 63 secondary industries and that over two-thirds of the industries were related to "woodworking." Prefabricated housing, which makes up over 10 per cent of the industries, is the second

SEVEN

Table 38. Commercial Businesses on Reserves Across Canada

Services	Indian business	Non-Indian business	Indians employed	Man years	Total earnings ($)	Average earnings ($)	Sales volume ($)
Amusement and recreation*	77	115	240	97	165,850	1,709	112,800
Buses, taxis, trucks, gas	324	54	438	282	1,797,400	6,373	1,084,700
Home, farm construction	120	24	195	127	507,700	3,997	368,700
Retail and related	148	29	235	189	511,600	2,842	1,983,350
Others	17	–	34	18	57,500	3,194	31,000
Total	686	222	1,142	713	3,040,050	2,678	3,580,550

Source: Department of Indian Affairs, *Annual Report 1970–71*. Reproduced by permission of Information Canada.

*e.g. golf course, movie theatre, swimming pool, etc.

Table 39. Industry on Reserves Across Canada

Secondary Industry (i) To March 31, 1969

Nature of secondary industry	No. of businesses	Existing Man years	Existing Indians employed	Existing earnings ($)	Average yearly earnings ($)	Short term potential Man years	Short term potential Earnings ($)	Financial input ($) DIAND	Financial input ($) Other
Woodworking and allied	40	72	117	302,400	2,586	72	302,400	136,433	68,850
Needle trades	1	21	21	59,000	2,810	30	103,000		
Prefab housing etc.	7	50	92	198,000	2,152	50	198,000		
Other	11	54	43	109,080	2,553	60	236,700		
Total	59	197	273	668,480	2,448	212	840,100	136,433	68,850
(ii) Since April 1, 1969									
Started									
Woodworking and allied	1	1	1	3,600	3,600	8	28,800		
Needle trades	2	17	17	42,120	2,808	37	130,830	11,500	75,840
Prefab housing etc.	1	100	100	500,000	5,000	200	1,000,000	700,000	2,417,000
Total	4	118	118	545,720	4,625	245	1,159,630	711,500	2,492,840
In negotiation									
Woodworking and allied	1		10		3,100	10	31,000		
Needle trades	2		50		3,936	50	192,400	10,000	196,820
Other	1		40		7,280	40	291,200		25,000,000
Total	4		100		5,146	100	514,600	10,000	25,196,820

largest single industry. However, prefab housing is not an indigenous profit industry. The houses produced are used for the reserve residents. This may bring money to the reserve but it obviously does not promote the group's development. Of the industries in Table 39, only "woodwork and allied" have any long-range potential. The federal government has not set up international trade restrictions (or even intra-Canadian restrictions) for "woodwork and needlework" articles as it has done with Eskimo artifacts. Many other nations such as Japan and Hong Kong produce "Indian" artifacts.[10] Since other "new" industries in Canada are protected by tariffs and taxes, BC Indians have urged the government to do the same for them, but so far without success.

6. *Treaty rights originally guaranteed by the dominant group must be upheld.* These include (*i*) water rights, (*ii*) rights under the Customs Act to bring duty-free goods into the country, (*iii*) rights under the Migratory Birds Convention Act and (*iv*) rights under the Fisheries Act. All of these rights are necessary for the "upgrading" of natives and their full community development. As MacGregor (1961) argues, creative development of any type will not emerge on the reserve until all forces (both conscious and unconscious) opposing Indian administration and social adjustments are significantly reduced. Indians must be given authority to act without fear of reprisals if their decisions clash with the dominant group's wishes.

How do Canadians react to these suggestions? Likely responses might include: "Everyone is equal in Canada; they don't need special treatment." "It will never work." And the racist comment: "They are incapable of development even if we gave them what they ask." Whites will make this a case of either/or—as Dixon notes:

> For example, if I am pro-Black, then I must be anti-white. If I am pro-White, then I must be anti-Black. Another way of stating the either/or concept is the two person, zerio sum game. According to the strategy of this game, if, for example, a sum of 100 units of some commodity is to be distributed between two people, then any change in a given distribution means that increasing one side causes a corresponding decrease in the other. Similarly, in the context of American race relations, any gain for Black is viewed as a loss for White and vice versa. *(1971:28)*

What is being done today toward economically developing reserves? Several are trying to progress now, before any of the demands have been achieved. The following article from *Time* (April 19, 1971) describes an attempt by a Blackfoot band in southern Alberta. It shows that with control over finance, an Indian group can develop its economic potential.

Indians: A New Stand at Standoff

The 351,575-acre Blood Indian reserve in Southern Alberta is the largest in Canada. A band of the Blackfoot nation, the Bloods once roamed the

---

[10]The creating, buying and selling of Eskimo art is carefully controlled by the federal government. It arranges for the collection of the rocks, allows only a certain number of prints to be made, destroys the originals and supervises the auctions at which they are sold.

area as splendid horsemen and canny fur traders. Eventually, as the North West Mounted Police noted in 1874, the white man's influence—especially his booze—reduced the Bloods "from the most opulent Indians in the West to abject poverty, in rags, without horses or guns." The fur traders' whiskey forts ultimately disappeared, but over the years the living conditions of the Bloods have only marginally improved. Until recent years, life on the reserve largely meant subsisting on the band's $1 million-a-year in gas royalties and land leases as well as federal welfare checks, and drinking up a storm in nearby Lethbridge on Saturday nights.

Now the Blood reserve (pop. 4,397) is in the midst of a remarkable economic and social rebirth that may serve as a model for other native communities. Even at their lowest ebb, the Bloods were not entirely down and out—or at least not all of them were. Five years ago, the band's leadership—Indians who were themselves successful as farmers and cattle ranchers—recognized that the band could never throw off its lethargy without providing decent jobs for its people. They formed an industrial development committee, hired Oblate Father Denis Chatain as an adviser, and went shopping.

Janitor to President—The objective was to find a manufacturer who would set up shop on the reserve and be prepared to train Indian workmen—and management. Said a member of the industrial development committee, Stephen Fox: "We wanted to be able to operate completely on our own, from janitor to president, within 15 years." After a broad search, the Bloods found their company in their own backyard: Lethbridge's HaiCo Manufacturing Ltd., a large builder of mobile homes.

An 80,000 sq. ft. plant on a sere bluff overlooking the reserve's main community of Standoff is now turning out one prefab house a day, and expects to increase its production to four a day by the end of the year. The Bloods borrowed $876,000 from Jean Marchand's Department of Regional Economic Expansion to build the plant; HaiCo is providing operating capital, on-the-job training and management for the first five years—when the Bloods have an option to take over the operation entirely. The prefabs will sell for $15,000–$20,000 each. Already a Lethbridge real estate firm has signed a contract estimated at $20 million to buy the plant's production run for the next three years.

But first the operation will turn out several hundred houses for a modern townsite at Standoff. The project has so far brought water, sewage, telephones and natural gas services to the town; soon it will employ 240 Indians and provide a payroll of $1 million a year. Says Father Chatain: "This is just the beginning. Imagine the rippling effect—the service industries needed, the possibilities for auxiliary manufacturing and so on." Among the ripples already being felt, the Safeway supermarket chain has opened a small market in Standoff, and the Bank of Nova Scotia has established a branch in the town—the first on an Alberta reserve. Plans are being formulated for nothing less than a subdivision with several hundred homes, a shopping center, schools, churches, and all of the other amenities of suburban life.

Off the Sauce—The quest for economic independence is mirrored in changing social attitudes among the Bloods. Fred Gladstone, a cattle rancher, a former North American calf-roping champion and the son of Canada's first Indian Senator, is president of Red Crow Developments, the band-owned company that is HaiCo's partner in the plant. He says: "Our motto is 'Get off the welfare line and on the production line.' " According to Father Chatain, the sentiment is more than a slogan. "People who never have worked have come in for a job," he reports. "Suddenly

it is the in thing on the reserve to quit drinking." Father Chatain predicts
that within two years there will be no unemployment on the reservation,
and "if everything goes as we project, we will be hiring Indians from
other reserves."

Federal Indian Affairs officials are both impressed and somewhat
startled by the Bloods' initiative in throwing off the Government's tutel-
age. Says Tom Turner, the department's district supervisor: "The excit-
ing thing is that it is their baby. They call us when they need us. Otherwise, what they want is for us to stay the hell out of the way, and they
make it just that plain."[11]

These Indians hoped to be able to take over the operation from HaiCo
after five years. This was a most necessary clause in the contract. By 1973
the project was in full operation. While operating expenses were still high,
a slight profit was realized in the first few months of 1973. In addition,
the employee turnover rate had stabilized at about 10 per cent—a rate
comparable to that of established industry. Unfortunately, capital gain had
not been sufficient to allow the Bloods to expect a takeover of the entire
operation at the end of the five year period.

This is a clear example of the unplanned, or "unbalanced" approach
described earlier. The Indians are concerned with only one major industry,
so a white food chain and other outside white industries and commercial
activities were moving in to establish franchise relationships with local Indians. Therefore, a big proportion of what the Indians would spend daily
on the reserve would leave the community. How can this pattern be broken
so that natives achieve control over their fate?

I am not advocating apartheid in reverse but support the strategy of
independence suggested by Sorenson and Wolfson (1969). With independence, the returns from the major proportion of the Indians' economic
activity would remain (initially) within the reserve. Indians could operate
industries employing only Indians and using money they had saved. But
this would be extremely slow and has to be rejected. Instead, Indians should
receive external aid in the form of capital grants. This would avoid completely separating Indians and whites. White control over Indian economic
development would be minimized by insisting on using Indian financial
intermediaries and outside credit (supplemented by local savings).

The natives have to make a crucial decision. Can they allow "outside"
interests (having decided which ones) to invest money in their development with "no strings attached" or can they go it alone? They are in a strik-
ingly similar situation to the newly emerging nations, seeking economic
independence but also high incomes for their people and quick capital.
Can these be achieved when outside entrepreneurs or companies invest?
The experience of the emerging nations has been that when individual entrepreneurs or companies are allowed to come in and stimulate economic
activity, it is only for a short period and for their interest, not the natives'.
Long-range studies show that when this happens, the country's economic

[11]Reprinted by permission from *Time*, The Weekly Newsmagazine; Copyright
Time Inc.

development actually decreases and subsequently depresses the per capita income.

Clearly, internal capital development is the answer. How would such
a native sub-economy work. It would have to trade with the surrounding
Euro-Canadian population but would not have to duplicate any existing
services such as highways and hydro power which would drain capital.
Therefore, the sub-economy would have an important "external trade"
factor. The composition of the sub-economy would be straightforward—
corporate structures owned and controlled by the native community. These
would supply other native industries and the Euro-Canadian industries
with many products but would not receive goods from the latter (Sorenson
and Wolfson, 1969). This modified sub-economy could not only survive,
but expand until natives became integrated and self-sustaining in the larger
economy.

REACTIVE ADAPTATION BY NATIVES

I have attempted to show why natives must reject individual entrepreneurship and what changes are needed if Indians are to improve their
position in society. If there is no change, if the status quo is maintained,
what will happen? Apart from accepting the status quo, Indians have a
choice between violence and non-violence. We shall now evaluate the likelihood of each—and the repercussions for the Canadian society if either
is chosen.

Non-Violence

The aim of non-violent action is to push demands by group confron-
tation without resorting to physical destruction. It can involve legal or illegal activities. Two major forms are:

Voting—Since Canadian Indians were not allowed to poll in federal
elections until 1960 (unless they relinquished their legal Indian status),
they have not had the chance to realize how useful the vote can be as a tool
for immediate social change. Even if they did appreciate its significance,
they do not have much political leverage on a population basis. Bloc voting
could be introduced, but this would take more time to achieve results than
the Indians can afford. However, bloc voting could be extremely useful in
provincial and local elections.

Demonstrations—The word these days can apply to small sit-ins or
massive protest parades. However, the planning and high cost have to be
weighed against what they achieve. Natives have tried to evaluate the effectiveness of sit-ins and other demonstrations in the US by blacks and they
have decided that such protests bring only negative results. They found
that the brightest, most articulate leaders of the minority group were removed, either by being co-opted or imprisoned. Also, protests and sit-ins
provide the opportunity for some people to "backlash" against the demon-

strators. They like to see Indians kept in their place and they become up-set when natives get "uppity." Non-violent passive resistance and semi-violent defensive resistance have been traditional techniques of Indian protesters. However, today the attitude on the use of violence is that it should be a "last resort." This means Indians will soon be claiming that "all else" has failed—the judicial system, voting and peaceful demonstrations. The time for the last alternative—violent action—will have arrived.

Today the stereotype of an Indian is often a lazy drunk. This view has developed over time. Because he is regarded as inferior it does not become a serious moral dilemma for white society to segregate and exploit him. Also, whites have for centuries attempted to inculcate the Indian with the belief that he is inferior. The cumulative effect is that the Indian tends to be inhibited in speaking out against white society.

Capitalism (including private property ownership and individual-ism) is foreign to Indian culture but nevertheless was introduced and the Indian has had to compete. Since democracy is predicated on equality and since everyone has "freedom of choice," it follows that hard work leads to success in the economic system. This freedom of choice has now been ex-tended to include the people one works with and for, the neighbors one has, *etc.* Given this choice, the economic system, and the stereotype of Indians, it should not be a surprise that Indians are not included in the larger society's commercial or industrial activities. A vicious cycle now keeps the Indian out of the economic system, reinforcing society's stereo-type of him. And the stereotype continues to keep him out of the labor force . . . (Franklin, 1969).

From this, Indians have an objective and subjective basis to apply a "last resort" rationale to their more militant activities. For example, this was a partial explanation given by Six Nations Indians who went to Cuba in 1958.

Violence

Violent action can be directed against property or people though gen-erally in any conflict, both suffer. Most Canadians are concerned about property damage and they consider it to be more objectionable than vio-lence involving people. Violence can be categorized by the way it is ap-plied, using conventional means or guerrilla action.

Technique of Application

		Conventional	*Guerrilla*
Direction of violence	Property	1	2
	Person	3	4

Native people reject strategies 1 and 3 (conventional violence against peo-ple and property) on pragmatic grounds. The existing dominant group clearly has the upper hand in firepower and could unequivocally defeat any subversive group which met them in this manner. Strategies 3 and 4 (personal violence using conventional or guerrilla methods) could be objectionable from a moral standpoint. Kwan and Shibutani (1967) say in their appraisal that killings arising out of collective violence are decisions that are rationalized to be the "best" outcome. Guerrilla attacks against property is the remaining possibility. It alleviates the moral and pragmatic objections and because it "hits where it hurts," would be most instrumental in bringing about meaningful social change. I agree with McNamara (1969), who points out that it is absurd to equate property with life, *e.g.* one cannot reject violence against property as absolutely immoral action without regarding property as an extension of the individual and thus as sacred as life itself.

Most Canadians embody the basic elements of the Protestant ethic, working hard to possess material goods in the belief that the harder one strives, the closer one will be to salvation. And in our society material goods are the prime source of prestige and status—the more one has, the higher one's status. Therefore it is considered a "status loss" if one has no material goods or if one loses them. Since entire social interaction patterns as well as power relationships are built on prestige and status differentials, changes in either of these may radically change interaction processes. Power relationships may be dissolved into peer interactions, and relationships which initially were "equal" may change to superordinate-subordinate ones or the entire process may reverse. We should note here that as an interaction, conflict is considered to be as natural as non-conflict. That is, we view conflict as a form of social behavior. Its consequences can be "negative" or "positive" depending on how it is viewed. If disruption is considered to indicate social change (and social change is viewed as good), then conflict will be viewed as positive. On the other hand, if conflict is regarded as "disruptive," then violence will be viewed as impeding society's functioning and consequently labelled "bad."

Violence is one form of interaction that can result when social groups have interacted over time. Unless a goal is clearly stated and quantified attempts to measure its degree of attainment are made, one cannot argue that conflict (violence) is "good" or "bad." It is argued here, however, that our society has set forth clear, long-range goals based on values of equality, human rights, and the belief in a right to a minimum standard of living (Jones and Lambert, 1967). Are these goals being met by all segments of Canadian society? The answer, based on the information presented in the first two chapters, is clearly no. Will natives engage in any type of violence? Most Canadians say no. Their answers are based on a variety of rationale but all show little understanding of the use of violence.

My contention that conflict will emerge is based on a thorough analysis of the violent activities in Canada and other nations. An attempt has been made to dig out the relevant variables and apply them to the contemporary scene. As Whiteside (1972) explained, several historical factors have prevented Canadian Indians from participating in violent activities. However, these are now being recognized and a turn of events is imminent.

Whiteside says that one of the major reasons why Indians have not indulged in aggressive activities is that they are directly controlled by the federal government in every aspect of life, including voluntary organizations. Secondly, he points out that because of the subtlety of genocidal practices against Indians, their enemy is less clearly defined than the tactics needed to overcome them. A third restraining factor against Indian violence has been the control held by the RCMP. It has been clearly demonstrated that the RCMP's most important role since its conception has been the control and subjugation of the natives. Potential conflict has been diffused to individual levels and group participation has never arisen. The last factor which Whiteside says has contributed to Indian non-agression is the role of the Indian agent. Since agents were civil servants, not political appointees, they were directly responsible to the federal government for all business and other transactions. Agents were also encouraged to control every facet of Indian life since this would indicate involvement and mean longer tenure of their jobs.

DEVELOPMENT OF CONFLICT

Perception is generally referred to as the process of "taking in stimuli." However, when this happens, it is to some extent a product of socialization processes. That is, people learn to perceive certain things. They become aware of some stimuli and not others. A result is that a lot of what goes on in the "outside" world never "registers" on our socializing senses. This has been demonstrated by many investigations utilizing cross-cultural data. (See Deutsch, 1968 for further discussion.)

The point is that various stimuli, depending on the social and cultural factors the individual is exposed to, will become apparent to him and to others. Thus, certain ethnic groups will perceive certain stimuli and ignore others. The correspondence between what is perceived by different ethnic groups will depend on the similarity of the social and cultural factors that have affected them. More central to our argument is that "true reality" can never be established; reality is in the mind. The importance of this proposition will be illustrated shortly.

W. I. Thomas proposed that: "If men define situations as real, they are real in their consequences." How the situations are defined (interpreted), of course, depends on several social and psychological variables. But the important point is that each situation which confronts a person requires an interpretation. The final concept, vocabulary of motives, refers to the type of interpretation made about the behavior or action being emitted by an individual or a group and perceived by another person or group. Motives are always inferential, thus, when behavior is observed, many motives can be imputed to the individual (or group) under observation.

Clearly these are three essential factors to be considered. Because all groups are exposed to particular structural factors—social class, occupation, *etc.*—their perception of behavior is "slanted." That is, people learn to see only certain kinds of behavior. Therefore, people impute motives (rightly or wrongly) to a group and then define the situation to meet their needs.

These principles are especially true when applied to the emergence of violence. When groups have been interacting for some time, they begin to define each other. Each defines roles in the society that the other should play. Thus, Japanese can be gardeners and run certain restaurants, blacks can be porters and Indians can be hunters and fishermen because these activities are congruent with white society's role expectations of them. Ethnocentrism emerges and certain activities are defined as not only appropriate for a certain group but "right or wrong." When these definitions and expectations are not met, people feel uncomfortable and are left in an ambiguous position about how to act. Eventually bipolarization develops and people see their group as good and other groups as bad.

Interestingly, all groups see each other in similar ways. Kwan and Shibutani (1967) refer to this as the emergence of "contrast conception." This process continues through "selective perception." Only stimuli that meet with a previous definition of a situation will be perceived. Thus, the motives that have been imputed to the other perceived appearance group are always upheld.[12] Sensory cues inconsistent with the initial definitions are overlooked. Once the contrast conceptions (seeing one's own group as good, sincere, *etc.* and the other group as evil, bad, *etc.*) are formed, several subsequent events culminate in an eventual act of violence.

Solidarity between the members of each group increases and negative comments about one's own group and positive comments about the enemy are prohibited (offenders would be charged with complicity). The situation which develops under these conditions is known as ethical dualism, meaning that members of one group can deviate from normal standards of behavior when interacting with the enemy, although they must adhere to the norms when interacting with members of their own group (Gladstone, 1959).

In dominant-minority group relations, minority groups make demands on the dominant group to change their position in the system. The dominant group must react to these demands by responding positively or negatively. The dominant group's response will be positive to minority demands up to a "critical point"—at which the status quo could be seriously disrupted (Lightbody, 1969). In other words, before this point, the minority group is working "within the system." However, beyond the critical point there is a period of increased tension. As the group makes additional demands (which must be subsequently denied by the dominant group), overt conflict will begin.

Before analyzing the demand functions further, let us look at the other dimension of the model—the dominant group's responses, which are

[12]Perceived appearance group refers to a group of people who are perceived by another group (or by themselves) as having distinct cultural and/or physiological attributes which distinguish them as "different" from other groups of people. The central point is that these people do not "objectively" need to have certain attributes, *e.g.*, color of skin, hair texture, *etc.*, but as long as these features are defined as being present, those making the definition will react in socially prescribed ways. An example is anti-Semitism. A non-Jewish person perceived to have a large, hooked nose, (even though he may not objectively have one), will be subject to discrimination and prejudice.

to be considered social control mechanisms. Again we must introduce the notion of critical point. Lightbody contends:

> Beyond [this critical point] the state must realign its institutional structures about a new ethnic configuration by either physically attempting culture, or through accepting the creation of the new political nationality, move itself toward being an ethnically homogeneous national group. *(1969:334)*

Thus depending on the dominant group's responses to the minority group's demands (coupled with the minority group's perception of the dominant group's reaction and its subsequent definition of the situation), the minority group will not pass the critical point. The distance between the critical point and an outbreak of violence will vary with the minority group. For natives, the distance has traditionally been great. Even though there has been tension for a long time, no violence has taken place. It will now be argued, however, that with the upsurge of Red Power, the distance is decreasing (there are more demands and the dominant group's responses are more negative). That is, the probability of violence is increasing.

SOCIAL CONTROL MECHANISMS

The dominant group has so far been successful in averting native violence because new and more sophisticated social control mechanisms have been developed to meet the changing times. These give the appearance that something is being done to alleviate native problems, thereby pacifying the Indians. But in reality, the social control mechanisms do nothing—thus serving the needs of the dominant group. How is this achieved? Gamson (1969) has delineated two general types of social control mechanisms. The first involves modifying an original decision to suit a particular minority group and the second involves controlling a minority group's desire for change. The dominant group is constantly making decisions affecting minority groups. Under certain circumstances, minority groups oppose a decision. Therefore, one control mechanism available to the dominant group is simply to modify its decision, placing the minority group in an "indebted" position. The second type of control mechanism (control of desire) suggested by Gamson can take three forms—insulation, sanction, or persuasion. Let us look at each.

Insulation—This involves the notion of keeping a particular group from "power positions." It can be seen in the federal and provincial programs to "help" natives. All of them are oriented toward semi-skilled and blue collar occupations. There have been no serious plans to place natives in universities or managerial and professional occupations.

Referring to our model again, one can see that natives have demanded more occupational opportunities, more participation in decision making processes and generally a louder voice in their destiny. The dominant group has responded by instituting programs which manifestly appear to "correct" the problem but which latently subjugate natives even further. This seems to solve the problem for natives (who think something is being done) and for the dominant group (who can see that these policies are not actually changing the social relationships). The result is that the minority group is prevented (insulated) from acquiring skills and knowledge which might threaten the dominant group.

Sanction—This refers to positive and negative rewards that can be given or withdrawn. These are more overt control techniques than the above. Reserves with no "trouble makers" are more likely to receive federal grants, to be allowed some control over finance, to elect their band leaders, and to have freedom in many other activities. However, these reserves must also "buy the line" of the federal and provincial governments. So if positive rewards fail, negative sanctions can be introduced. Leaders can be jailed, bands can have finance held back, *etc.* All of these techniques have been repeatedly demonstrated. For example, when Cardinal was accused of being insubordinate by Indian Affairs and Northern Development, all funds were cut off to the Indian Association of Alberta. It should be noted that the definition of "responsible" and "irresponsible" behavior on the reserve is always made by the dominant group.

Persuasion—The dominant group uses two forms of persuasion in its method of controlling Indians. The first, called "activation of commitment", involves any attempt by the dominant group to highlight a commitment the minority group may have to the existing social system. Minority groups are told that despite any "temporary setbacks" they may strike, in the long run it is for the best. Indians are continually told that change is slow and cannot come overnight. They must wait for change but while waiting, they must not engage in any tactics to upset the dominant group.

The second form of persuasion, selective-participation, is the method of allowing members of Indian bands to participate selectively in the dominant group's decision-making. Certain Indians sympathetic to the dominant group's position are allowed to "help" make a decision—if it is not important. However, Indians always have a less powerful position in the decision making than their white counterparts. When whites say that Indians do participate in "decision making" which affects them, they do not admit that those Indians are generally sympathetic to the white position. Also, Indians could not override the decisions made by whites even if they voted in bloc. For example, a committee may consist of ten people—three Indians and seven whites—so it would be impossible for the Indians to out-vote the dominant group. But this representation prevents minority groups from claiming that they are not able to "determine their destiny." It is always argued that Indians do participate—but the extent is never detailed.

One of the most intriguing and complex of social controls is co-optation. This involves a "yielding" process and is generally not used unless the previous techniques have failed. While it clearly involves certain risks for the dominant group (in allowing Indians access to power) it eventually works to the whites' advantage. The dominant group allows Indians to enter the larger power structure, giving members of the minority group access to information they otherwise would not have. This information could be used against the dominant group to bring about changes in their relationships between each other. However, the dominant group calculates (generally correctly) that it will not be used. Why? First, if the native enters the dominant group, he is still subject to its sanctions. While these may be different to those he is used to, they are still sanctions. Second, the native who moves into the dominant group structure risks losing credibility. Other Indians are less likely to see him as "one of us" and may charge him with "selling out." They would pay little heed to the advice and information he might pass out, which objectively could help them. Third, the whites are able to obtain the most talented and vocal members of the Indian community by pulling them into the dominant structure. In this way, the Indian community loses technical expertise and leaders.

All of the techniques described have been practised against Indians, but insulation is the most predominant and widespread social control mechanism in use. However, as society changes, the dominant group will assess its position (perhaps by another survey, like Hawthorn's) and decide whether it needs to change its control methods. As Gamson (1969) points out, when the dominant group defines a minority group as having no faith in its (the dominant group's) quest for goals, then insulation will be the mechanism of social control.

8

Red Power

WALTER STEWART

AN INDIAN CHIEF called his tribe to the long-house and said, "My people, I have always spoken to you with a straight tongue. When I had a good thing to say, I said it; when my tidings were bad, I told them without delay. Today I have some good news and some bad. I will tell you the bad news first. The white man has decided he can no longer afford to feed his red brother. From now on, we will have to eat buffalo dung."

There was a moment of silence, then a brave arose at the back of the hall. "That is the bad news," he said. "What is the good?"

"There's plenty of buffalo dung," the chief replied.

This blunt little joke, which I heard recently in half a dozen versions in half a dozen Indian communities across Canada, reflects in a few words the new face of bitterness Canadian Indians are turning to the white man. All across Canada, the natives are restless. They are fed up with oppression and want, with polite prejudice

*From *Star Weekly*, May 11, 1968. Copyright 1968, *Star Weekly*. Reprinted with permission.

and gentle apartheid; they are fed up with being pushed around and they
are ready, now, to start pushing back. And so, all across the land, Indians
are launching lawsuits, and talking back to agents of the Indian Affairs
Branch, and painting placards, and plotting marches. Some Indians—the
timid, the elderly, the ones we like to think of as "responsible"—call this
new aggressiveness "self-determination;" others, bolder, younger and more
determined, call it Red Power.

Red Power invites comparison with Black Power in the U.S., con-
jures up visions of howling mobs, burning buildings and looted stores;
therefore, many Canadian Indians reject the term, and say comforting
things—"We don't want violence;" "This is not Alabama;" "We have
nothing against whites"—things like that. Others, more of them every day,
accept both the term and its implications, and their words hold less comfort for the white majority. They say, with Tony Antoine, 27, an Okanagan
from the interior of B.C., "Well, violence is part of our society; if it has to
come, it has to;" or, with George Monroe, 23, a Manitoba Metis, "Sympathy is for the weak; I have never seen in history where sympathy allev-
iated poverty. If the Indian wants something, he is going to have to take
it;" or, with Duke Redbird, 29, a Saugeen now living in Toronto, "There
are terrible things happening every day to Indians in Canada . . . there are
many, many communities like powder kegs, ready to blow up."

It would be comforting to say that these young hotheads represent
only a tiny minority of the Indian population, but it would not be true. In
recent travels among the Indians, in cities and villages and reserves, I found
the strong talk of the militants far more common than the whispers of the
conservatives, especially among Indians under 21—who represent about
60 per cent of the native population. I found that, despite vigorous denials
when the subject was raised in the House of Commons a few months ago,
some Canadian Indians are, in fact, in touch with revolutionary native
groups in Latin America, as well as with Black Power advocates in the U.S.,
and that, while many of the young people look to Martin Luther King as
a martyred folk hero, just as many prefer the style of Che Guevara. One
young Indian, writing to Dr. Howard Adams—a Metis, and a Red Power
advocate at the University of Saskatchewan—began his letter, "Dear Sir:
Let me introduce myself; I am a revolutionary."

I short, there may be a parallel between Red Power in Canada and
Black Power in the U.S. Not that the parallel is exact. American Negroes
represent about 10 per cent of the U.S. population; Canadian Indians represent 2 per cent of ours. Our natives are split by language, tribal and
religious differences largely absent in the U.S., and they are not subject
to the same crude and open oppression. "In the United States," says Larry
Seymour, 21, a Cowichan from Duncan, B.C., "the coloreds get a shot in
the mouth; here we get a pin in the back."

Just the same, Red Power has this overwhelming similarity to Black
Power: A minority people is held down, despised and oppressed, on racial
grounds, and that minority has decided not to take it any more. Larry Seymour, who travelled to the U.S. to study Black Power there, warns, "Canadians like to look across the border and say it can't happen here; but what

is going on down there is what happens when people have nothing to lose."

If that statement sounds too strong, look for a moment at Canada's Indians. There are about 415,000 of them. There are 215,000 on the rolls of government registers—and thus eligible for $5 a year in Treaty money —of whom 155,000 live on reserves, 20,000 on crown land, and the rest dispersed among the general population, mostly in slums. There are about 200,000 Metis—half-breeds—in settlements and slums. As a people, the natives are poorer, sicker, worse housed, less educated and more delinquent than the rest of us. Over 40 per cent of the Indian population is unemployed, and the situation is getting worse, not better. In 1964, 37.4 per cent were on relief; in 1966, the figure was 40 per cent. About 47 per cent of Indian families earn less than $1,000 a year—that is, about half the people have total family earnings of less than $20 a week. Nearly 60 per cent live in houses of three rooms or less, compared to a national average of 11 per cent, and only 9 per cent of these houses have indoor toilets. Their mortality rate is eight times the white rate for preschool children, three and a half times the white rate for adults. About 24 per cent are functionally illiterate. They spend much more time in jail than whites; although national figures are not kept on racial grounds, regional studies reveal that the tiny Indian population fills a huge proportion of jail cells. In Saskatchewan, for instance, where the Indians comprise three per cent of the general population, they make up 80 per cent of the inmates of reform institutions for females.

The Canadian Corrections Association, in a study on Indians and the law, noted that for many of them, the only place that they felt at home was in jail.

Looking at these figures, Dr. Howard Adams, a Metis, says, "Don't ask whether there will be racial violence in Canada; it is already being practised against us; the question now is whether we are going to fight back."

There is nothing new in the facts of Indian degradation; what is new is the Indian determination to change those facts, a determination reflected in an astonishing variety of ways across the country:

In British Columbia, a group of Indians is suing for recovery of 7,000 square miles of their land, or for suitable compensation, since the land was simply snatched away without benefit of treaty.

In the same province, a group of Indians asked for housing help, were turned down, and promptly organized a march on the Indian agent in Vancouver. They got by threat what they couldn't get by reason; the houses were promised and the march was called off.

At Edmonton this March, a group of Indian women heard that health services were going to be cut back to save the federal government money; they marched on the legislature with angry placards, won provincial support and an eventual promise from Ottawa not to make the cuts (a hollow victory, perhaps, since the restored services are still grossly inadequate— but a victory of sorts).

Also in Alberta, a group of Saddle Lake Indians getting ready to leave for an agricultural training course found the trip was cancelled at the last minute, because two government departments couldn't decide which should pay the tab. An Indian put in a long-distance phone call to an opposition MP at Ottawa and, within minutes, the money was found and the project restored.

At Fort William, Ont., Indians on the Mission Reserve, who have been receiving an average $1,500 a year for water rights—most of the city's water supply is on tribal property, and Indians are denied use of the watershed—called in a management firm, produced a fair-price estimate of $66,000 a year for the water and presented the city council with a bill for that amount. "Or else," said an Indian spokesman gravely, "we would have to consider alternative utilization of the watershed." The reaction of the white burghers was interesting; a number argued against paying the price, not because it is too high—it is lower than the average for 10 comparable cities—but because "the Indians would only spend the money on wine." This is like shortchanging a customer on the grounds that he'd only spend the difference on cocktails. Incidentally, the Indians plan to use the money to develop tourist facilities.

At Cornwall, Ont., Mohawks are bringing a lawsuit for land despoiled for the St. Lawrence Seaway, and Montreal Indians are looking over the possibilities of a suit.

In northern Quebec, natives are carrying a test case against the game laws, arguing that they are not bound by the white man's new rules, but by the old treaties, which promised unlimited hunting.

In New Brunswick, an Indian wouldn't move out of the way of the Mactaquac Power Project, and nearly brought the giant complex to a halt before his house could be shifted.

So far, this new aggressiveness has been peaceable, at least on the Indian side. (Not on the white, of course. When Peter Kelly, 31, and his brother Fred, 25, began stirring up fellow Indians in Kenora, Ont., they were jumped by a group of whites on the street and thrashed.) Will it stay that way? Frankly, I don't see how it can.

To assess the potential for violence, put yourself in the place of a Canadian Indian for a few minutes, and ask yourself how you'd react.

Project yourself into the tawny skin of Rod Bishop, 30, at Green Lake, in north-central Saskatchewan. You are a Metis, and all your life you have known, because you have been told, that your people are dirty, lazy drunks. You received little schooling, and find jobs hard to get and harder to hold. You were fired once for roughhousing with two whites in a company cafeteria, although the whites were not fired. You went back to school last winter, and watched a white teacher, younger than yourself, come bursting out into the schoolyard to order grown-up natives to stop speaking Cree, their native tongue . . . and you saw them stop. You are an adult, with a wife and four children, but have no say in running your community. Although there are six elected native councillors, their role is advisory; the decisions are made by white civil servants. Not long ago, the whites condemned some Metis homes, and moved the natives into government houses. The Metis were not asked, of course, what kind of houses they would like, or where they should be placed, or how they should be painted—even though they will be buying them. Some Metis wondered if their old homes couldn't be fixed up for less than the $7,500 cost of the new ones, but the whites said that was impractical, the old houses were beyond repair. Now they have been sold, to a white man, who is fixing them up. There may be an explanation for this, but you have not heard it; and when the council protests, the protest is not even recorded in the council minutes, which are kept by the whites. What would you do?

For a few minutes, become Geraldine Larkin, a pretty little girl who went to school at Alert Bay, near Vancouver. You learned to be called "squaw" and to be followed by the white boys and teased about what an easy make the squaws are—all in fun, of course. You met a nice white boy and he used to take you out; then one day he came to explain he couldn't see you any more; he wanted to become an accountant, see, and personally, he has nothing against Indians, but it just wouldn't look right. You understand? You do, of course, and later you marry a nice white boy and have a lovely baby, but do you ever forget your humiliation?

Stand for a time in the shoes of Matthew Bellegard, 20, at Little Black Bear Reserve in southern Saskatchewan. You have a white friend, too, an okay guy who doesn't mind coming to the reserve, doesn't mind the poor houses and strange smells. You drive around town a lot, and people stare at the white kid riding with an Indian, in a town where whites and Indians have lived since 1908, but nobody says much until your friend starts to date an Indian girl, and then the remarks begin. One day, on the street, a white boy comes up to you both and says, "Hey, Matt, who's the Indian-lover?" So you bust him one, and a fight breaks out, and it gets pretty nasty. You know it was a stupid thing to do, busting him, but didn't it feel good?

Almost every Indian I talked to carries the memory of some racial incident burning in his gut. Larry Seymour remembers sitting in the Indian gallery in the theatre in Duncan, B.C., so he wouldn't contaminate the whites. Terry Lavallee, 20, a Cree from Broadview, Sask., remembers being called "chief" and watching faces go dead when he said no, he was not an Italian, with his dark skin—as a matter of fact, he was an Indian. Duke Redbird remembers being told in the nine foster homes he drifted through that he would come to no good, because everyone knows Indians are depraved. He remembers, too, being turned out of a hotel when a group of Indians came to visit his room while he was working for the Company of Young Canadians, because, once they knew what he was, the hotel was sure he wouldn't pay his bill. Stan Daniels, 42, president of the Alberta Metis League, remembers the favorite sport in the Edmonton area where he grew up—"kicking the asses of the half-breeds all the way to school." He carries a scar on his buttock from a white man's knife.

None of these people is going to burn down a store because of what happened to him, but for all of them the past has a bitter aftertaste. The goodwill that would keep violence down if a crisis came was used up years ago; and whites who think no harm can come to Canada because the Indians are our friends have never talked to an Indian.

Bitterness is perhaps the only bond linking the natives of Canada, who live such different lives in cities and towns, on farms and in the bush. Bitterness makes them wary of even the most helpful whites, and keeps the Red Power movement from being hugged to death by white liberals who want to make sure it doesn't get violent and doesn't do much—who want to lead the marches themselves, just to show these poor children of nature how it is done, so that we never have to give up that wonderful, smug feeling of stooping to help an inferior race.

Red Power is being exercised when the Indians of B.C. sue for the return of their land; it is also being exercised when a nervous 19-year-old, chairing an Indian-Metis youth conference in Winnipeg, finally asks a middle-aged white woman, who can't help butting in with worthwhile suggestions, to be quiet, please, since she is not a delegate, and sticks to his guns while she humphs to her seat in a fury. Finally, Red Power is being wielded when Indians begin to assess frankly the chances of violence.

Dr. Howard Adams told me, "I deplore the thought of violence; it would set us back 20 years," and then he acknowledged, "I'm rapidly changing my mind on the possibility of its coming, though. A year ago, I would have said never, not in Canada. Now . . . well, look around."

Looking around, I am astonished that violence has not flared long since. Two years ago, at Inuvik, in the Northwest Territories, I stood and gazed in wonder along a utilidor carrying heat, water and sewer services for the white folks' homes, past the crude huts of the Indians. Civil servants rented three-bedroom apartments for $125 a month, with all services; Indians could have the services put into their shacks for $120 a month. They couldn't afford it, of course, although the utilidor ran right through their village. I asked some Indians if they ever thought of blowing up the utilidor, but I was told that would only lead to trouble. I don't know whether such acceptance is noble and rational or meek and foolish; I only know that if I squatted in a shack and watched my children shiver with cold and disease a few feet from such a symbol, my reaction would not be passive.

I also know that the days are fast fading when Indians will remain passive. With increasing education, with a modicum of prosperity, with the ability to travel and see other people, to watch TV and read books, a new generation of natives is growing up impatient with the acquiescence of the old. Just as in the U.S., expectations are rising far faster than conditions can be improved, and impatience is greatest among the very people who have made some strides, and now know how far they have to go.

The efforts of the Indian Affairs Branch to win the affection of the natives with better schools and more welfare are welcome to the old folks, like Walter Deiter, president of the Federation of Saskatchewan Indians. He says that "things are getting better all the time." To the young, like Duke Redbird, the new concessions merely mean that the white man is shifting his grip on the club.

I asked Redbird, "Why are you pressing so hard? Haven't we promised to improve the Indian Act?" He smiled and asked in turn, "Why should there be an Indian Act?"

There must be a reason. There is no White Act, of course, no Poor Act, or Deprived Italians Act; only the Indians are singled out this way. It must be for their protection, so that we can help them. If that is so, how come—after so many years of such help—they are still so squashed and poor? If we really are spending $104 million a year for the benefit of the natives, and not just to maintain a bureaucracy of 3,000 whites, why isn't the money turned over to an Indian Development Corporation, run by natives, to be used as they decide? That is really a naive question, because the Indians are not even allowed to spend their own band moneys without white approval, and the reason given is that the natives are not ready, yet, to run their own affairs. In 1854, Lord Elgin argued that if paternalism worked, the Indians were surely ready to govern themselves after hundreds of years of it, and if it didn't work, it should be scrapped. He suggested that Canadian Indians be given control of their own funds at once. The white government felt, of course, that the natives weren't ready for that and now, 114 years later, neither the challenge nor the reply has changed a jot.

In the meantime, we tell the Indians what to do and where to go, where the children must go to school—the Indian Act provides that the minister can send an Indian child to school anywhere in the country, and dispatch an RCMP officer to enforce the order if the child's parents object to having their child snatched away from them—and what language they must speak and what gods they must worship and how they must spend their own money.

All for their own good, of course.

We have given them 6,000,000 acres of their own land for reserves, most of it tucked safely away in the bush, so we won't have to see or smell the odious creatures; we have made it almost impossible for them to develop this land, not only by keeping them poor and ignorant and demoralized, but by making it illegal to raise mortgages on reserve property; and then we ask them, in the voice of Arthur Laing, our minister of Indian affairs, "Why don't you stop feeling sorry for yourselves, get to work and develop your heritage?"

The trouble is, we have been found out. It was all right in the old days to patronize the proud Indian, to admire his war bonnet and steal his land; to make him drunk, then chide him for drinking; to drive off his game, then rebuke him for being hungry; to destroy his religion, debauch his children, rape his women, then reprimand him for a savage. That was all right in the old days; but now a whole generation of educated Indians is springing up and, instead of falling on our necks for all we have done, the ungrateful wretches call us thieves and corrupters and racists—all terrible charges, and all true. These young upstarts are elbowing the old, safe leaders aside, and they are not even using their education to glorify our way of life. "We have difficulty adjusting to the white society," Geraldine Larkin told me gravely. "It is not our custom to get up by stepping on each other's faces."

These young whippersnappers should be brought to heel; they are a danger to white supremacy (and if it is not white supremacy we are trying to preserve, someone else explain it to the Indians; I have tried, and I cannot). They will not stick to the rules of the game; that is, they will not take all their grievances to the Indian Affairs Branch, where they can be discussed and filed and forgotten. As a matter of fact, even though the Indian Affairs Branch is making a valiant attempt to reform, the Indians simply don't trust it, and that is a very hurtful thing.

In Ottawa, a senior IAB official told me, "There have been terrific changes here; the Indians must see that."

What the Indians see is that when a government man really tries to help, he is soon shuffled aside. When William Grant, the Indian agent for the Yukon, cut through red tape to use social welfare funds for Indian housing, he was fired and prosecuted in court. When the judge who heard his case praised him, and imposed a minimum fine, the Crown appealed the sentence and obtained a harsher one. When Gerry Gamble, a community development officer, helped Indians in the Cornwall area air their grievances, he was dismissed for "failure to form positive relations with officials of the branch". When Anton Karch, another community development officer, helped Cowichan Indians organize their march in B.C., he was transferred to remote Fort St. James, and quit. When Mrs. Jean Goodwill, an Indian, and co-editor of the IAB house organ, Indian News, joined the Alberta protest last month, she found herself out of a job.

The natives, suspicious fellows, see a pattern in all this, so they have turned their backs on the branch and intend to get what they want on their own, even if it means taking to the streets. In at least two towns that I know of, tensions are already so high that whites are beginning to form safety committees, and look to their weapons. That kind of tension is not going to be brought off with pious hopes that Canada is different from the U.S.

"Whatever happens from now on," said Stan Daniels of the Alberta Metis League, "the Canadian Indian will never go back into his shell."

What Canadian whites must decide is whether that emerging Indian will be met with a handshake and a fair deal or a club and a clutch of cliches about giving him power when he is ready for it. If we choose the second course, we may well have our own Canadian version of the long, hot summer, and no one but ourselves to blame.

Bibliography

ABERLE, D. F. ET AL. "The Functional Prerequisites of a Society." *Ethics* 60 (1960): 100–111.

ABLON, JOAN. "American Indian Relocation: Problems of Dependency and Management in the City." *Phylon* 26(Winter, 1965): 362–371.

AGRICULTURE INSTITUTE OF CANADA. Background Documentation for AIC Conference on Indians. Jasper, Alberta, 1968.

ALLAN, D. J. "Indian Land Problem in Canada." In *The North American Indian Today*, edited by C. T. Loram and T. F. McIlwrath. Toronto: University of Toronto Press, 1943.

ANDERSON, DAVID AND ROBERT WRIGHT. *The Dark and Tangled Path*. Boston: Houghton Mifflin Co., 1971.

ANDRIST, RALPH. *The Long Death*. New York: Macmillan Company, 1964.

ATWELL, P. "Kinship and Migration Among Calgary Residents of Indian Origin." Master's thesis, 1969.

BARNETT, M. L. AND D. A. BAERREIS. "Some Problems Involved in the Changing Status of the American Indian." In *The Indian in Modern America*, edited by D. A. Baerreis. Wisconsin State Historical Society, 1956, pp. 50–70.

BEAR ROBE, ANDREW. "A Study Tour of Canadian Friendship Centers." Vols. 1 and 2. Ottawa: Steering Committee for the National Association of Friendship Centers, 1970.

BLAUNER, ROBERT. "Internal Colonialism and Ghetto Revolt." *Social Problems* 16 (Spring, 1969): 393–408.

BIENVENUE, RITA AND A. H. LATIF. "The Incidence of Arrests Among Canadians of Indian Ancestry." Paper presented at Canadian Sociology and Anthropology meetings in Kingston, 1973.

BOEK, W. E. AND J. K. BOEK. "The People of Indian Ancestry in Greater Winnipeg. Appendix 1: A Study of the Population of Indian Ancestry Living in Manitoba." Manitoba Department of Agriculture and Immigration, 1959, p. 132.

BOYCE, G. A. "New Goals for People of Indian Heritage." Sixth Annual Conference on Indians and Metis. Welfare Council of Greater Winnipeg, 1960, p. 8.

BROWN DEE. Bury My Heart at Wounded Knee. New York: Holt, Rinehart and Winston, 1971.

BROWN, G. G. "Culture, Society and Personality: A Restatement." *American Journal of Psychiatry* 108 (1951): 173–75.

BUCKLEY, HELEN, J. KEW AND F. HAWLEY. "The Indians and Metis of Northern Saskatchewan." Saskatoon: Saskatoon Center for Community Studies, University of Saskatchewan, 1963.

CALDWELL, GEORGE. "Indian Residential Schools." Ottawa: Department of Indian Affairs and Northern Development, 1967.

Canada Year Book. 1962–70. Ottawa: Queen's Printer.

CARDINAL, H. *The Unjust Society.* Edmonton: Hurtig Publishing Co., 1969.

CARSTENS, PETER. "Coercion and Change." In *Canadian Society*, edited by Richard Ossenberg. Scarborough, Ontario: Prentice-Hall of Canada, Ltd., 1971.

CASTELLANO, MARLENE. "Vocation or Identity: The Dilemma of Indian Youth." In *The Only Good Indian*, edited by Waubageshig. Toronto: New Press, © 1970.

CHANCE, NORMAN. "Developmental Change Among the Cree Indians of Quebec." Ottawa: Summary Report, ARDA Project 34002. (Reprint 1970) Department of Regional Economic Expansion, pp. 33–35.

CHRETIEN, J. "Indian Policy ... Where Does It Stand?" Speech at Empire Club, Toronto, October 16, 1969.

COUES, E., ED. *Manuscript Journals of Alexander Henry and David Thompson.* Vol. 1. New York: Harper and Row, 1897.

CUMMING, G. GRAHAM. "The Health of the Original Canadians 1867–1967." *Medical Service Journal* 13 (February 1967): 115–166.

CUMMINGS, PETER. "Indian Rights—A Century of Oppression." Toronto: Indian-Eskimo Association of Canada, mimeo 1969.

CUMMINGS, PETER AND NEIL MICKENBERG. *Native Rights in Canada.* 2nd ed. Toronto: Indian-Eskimo Association, 1972.

DAVIS, ARTHUR. "Edging Into Mainstream: Urban Indians in Saskatchewan." Bellingham: Western Washington State College, 1965.

———. "Urban Indians in Western Canada: Implications for Social Theory and Social Policy." Transactions of the Royal Society of Canada, 6 (series 4, 1968): 217–28.

DENTON, TREVOR. "Migration From a Canadian Indian Reserve." *Journal of Canadian Studies* (1972): 54–62.

DEPARTMENT OF INDIAN AFFAIRS AND NORTHERN DEVELOPMENT *Annual Report 1966–67; 1967–68; 1968–69; 1969–70.* Ottawa: Queen's Printer.

DEPREZ, PAUL AND GLENN SIGURDSON. "Economic Status of the Canadian Indian: A Re-examination." Winnipeg, Manitoba: Center for Settlement Studies, University of Manitoba, 1969.

DEUTSCH, CYNTHIA. "Environment and Perception." In *Social Class*, Irwin Katz, and Arthur Jensen. New York: Holt, Rinehart and Winston, Inc., 1968.

DIXON, VERNON. "Two Approaches to Black-White Relations." In *Beyond Black or White: An Alternative America*, edited by Vernon Dixon and Badmer Foster. Boston: Little, Brown and Co., 1971.

DOSMAN, EDGAR. *Indians: The Urban Dilemma.* Toronto: McClelland and Stewart Ltd., 1972.

DuBois, W. E. *Dusk of Dawn.* New York: Harcourt, Brace and Co., 1940.

Dunning, R. W. *Social and Economic Change Among the Northern Ojibwa.* Toronto: University of Toronto Press, p. 217, 1959.

———. "Ethnic Relations and the Marginal Man in Canada." *Human Organization* 18, 3 (1959a): 117–22.

———. "Rules of Residence and Ecology Among the Northern Ojibwa." *American Anthropologist* 61 (1959b): 806–16.

———. "Indian Policy—A Proposal for Autonomy." *Canadian Forum,* (December 1969).

———. "The Indian Situation: A Canadian Government Dilemma." *International Journal of Comparative Sociology* XII (June 1971): 128–34.

Fellner, W. *Trends and Cycles in Economic Activity.* New York: Holt, Rinehart and Winston, 1956.

Fidler, Dick. *Red Power in Canada.* Toronto: Vanguard Publishers, 1970.

Fisher, A. D. "White Rites Versus Indian Rights." *Transaction* 7 (November 1969): 29–33.

Fitzgerald, P. K. *Introduction to The Indian in Modern America,* edited by D. A. Baerris. Wisconsin State Historical Society, 1956.

Fitzgerald, J. P. "The Adjustment of Puerto Ricans to New York City." *Journal of Intergroup Relations,* (1960): 43–51.

Franklin, Raymond. "The Political Economy of Black Power." *Social Problems* 16 (Winter 1969): 286–301.

French, B. F. *Historical Collections of Louisiana.* Dublin: Part 3 Arbers Annals, 1851.

Frideres, James. "Indians and Education: A Canadian Failure." *Manitoba Journal of Education* 7 (June 1972): 27–30.

Fuchs, Estelle. "Time to Redeem an Old Promise." *Saturday Review,* January 24, 1970: 53–58. © 1970 by Saturday Review Co. Used with permission.

Gamson, W. *Power and Discontent.* Illinois: Dorsey Press, 1968.

Gladstone, A. "The Conceptions of The Enemy." *Journal of Conflict Resolution* 3 (1959): 132–37.

Green, Jerome. "When Moral Prophecy Fails." *Catalyst* 4 (Spring 1969): 63–79.

Harrison, G. S. "The Alaska Native Claims Settlement Act: 1971." *Arctic* 25 No. 3 (September 1972): 232–33.

Hatt, Fred. "The Metis and Community Development in Northeastern Alberta." In *Perspectives on Regions and Regionalism and Other Papers,* edited by B. Y. Card, pp. 111–19. Edmonton: University of Alberta, 1969.

Hawthorn, H. B. et al. *The Indians of British Columbia.* Toronto: University of Toronto Press, 1958.

———. *A Survey of the Contemporary Indians of Canada.* 2 Vols. Indian Affairs Branch. Ottawa: Queen's Printer, 1966–67. Excerpts reproduced by permission of Information Canada.

Hearne, Samuel. *A Journey to the Northern Ocean.* Edited by R. Glover. Toronto: Macmillan Co. of Canada, 1958.

Heilburn, James and Stanislaw Wellisz. "An Economic Program for the Ghetto." In *Urban Riots,* edited by Robert Connery. New York: Random House, 1969.

Hertzberg, Hazel. *Search for an American Indian Identity: Modern Pan Indian Movements.* Syracuse, New York: Syracuse University Press, 1971.

Hirschman, Albert. *The Strategy of Economic Development.* New Haven: Yale University Press, 1958.

Hoebel, E. A. "To End Their Status." In *The Indian in Modern America,* edited by D. A. Baerreis. pp. 1–15. Wisconsin State Historical Society, 1956.

HONIGMAN, JOHN. *Personality in Culture.* New York: Harper and Row, 1967.

HUNT, GEORGE. *The Wars of the Iroquois: A Study in Intertribal Trade Relations.* Madison: University of Wisconsin Press, 1940.

INDIAN ASSOCIATION OF ALBERTA. *The Native People.* Edmonton: (June 1971).

INDIAN TRIBES OF MANITOBA. *Wahbung (Our Tomorrows).* Winnipeg: Manitoba Indian Brotherhood, 1971.

JACK, HENRY. "Native Alliance for Red Power." In *The Only Good Indian,* edited by Waubageshig. Toronto: New Press, © 1970.

JAMES, BERNARD. "Social Psychological Dimensions of Ojibwa Acculturation." *American Anthropologist* 63 (August 1961): 728–44.

JENNESS, DIAMOND. "The Indian Background of Canadian History." Ottawa: Department of Mines and Resources *Bulletin No. 86, Anthropological Series No. 21,* 1937.

———. *Indians of Canada.* 7th ed. Ottawa: Queen's Printer, 1967.

JONES, FRANK AND WALLACE LAMBERT. "Some Situational Influences on Attitudes Toward Immigrants." *British Journal of Sociology* 18 (March 1967): 408–24.

KAEGI, GERDA. *The Comprehensive View of Indian Education.* Toronto: Indian-Eskimo Association of Canada, 1972.

KARDINER, ABRAHM AND LIONEL OVESEY. *The Mark of Oppression.* New York: N. W. Norton and Company Inc., 1951.

KENNEDY, RAYMOND. "The Colonial Crisis and the Future." In *The Science of Man in the World Crisis,* edited by Ralph Linton. New York: Columbia University Press, 1945.

KING, CECIL. "Sociological Implications of the Jeannette Corbiere Lavell Case." *The Northian* 8 (March 1972): 45–55.

KWAN, K. M. AND TAMOTSU SHIBUTANI. *Ethnic Stratification.* Toronto: The Macmillan Co., 1965.

LAGASSE, JEAN. "Community Development in Manitoba." *Human Organization* 20 (Winter 1962): 232–37.

LAING, A. *Indians and the Law.* Ottawa: Queen's Printer, 1967.

LA RUSIC, IGNATIUS. "Hunter to Proletarian." Research paper for Cree Development Change Project, 1968.

LA VIOLETTE, F. E. *The Struggle for Survival.* Toronto: University of Toronto Press, 1961.

LEACH, E. R. "The Epistemological Background to Malinowski's Empiricism." In *Man and Culture,* edited by Raymond Firth, pp. 119–37. London: Humanities Press, 1957.

LEECHMAN, DOUGLAS. *Native Tribes of Canada.* Toronto: W. J. Gage Ltd., 1956.

LEIGHTON, A. H. "My Name is Legion." Foundations for a Theory of Man's Response to Culture. © 1959 by Basic Books, Inc., New York.

LEWIS, W. A. "Theory of Economic Growth." *Economic Journal* 66 (December 1956): 694–97.

LIGHTBODY, JAMES. "A Note on the Theory of Nationalism as a Function of Ethnic Demands." *Canadian Journal of Political Science* 2 (September 1969): 327–37.

LINDESMITH, ALFRED AND ANSELM STRAUSS. *Social Psychology.* New York: Holt, Rinehart and Winston, 1968.

LOWER, A. *Colony to Nation: A History of Canada.* Toronto: Longmans, Green, 1957.

LURIE, NANCY. "The Contemporary American Indian Scene." In *North American Indians In Historical Perspective*, edited by E. B. Leacock and N. Lurie. New York: Random House, Inc., ©1971.

LYON, LOUISE, J. FRIESEN, W. R. UNRUH AND R. HERTOZ. *Inter-Cultural Education.* Calgary: Faculty of Education, University of Calgary, 1970.

MCINNIS, E. *Canada: A Political and Social History.* New York: Holt, Rinehart and Winston, 1959.

MCNAMARA, ROBERT. "The Ethics of Violent Dissent." In *Urban Riots*, edited by Robert Connery. New York: Random House, 1969.

MELLING, J. "Recent Developments in Official Policy Towards Canadian Indians and Eskimos." *Race* 7 (1966): 382–89.

MICKENBERG, NEIL. "Aboriginal Rights in Canada and the United States." *Osgood Hall Law Journal* 9 (1971): 154.

MILLS. C. W. *The Sociological Imagination.* New York: Oxford University Press, 1961.

MORRIS, ALEXANDER. *The Treaties of Canada With the Indians of Manitoba and the North West Territories.* Toronto: Belfords, Clarke and Co., 1880.

MORTON, W. L. *The Kingdom of Canada: A General History from Earliest Times.* Toronto: McClelland and Stewart Ltd., 1963.

NAGLER, MARK. *Indians in the City.* Ottawa: Canadian Research Center for Anthropology, St. Paul University, 1970.

NAMMACK, GEORGINA. *Fraud, Politics and the Dispossession of the Indians.* Norman, Oklahoma: University of Oklahoma Press, 1969.

NEILS, ELAINE. *Reservations to City.* Chicago: University of Chicago Press, 1971.

NURKSE, RAGNAR. *Problems of Capital Formation in Underdeveloped Countries.* New York: Oxford University Press, 1953.

PARSONS, T. "Malinowski and the Theory of Social Systems." In *Man and Culture*, edited by Raymond Firth, pp. 53–70. London: Humanities Press, 1957.

PATTERSON, E. PALMER. "The Canadian Indians: A History Since 1500." Don Mills: Collier-Macmillan Canada Ltd., 1972.

PELLETIER, W. *Two Articles.* Toronto: Neewin Publishing Co., n.d.

PERROUX FRANCOIS. "Note sur la notion de 'pole de croissance'." *Economie appliquée* 8 (January–June 1953): 307–20.

PETERS, OMAR. "Canada's Indians and Eskimos and Human Rights." Paper presented to the Thinkers' Conference on Cultural Rights, 1968.

PIORE, MICHAEL. "Public and Private Responsibility in On The Job Training of Disadvantaged Workers." Department of Economics Working Paper. Massachusetts: MIT Press, 1968.

PRICE, JOHN. "U.S. and Canadian Indian Periodicals." *Canadian Review of Sociology and Anthropology* 9 (May 1972): 150–62.

RENAUD, A. "Indian Education Today." In *Anthropologica* 6 (1958): 1–49.

Report on the Affairs of the Indians in Canada. "History of the Relations Between the Government and the Indians." *Journals*, section 1. Ottawa: Queen's Printer, 1844.

RICH, E. E. "Trade Habits and Motivation Among the Indians of North America." *Canadian Journal of Economics and Political Science* 26 (1960): 1: 35–53.

RICHARDSON, B. "James Bay." San Francisco: Sierra Club, 1972.

RICHARDSON, J. "Law and Status Among the Kiowa Indians." American Ethnological Society, Monograph 1, 1940.

ROBERTSON, HEATHER. *Reservations are for Indians.* Toronto: James, Lewis, and Samuel, 1970.

ROSENSTEIN-RODAN, P. N. "Problems of Industrialization of Eastern and Southeastern Europe." *Economic Journal* 53 (June–September 1943).

SCHUMIATCHER, MORRIS. *Welfare: Hidden Backlash.* Toronto: McClelland and Stewart Ltd., 1971.

SCITOVSKY, TIBOR. "Two Concepts of External Economies." *Journal of Political Economy* 62 (April 1954): 143–52.

SHEA, I. G. *Charlevoix's History of New France.* New York: Colonial Documents, Vol. 2, 1879.

SNYDER, PETER. "The Social Environment of the Urban Indian." In *The American Indian in Urban Society,* edited by Jack Waddell and O. M. Watson. Boston: Little, Brown and Co., 1971.

SORENSON, GARY AND MURRAY WOLFSON. "Black Economic Independence: Some Preliminary Thoughts." *The Annals of Regional Science* 3 (December 1969): 168–78.

Special Senate Committee Hearing on Poverty. Proceedings. Vols. 13–14 (January 1970).

SPENCER, ROBERT AND JESSEE JENNINGS. *The Native Americans.* New York: Harper and Row, 1965.

STANLEY, GEORGE. "The Indian Background of Canadian History." *Canadian Historical Association Annual Report,* 1952.

SURTEES, R. J. "The Development of an Indian Reserve Policy in Canada." *Ontario History* LXI No. 2 (June 1969): 87–98.

TABB, WILLIAM. *The Political Economy of the Black Ghetto.* New York: © 1970 by W. W. Norton and Company Inc.

TAX, SOL. "The Social Organization of the Fox Indians." In *Social Anthropology of North American Tribes,* edited by Fred Eggan, enlarged edition, pp. 243–82. Chicago: University of Chicago Press, 1935.

The Canadian Superintendent. The Education of Indian Children in Canada. Toronto: Ryerson Press, 1965.

THOMAS, CYRUS. "Indian Land Cessions in the United States." *18th Annual Report of the Bureau of American Ethnology,* Vol. 2 (1896).

THOMAS, W. I. *The Child in America.* New York: Knopf, 1928.

TRIGGER, BRUCE. "The Jesuits and the Fur Trade." *Ethnohistory* 12 (Winter 1965): 30–53.

TRUDEL, MARCEL AND GENEVIERE JAIN. "Canadian History Textbooks." *Studies of the Royal Commission on Bilingualism and Biculturalism,* No. 5. Ottawa: Queen's Printer, 1970.

VANDERBURGH, ROSAMOND. "The Canadian Indians in Ontario's School Texts: A Study of Social Studies Textbooks Grades 1 Through 8." Report prepared for the University Women's Club of Port Credit, Ontario, 1968.

VINCENT, DAVID. "An Evaluation of the Indian-Metis Urban Problem." University of Winnipeg, 1970.

WADDELL, JACK AND O. M. WATSON. *The American Indian in Urban Society.* Boston: Little, Brown and Co., 1971.

WALSH, GERALD. *Indians in Transition.* Toronto: McClelland and Stewart Ltd., 1971.

WALKER, JAMES. "The Indians in Canadian Historical Writing." Paper delivered at Canadian Historical Association meetings, 1971.

WASHBURN, WILCOMB. "Indian Removal Policy: Administrative, Historical and Moral Criteria for Judging its Success or Failure." *Ethno-History* 12 (Winter 1965): 274–78.

WAUBAGESHIG. *The Only Good Indian.* Toronto: New Press, ©1970.

WAX, ROSALIE AND R. THOMAS. "American Indians and White People." *Phylon* 22 (Winter 1961): 305–17.

WHITESIDE, DON. "A Good Blanket has Four Corners: An Initial Comparison of the Colonial Administration of Aboriginals in Canada and the United States." Paper presented at the Western Association of Sociology and Anthropology, Calgary, Alberta, 1972.

WILLHELM, SIDNEY M. "Red Man, Black Man and White America: The Constitutional Approach to Genocide." *Catalyst* 4 (Spring 1969): 3–4.

WUTTNEE, W. *Ruffled Feathers.* Calgary: Bell Publishing Co., 1972.

Index